Consuming Cultures: Globalization and Local Lives

Jeremy Seabrook

Consuming Cultures:
Globalization and Local Lives

First published in the UK by
New Internationalist™ Publications Ltd
Oxford OX4 1BW, UK
www.newint.org
New Internationalist is a registered trade mark.

Cover photo: Chris Stowers/Panos Pictures

Design: Andrew Kokotka/Ian Nixon

Typesetting by Avocet Typeset, Chilton, Aylesbury, Bucks

Printed on recycled paper by T J International Ltd, Padstow, Cornwall, UK.

British Library Cataloguing-in-Publication Data.
A catalogue record for this book is available from the British Library.

ISBN 1-904456-08-1

Contents

Part 4 RECLAIMING HEARTS AND MINDS

List of Plates

PART 1

Consuming
Cultures

Setting
the scene

Globaliza
and Local
Lives

1 Introduction: another sunrise

'I love markets. I love my local market where local subjees (vegetables) are sold, and one can chat with the women. The tragedy really is that the market is being turned into the only organizing principle for life, and Wall Street is being turned into the only source of value, and it's the disappearance of other markets, other values that I am condemning.'

Vandana Shiva[1]

Muktagacha is a small market town in North Bangladesh. The richness of local produce is astonishing – goats, cows, chickens, ducks, skins, rice, green vegetables, gourds, cucumbers, bamboo, paddy. In the flare of kerosene lamps, a smoky shifting light plays over the piles of goods, which encroach far into the road, leaving only a narrow passage for vehicles to pass. Fodder, rice-straw, fawn grasses and reeds, tamarind in rusty brown pods with feathery leaves, pink-blush *pomelos*, several kinds of squat *deshi* (local) bananas with mildewed skins, eggplants, ladies' fingers, ripening tomatoes, papery opals of garlic, onions the colour of indelible ink, green peppers, fiery flames of red chilli; fish-traps, bowls, containers, great globes of woven bamboo, musical instruments, ornaments, earrings. Here is the market at its most basic and elementary – embedded in all societies and cultures, noisy, energetic, disputatious. It is from this simple, homely image that the idea of a world market borrows a kind of legitimacy. Here, everything is local, nothing that grows is wasted.

Nothing comes further than a walk, or a cycle ride away.

But Muktagacha is not only a market; its products represent a whole way of life; in fact, a culture. And like local markets worldwide, it is under threat of invasion and usurpation from elsewhere. The replacement of locally made goods by industrial artifacts of plastic and metal cannot leave untouched the culture that grew out of and celebrated these indigenous markets: the songs of the paddy fields, the celebrations of harvest, the festivals that marked the passing of the seasons – the deepest purposes of the society are undermined by the effacement of their rooted tradition and custom.

Globalization declares war

For globalization has declared war upon all other cultures. And in cultural wars, there are no non-combatants. No innocent bystanders. We are all involved, by virtue of where we are born, and by the actions and choices we make every day of our lives.

Globalization has declared war upon all other cultures

The word 'globalization' is usually taken to refer to the emergence of a single world-wide economy. This process does not obligingly halt at some vague frontier between economics, society and culture. It generates its own inner compulsions. It imposes its own culture, which profoundly influences the lives of people everywhere.

So what is this 'globalized culture'?

The word culture originally evolved from Latin, *colere*. This had a range of meanings that subsequently separated into 'cultivate' (as in tending the earth), 'cult' (as in worship) and 'colony' (meaning to inhabit).

The word 'culture' now has two distinct meanings in English – three, if we count the reference to 'tissue culture' or any other laboratory cultivation.

One suggests a particular way of life, of a people, a group, and includes every aspect of that life – its social and moral structure, its division of labor, its domestic arrangements, and relationships between people.

The second refers to the works and practices of artistic and intellectual activity – music, literature, painting, and scholarship. This extends in recent Western discussions to include 'popular culture', a development which, strictly speaking, means a culture consumed through the market, since it is not initiated by the people themselves, like older folk cultures. Indeed, it replaces these. This has led to the spread of a global 'popular culture', which is rooted, not in the lives of the people, but in commerce and the market. This 'globalized culture' has now become a major influence on the lives of people all over the world, especially the young.

Global and local

By definition, globalization makes all other cultures local. But to billions of people all over the world, their culture is not local. It is central to their lives and who they are. At a stroke, a globalized culture diminishes and marginalizes all other ways of life.

Ideally, peoples would retain the best of traditional societies, while jettisoning practices and customs that are harmful. At the same time, they would take what is advantageous from the modern world, while rejecting those elements which are damaging or injurious to human wellbeing. But culture – like the economy, like society – comes as a package, in which you have to take all or nothing.

No aspect of social life, traditional practice or behavior remains the same under the impact of globalism. It leaves nothing untouched, but reshapes all elements of culture so that these conform to the demands of a global market. In other words, what it cannot turn into some commodity is allowed to lapse or is suppressed.

Economy, society and culture do not operate in separate spheres. Peasant

A history of culture and civilization

At the time of the Enlightenment, in the 18th century, 'culture' was used to describe the development of human societies. This was generally taken to mean a form of progress: cultures grew out of 'primitivism' or 'savagery' towards the high point of European civilization in the 18th century.

German philosopher Johann Gottfried von Herder, in his *Ideas on the Philosophy of Mankind* (1784 – 91) was the first to question this assumption. He attacked European subjugation of the globe:

'Men of all the quarters of the globe... you have not lived solely to manure the earth with your ashes, so that at the end of time your posterity should be made happy by European culture. The very thought of a superior European culture is a blatant insult to the majesty of Nature.' Herder insisted it was necessary to talk of cultures in the plural; a view which collided with ideas of European providential cultural superiority.

But in the 19th century, the word 'culture' was used by anthropologists to describe the 'primitive' societies they studied. This contrasted with the 'civilization' to which they, the 'civilized' anthropologists, belonged. 'Culture' referred to the aggregate of values, beliefs, customs and practices of the group under consideration.

In 1963, Fernand Braudel, in his *History of Civilizations*, observed that civilization, as a singular noun, was no longer in use: it was a relic of colonialism to oppose one single civilization to barbarism or primitivism. The plural, 'civilizations', is now often used as a synonym for 'cultures'. But this does not necessarily mean that the certainties of 19th century imperial anthropologists have been laid to rest. Quite the contrary. Indeed, in the US in the early 21st century, (President) George W Bush regularly referred to what he called 'the civilized world.' This was meant to distinguish the US and its allies from 'terrorism' or 'failed states'; but it was clear that the idea of a single, universal 'civilization' had been rehabilitated.

The humility of the West identified by Braudel was only transient.

cultures, based upon particular strains of rice, maize or wheat, grew organically out of preparing the earth, planting, tending and harvesting the crops that sustained them. Rituals, celebrations and work-songs were an aspect of whatever provided sustenance. Gods had to be propitiated in order to ensure the fertility of the soil, certain rites were indispensable to sufficient rainfall; and when harvests failed, expiatory or sacrificial offerings were made. Indeed, the source of material survival was sacralized, so that religion, too, was inseparable from economics; although of course, subsistence was not called economics. Bengali writer Rabindranath Tagore stated that 'the culture of the forest has fuelled the culture of Indian society. The culture that has arisen from the forest has been influenced by the diverse processes of renewal of life which are always at play in the forest, varying from species to species, from season to season, in sight and sound and smell.' Tagore believed this principle animated the whole of Indian society.

A kind of magic

Because of its power to create wealth, global capitalism assumes its own kind of magic: one that permits it to sweep aside all other human societies, all existing institutions, and all searches for meaning in the world.

Globalization represents dominance. Dominance is no new thing in the world, as the fight for supremacy of rising and falling empires has shown.

Civilizations (or cultures) are always borne up by systems of belief or faith, which are, at least potentially, at war with one another. It goes without saying that virtually all of them seek to vanquish, absorb or influence smaller cultures in their midst or on their periphery.

What does change from time to time are the mechanisms through which powerful cultures transmit themselves. Sometimes military might gives way to religious evangelism. Occasionally, economic power speaks for itself. During the period between defeat in Vietnam and 'victory' in Iraq, the US, for instance, while by no means abandoning its use of force, preferred to promote an economic system which spoke to the peoples of the world of untold wealth. This appeared a more persuasive vehicle for the spread of a single global culture than invasion, conquest and demands for tribute.

For at the heart of the Western culture has lain a promise – the same promise which gained the assent of the majority of the people in the West to a violent and disruptive industrialism 200 years ago – that is, a pledge that the industrial system, with its limitless ability to produce and to provide, would mean an end to poverty.

And what a promise that is! It holds out the possibility that human beings will no longer be at the mercy of lean seasons, famine and loss, the vagaries of climate, the ruin of one season's crops, times of want and the dread of destitution. This is, surely, what humanity has craved since human beings first conceived of the security embodied in the sanctuary, the shrine and the stronghold of their earliest settlements. Delivery from poverty and insecurity; that most ancient of human dreams.

At the heart of Western culture is a promise: an end to poverty

What is difficult to understand, especially for people in the West, is that the present worldwide economic system is the triumph of what was formerly merely one local culture. Ruth Benedict, the American anthropologist, expresses this clearly in her book, *Patterns of Culture*. She was writing in 1943, before the dissolution of the European colonial empires, and long before the eclipse of Communism, and the subsequent expansion of the Western development model into almost every country on earth:

'Western civilization, because of fortuitous historical circumstances, has spread itself more widely than any other local group that has so far been known. It has standardized itself over most of the globe, and we have been led, therefore, to accept a belief in the uniformity of human behavior that under other circumstances would not have arisen.

Even very primitive peoples are sometimes far more conscious of the role of cultural traits than we are, and for good reason. They have had intimate experience of different cultures. They have seen their religion, their economic system, their marriage prohibitions, go down before the white man's…The psychological consequences of this spread of white culture has been out of all proportion to the materialistic. This worldwide cultural diffusion has protected us as no man had ever been protected before from having to take seriously the civilizations of other peoples: it has given to our culture a massive universality that we have long ceased to account for historically, and which we read off rather as necessary and inevitable.'

Responses: the fatalistic and the resistant

The view that globalization – and all that comes with it – is inevitable, unstoppable, is a counsel of despair, since it evokes human helplessness in the presence of our own creation. Belief in its irreversibility ('you can't turn the clock back') is also connected with a profound faith in 'progress' (which is purely material, the moral, social and spiritual advances of humanity since the industrial era having been far less conspicuous.) This suggests a passivity and fatalism which are far from the busy optimistic can-do language of capitalism. The truth is, this fatalism is the fatalism of the rich, who see their own power and privilege growing in perpetuity under this benign dispensation. It is self-serving and disingenuous, for the only hope it offers to the poor is the cliché that 'a rising tide lifts all boats'; a much-abused metaphor which, interpreted, means that the poor may, in this order of things, become a little less poor on condition that the rich are permitted to grow inordinately, abusively, rich.

There have been, broadly, two principal responses in the world to the speed and intensity of globalization – the fatalistic and the resistant. Among the most fatalistic have been the leaders of the most industrialized countries. Former US President Clinton stated 'Globalization is a fact not a policy choice.' Tony Blair called it 'inevitable and irreversible.' It is perhaps a paradox that the leaders of the most dynamic, expanding economies in the world offer such a passive and unchallenging view of what are, after all, only human-made arrangements. These are among the richest and most powerful countries, who can wage endless war upon the great abstraction that is terror, who can topple regimes, either clandestinely or with overwhelming force, as in Iraq, who can lay down one World Trade Organization (WTO) law for the poor and another for themselves. Who can believe in their helplessness in the presence of these economic and cultural upheavals?

The dynamic thrust of global- ization is towards growing inequality

'Progressives' in this conservative time try to refine this contemporary version of *laissez-faire*, believing that 'we' can intervene constructively, to make globalization 'work for the poor'. Some of the growing inequality it produces may be tempered; some of the institutional injustice may be addressed. 'We' cannot alter the sacred laws of economics, but we can assuage some of the malign effects of their workings.

But the dynamic thrust of globalization is towards growing inequality. The resolutions, declarations, initiatives and targets falter against the irrationality of market-distributed rewards, which spread their bounty and withhold their treasures with the arbitrariness and caprice of the most despotic, arbitrary dictator the world has ever seen.

Resistance takes at least two principal forms. One of these has been the re-assertion of local cultural identities. There has been a significant work of conserving and protecting, of guarding from extinction small-scale cultures, dying languages and folklore. This is the counterpart of efforts to save the 12,000 or so species of plants and animals on the edge of survival. The preservation of biodiversity also includes the safeguarding of human cultures threatened with dissolution.

Reclaiming the local is often concentrated in the field of cultural retrieval – music, song, dance, drama, handicrafts, artefacts, pottery and folk culture. There has been an attempt to quarantine local life-ways from the consequences – perhaps from the fallout might be an appropriate metaphor – of economic integration; a kind of *cordon sanitaire* set up around a dwindling culture. The problem with this is that it makes easier the transformation of these things into commodities: they become embalmed, something folkloric or picturesque, and are then readily absorbed into the global market which was the agent of their marginalization in the first place.

Some people believe it is possible to gain the best of both worlds – to accept the economic benefits of globalization, while at the same time maintaining what is of value in language, tradition and custom. This is the benign response.

The other has become only too familiar: a reaction of violence. The hatred engendered by globalization is not 'hatred of freedom', as George W Bush stated, but because many people feel the effects on culture and religion of what are sometimes falsely projected as 'only' economic processes as a violation of the core of their being.

The resentment of many Muslims (not just extremists) towards America, and the defensiveness of Hindu fundamentalism, opposed both to Islam and globalization (with its distant connection to Christianity) are the most vivid symptom of this. The appearance of Christian fundamentalism in the very heartland of the globalizing forces suggests that even the beneficiaries of the process are troubled by a sense that values, beliefs and faith are being sacrificed, and they seek to salvage something of their cultural heritage.

The failings of the powerful

An inability to acknowledge the profound, painful social and religious disruptions that are inextricable from globalization has been the most grievous failing on the part of the powerful of the earth. Their obsession with pushing economic 'reforms' onto the whole world has had repercussions, which reshape not only the contours of economies but also the heart and psyche of the people, reforming their value-systems and remaking them in conformity with the values of the global market.

This is how ancient virtues are disgraced – frugality, sparingness, the husbanding of resources, conserving water and soil fertility, cherishing the elements that sustain life, upholding reverence for habitats that have nurtured people for millennia. Of course, these developments appear to have nothing to do with the dry, bureaucratic prescriptions drawn up by development professionals, financial specialists and economic experts in the sequestered luxury of five-star hotels in capital cities.

Yet these projects of ruinous enrichment impact violently upon the lives of the people. When popular anger bursts forth, this is greeted with a display of indignant incomprehension.

The West was enabled to absorb the somber lessons of capitalism over generations, and to modify its culture accordingly. In 1926, R H Tawney, in his *Religion and the Rise of Capitalism*, followed the resistance of the Christian church to the values of the market, and showed how it was worsted in the struggle, principally by the self-evident wealth which managed to transform ancient Christian vices into modern virtues. The doctrine of the 'just price' was overtaken by what the market would bear; the 'fair day's wage' was eclipsed by the availability of despairing laborers who would offer themselves at below subsistence wages. The ancient sin of usury became a mechanism for increasing profit; and in this way, people learned to transform vices into virtues, and ceased to call them by their proper names: usury and exploitation became enterprise and adventurous risk-taking.

When these values are diffused globally, unmediated either by the long gestation period of their rebirth in the West, and untempered by any insight into the context in which these messages go forth into the world, few can foresee how violently this will strike at the sensibilities of others. It seems astonishing that so little thought was given to the gratuitous onslaught this represents, what an injury to rooted identities and values.

The question remains, who declared the cultural war which accompanies the economic re-ordering of the world? Who promulgated the terrible doctrine that only by the arbitrary and profane grace of a global market might each individual on earth expect to survive each day to see another sunrise?

2 What is global culture?

'The Cherokee word for land also means history, culture and religion. We have no history and no culture if we have no land for them to come from. We cannot think of ourselves as existing without existing directly in the land. Land for us is not property, or even a place to build a house or plant crops. It is something truly sacred in the most profound sense, and it is part of ourselves.'

Jimmie Durham[1]

Human lives are everywhere the same, although the conditions in which they are played out differ widely. Human needs are also stark in their simplicity. Birth, growth, maturity, procreation, ageing and death – these are the inevitable necessities with which all cultures must come to terms. Cultures could be described as the ways in which people decorate or embellish these inescapable realities, in order to make them more acceptable: our social lives veil existence: who wants to stare reality in the face every day of our lives?

First comes the creation of meaning: it cannot all be without purpose. We must be going somewhere – that somewhere may be an afterlife with the ancestors, the golden realm of paradise or a future inscribed in myths of progress. Then comes the need to understand and manipulate our environment, to ensure that it continues to sustain future generations. The anthropologist Bronislaw Malinowski states: 'There are no peoples however primitive' (he might also have said however 'developed') 'without religion and magic.

Nor are there, it must be added, any savage [sic] races lacking either in scientific attitude or in science, though this lack has been frequently attributed to them. In every primitive community... there have been found two clearly distinguishable domains, the Sacred and the Profane; in other words, the domain of Magic and Religion and that of Science.'[2]

This is no less true of 'advanced' societies, as will appear in due course.

Human beings have always sought to control the course of nature for practical ends, by ritual or magic spells, by compelling the elements, forcing animals or growing things to obey their desires. Magic is inseparable from controlling the natural world: if only the right formula can be found, if only the necessary sequence of actions is performed. Religion begins where the limitations of magic are recognized: it acknowledges that there are indeed things beyond our competence, forces we cannot control, no matter how elaborate the propitiatory rituals may be.

The cycle of life gives rise to an extensive repertoire of reactions. Birth customs, taboos around women who have recently given birth, and purification rituals, celebrate the successful passage to earth of new life. Even in the West it was common until recently for women to be 'churched' after childbearing. The uses of the umbilicus are varied: it may given to the children to ward off sickness, buried to destroy evil spirits. In living memory, the caul of a newborn child (a membrane which sometimes covers the face of a baby) was bought by sailors, who believed it would protect them against drowning at sea.

The passage of children into puberty and their initiation into adult life gave rise to a wide range of responses. Circumcision, isolation at the time of menstruation, the tests and trials of man- and woman-hood all engender powerful rites of passage. The taboos around menstruation have only recently been lifted. When I was a child, my mother kept a butcher's shop. When her husband deserted her, many people withdrew their custom, some as a signal of their disapproval of divorce, but some because they believed that a menstruating woman handling meat would make it go bad.

Apprenticeship, the test of warrior status, betrothal, preparation for adult life, are all marked with new humiliations to be endured, in order to acquire new powers and responsibilities. Unions of men and women have always been attended by fertility rites; and the throwing of rice and confetti at weddings today are the last vestiges of this practice in Western society. Sometimes it was possible to predict the sex of the child before birth; a process rendered easier by amniocentesis, with the consequent large number of abortions of girl-children, both in India and China, where boys continue to be preferred, since it is their duty to take care of aged parents. Prohibitions on sexual relations with kin have also varied from society to society: at the beginning of the Church of England Prayer Book with which we were issued in school, there was a fascinating table of those with whom marriage was strictly prohibited.

Cultures have been transmitted by the living example of flesh and blood

The relationship between human conduct and the natural world remains in many cultures; and even in Britain it did not vanish with the coming of industrialism. This everywhere created a rich reservoir of lore, superstition and legend. At the time of a big earthquake in Skopje in the former Yugoslavia in the 1960s, I can remember an old countryman who lived close to us saying it was a visitation of God 'because of the wickedness of folks'.

The relationships with nature were by no means all superstitions. The know-how required to produce food and to optimize the conditions for growing it depend upon observation and a deep understanding of the cycle of the year, the timing of the rains, the sowing of seeds, planting and transplanting, reaping and harvesting. A knowledge of where famine foods were to be found when crops failed accompanied all vulnerable societies which lived within the constraints of bare sufficiency.

In Britain, the ways in which children were instructed did not wait for the coming of education acts in the 19th century: by observation and imitation, a new generation learned to be worthy of the one that preceded it. This is how cultures have been transmitted through time – by the living example of flesh and blood rather than the specialization of professionals. Even so, certain exceptional individuals, or those who had inherited the role of shaman, healer, or intermediary between the worlds of the living and the dead, were often singled out for particular instruction.

The rituals around dying are as varied as those called forth by all the other points of transition in human lives. Because death has always been a constant companion of the living in most societies, omens, fears and propitiatory rites have always assumed particular importance. When I was a child, I counted up to 30 common omens of death in my family: these included a bird tapping at the window-pane, the flight of a solitary crow, cinders dropping onto the hearth (called coffins or cradles, according to their shape), a picture suddenly falling off the wall.

What happened to bodies after death produced great diversity of belief. Whether the remains were burned or buried separated great civilizations, while the Zoroastrians believed they should not be touched by the sacred elements, and were left for the vultures to devour. Status lingered into death, and this determined whether bodies would be preserved or mummified, buried with the material goods required for the afterlife. Did they take gifts for those who had preceded them in death, or were they dispatched in the state of material nakedness in which they had entered the world? When my grandmother died in 1948, all perishable foods in the house at the time were thrown out; death contaminated the sustenance of the living.

Just as the passage of the significant moments in human life were attended with a ceremonial which linked them to higher purposes, so the passing year was also accompanied by its appropriate rituals and to the gods whose benevolence was required to ensure survival – the songs of seed-time and harvest, the sacrifices to spirits and supernatural beings on whose goodwill the success or failure of crops depended. These annual rites reflected and replicated those that attended the coming and going of human lives.

All this forms the bedrock of cultures. Upon these simple and constantly repeated events enormous edifices of practice and custom are constructed. Men regard themselves as the custodians of cultures, but women are the transmitters.

Sometimes the rituals obscure the original purpose. They evolved, both from within, and equally, under the influence of outsiders, who came as conquerors, traders, or simply as bearers of more convincing accounts of human destiny than those which had hitherto prevailed.

Culture and place

Cultures arise out of strategies for survival in particular localities. They celebrate the collective human experience, and develop around the ways in which basic needs are answered by the places in which they grow.

The US anthropologist, Clyde Kluckhohn, in his *Mirror for Man*, written in 1952, gave a list of a dozen meanings for what a culture is. Among them are 'the total way of life of a people', 'the

Cultures are rooted in a particular space, in a particular environment

social legacy the individual acquires from his group', 'a way of thinking, feeling and believing', 'a storehouse of pooled learning', 'a mechanism for the normative regulation of behavior', and a 'precipitate of history.'

Cultures are bound up with place; more often than not, rooted in a particular space, in a particular environment. This usually means land, although it can
be either a specific locality or an imagined one. Cultures are the consequences
of geography as well as of history, perhaps primordially so. The sites in which
they evolve are also invested with sacred significance. Even cultures that travel
and make conversions in distant places – that become 'civilizations' in the
sense understood by Samuel Huntington – retain a mythic sense of a place of
origin: Mecca retains its holy status for Muslims in Jakarta or Johannesburg or
Buenos Aires.

In his 1993 book *On the Natural History of Destruction*, German writer W G
Sebald says of the Jewish writer Jean Amery: 'The destruction of someone's
native land is as one with that person's destruction. Separation becomes
dechirure, (tearing apart), and there can be no new homeland.'

Amery himself, brought up in provincial Austria, is quoted: 'Home is the
land of one's childhood and youth. Whoever has lost it remains lost himself,
even if he has learned not to stumble about in the foreign country as if he
were drunk.' Sebald observes: 'When he crossed the border into exile in
Belgium, and had to take on himself the Jewish quality of homelessness, of
being elsewhere, *être ailleurs*, he did not yet know how hard it would be to
endure the tension between his native land as it became ever more foreign and
the land of his foreign exile as it became ever more familiar.'

Fascism is an extreme example of a political and cultural revolution, which
made alien those it had alienated, and compelled many of its victims into exile
to avoid it. But such stories are repeated times without number by those who
have been forced out of their homeland by political enemies, by tribal or
ethnic strife, by torture and imprisonment; by natural calamity, and even,
although with lesser intensity, by being forced to seek livelihood in a hostile
elsewhere.

If place is essential to culture, the culture associated with globalization will
be the more powerful, for it is *everywhere*. Perhaps its greatest strength is its

capacity to dematerialize, and to inhabit, like a jinn or spirit, other cultural spaces, to make itself at home anywhere in the world. It is both ubiquitous and fugitive; and this makes it a very radical force indeed, since it is a negation of the very rootedness that has been a feature of most traditional cultures.

Land usually provides the resource-base for the survival of the social group which celebrates its culture – its rituals, festivals, ceremonies and initiations. Cultures endure as long as the link with the environment that produces them remains unbroken. The link may be tenuous. The life of shifting cultivators or nomads, for instance, may appear to deny this; although in practice, these usually move in certain prescribed spaces, returning to the same place after an interval during which the fertility of the soil has regenerated. For the most part, the bond is with the earth – the provider of the means of subsistence, the instrument of survival. Mother earth, the fatherland or motherland, mother country – place is linked to the generation of life, and expresses itself in the mother-tongue; the 'native place' is the root of nationalism.

Cultures endure as long as the link with the environment remains unbroken

Cultures which have lived on, even when the people have been evicted from the sites in which those cultures arose, are still haunted by a sense of place, even if in the negative image of exile. The Jews, sustained by an ancient promise of land, have lived in exile, preserving the dream of return from the places they have been compelled to occupy, sometimes the extreme dystopias of ghettos and concentration camps. The home-place, the Land (and the idea of recovering the land) remained in the diasporic Jewish psyche; and although place is a major determinant of culture, that place occupies the psychological spaces as much as the material ones. Indeed, much of the strife created by setting up the state of Israel derives from conflict between the ideal of a land bestowed by the Creator, and land when it becomes actual territory; the more so when its occupancy is also disputed. Myths realized are a contradiction in terms.

One of the rare cultures which has no clear territorial link is that of the gypsies: people who have been everywhere marginalized, persecuted and despised for that very reason. The gypsies are a kind of object-lesson in the fate of landless cultures. It is their destiny to be evicted, moved on, in a condition of perpetual homelessness. In the Europe of the 21st century, the Roma people remain the most persecuted on the continent. Their beginning is in an undefined realm; the absence of homeland becomes the distinctive definition of this almost unique cultural experience; although in one sense, their condition prefigures the state of the placeless subjects of globalism.

Myths of sacred spaces are central to cultures; even the after-life is colonized as place, the site of reward, of justice, of the achievement of all that has not been possible in the social spaces of this life. What Lewis Mumford said in *The City in History* may also be said of human cultures: both heaven and utopia had a place in their structure. The earthly paradise, the *pays de cocagne*, the land of milk and honey, the desert that blooms, the garden of Eden, the new Jerusalem, the city on the hill, are a few of the images that have accompanied an equally persistent desire – the longing to establish the hereafter in the here-and-now. This has remained a distant dream; until now, that is. And this is the promise enfolded within the cult of consumerism.

Cultures have sacralized the resources on which they depend. Animist societies, which endow rivers and forests with supernatural characteristics, ensure the survival of the sustaining ecological sites on which they depend. There is usually a direct relationship between culture, and what the modern world calls the economic arrangements that underpin it; although this relationship sometimes exists in story, myth or memory, rather than in the material world. The tenacity and endurance of the Jews have been a result of *rootedness* in the sacred

land, which is, of course, quite the opposite of how they have been portrayed
– as mobile outsiders, perpetually expelled and settling only provisionally here
or there. The possibility of *going back* has, perhaps, an even more powerful
appeal than the immemorial occupancy of land.

The roots of belonging

Cultures have impressed their accumulated wisdom, their traditions and rituals,
upon succeeding generations. They have offered both security and discipline.
They have clearly defined the limits of the possible for any individual. The
intensity of passionate commitment which this has generated depends upon
the constraints within which it operates: you love your country or language or
traditions because they are yours, and because these distinguish you from the
uninitiated and unprivileged of other, and generally lesser, cultures.

A major determinant on the social beings we are is where we happened to
be born, and the customs, expectations and traditions, as well as the language
which this has given us. The very randomness of this must be given significance, since it gives us meaning: the parcel of land which had the wisdom to
lodge us is elevated, even worshipped; and it remains the misfortune of others
that they didn't have our privileges.

The values and beliefs of the locality which bred us are absorbed during
childhood. This has always been the (often poisoned) gift of culture to a new
generation. That is to say, it has anchored them in a particular place, has
provided them with an interpretation of the world, has bestowed upon them
the incomparable blessing of the meaning of the cosmos they have inherited.

A blessing and a curse

All cultures aspire to be universal. There is no traditional culture, however
small, that has not seen itself as the essence of humanity, the central embodiment of creation. In this sense, too, all cultures have a spiritual basis. All
peoples have seen themselves as the centre of the universe. 'Outside of the

closed group', writes Ruth Benedict, 'there are no human beings.'

If it can be said that the culture we inherit is a blessing, there is also a sense in which that culture is also a curse: to be socialized into this or that set of values, rituals and beliefs is the necessary price to be paid for living. In other words, culture, as well as a benediction, has also been a kind of punishment, in the sense that the beliefs of one society automatically exclude the faiths, traditions and customs of all the others. Although no societies are impermeable to external cultural influences, their spiritual health depends upon belief: in the exclusiveness of their gods, the correctness of their practices and the inevitability of their way of life. In every culture, there will be unfortunates whose personality is at odds with the values she or he will have acquired. If such individuals are lucky, they may be singled out as especially gifted, even holy; if not, they may be seen as intolerably deviant, fit only to be killed as witches, or incarcerated as mad.

'Outside of the closed group there are no human beings'

Land and spiritual space – the material and mystical – have always been entwined in the etiological myth of cultures. The sites in which they evolve have been major determinants upon their growth and development. The rituals and customs are intimately connected with the protection and conservation of the places in which they are grounded.

Landscapes of the mind

This is why the very idea of a global culture is extremely radical. A culture that claims a whole world as the arena for its practices and beliefs contradicts everything that we know, or thought we knew, about the links between culture and environment.

'Global market culture' represents a reversal and negation of all earlier cultures, primarily because it operates everywhere, but is rooted nowhere. This appears to confer upon it a kind of *placeless ubiquity*. Or perhaps it is simply that the site of its operations is not in the world at all: the places in which the globalizing culture works are in the heart and imagination of people. This is its most powerful defense. Its topography is not that of mountains, forests or plains, but the internal landscapes of the mind and spirit. Precisely because it does not have a specific location where it sets up its shrines and places of worship, it is both more beguiling and harder to resist. The sense that it is everywhere, yet, at the same time, strangely inaccessible, creates enormous frustration in those who see globalization as a renewed imperial assault upon the peoples of the world and their traditional cultures. Unlike the resistance which developed to earlier occupying powers, it is harder to set up a liberation movement or a freedom struggle, since the adversaries are impalpable, dissolving and regrouping all the time, the better to take the citadels of faith and custom from within. These attack the subjective sense of who people are, rather than imposing practices and customs of the outsider upon their territory.

Power and promises

The power of the global market culture lies in the promises it makes to the world. Not only does its imagery of plenty imply the end of an ancient poverty, but it also suggests escape from the limiting influences of place-bound habit and beliefs. It is, of course, nothing new for conquerors to present themselves as agents of liberation (the US did so in Iraq), but freedom from the limitations of this or that culture itself is a far more appealing – and, at the same time, threatening – proposition.

The world market culture involves, not the imposition of one set of values and beliefs, but on the contrary, *an apparent freedom from these things*. It promises a new form of deliverance, whereby the individual will become the agent of her or his own cultural creation. This means the freedom to construct, out of a plethora of styles, experiences, services, goods and artifacts, a self-made identity, determined, not by tradition, not by antecedent, not by those who have gone before, but by what can be bought in the existential hypermarket.

But before this triumphant metamorphosis can occur, certain conditions have to be met: the individual must be pared down. As many traits and characteristics as possible must be erased. The individual at the heart of these transformations has to be prepared, in such a way that the acquisition of the symbols and identifiers that make up a new philosophy of belonging, come to constitute a parody of deliverance. This requires a *processing* of humanity, not so very different from the processing of any raw materials that go into the making of any other industrial product.

The individual must be washed clean of all inherited cultural impurities

In order for the human being to be reshaped in readiness for this version of liberation, she or he is cleansed of all social and cultural features, except the most irreducible characteristic. It is clear that ethnicity, and to a lesser extent, gender, cannot be eliminated; language, and sometimes faith, are also not so easily wiped out. But a person is black or white, male or female, gay or straight, old or young: this becomes the overriding source of selfhood. Instead of inheriting the defining elements of culture, the individual is stripped of all cultural accretions, so that she or he may be inducted into the culture which has superseded all local acculturations – one which is bought in, acquired from the universal market. Hence the insistence upon 'choice' in market culture: we shall make ourselves.

Cancelled birthrights

What has always been regarded as the birthright of human beings – that they inherit a culture acquired during infancy and childhood, transmitted unreflectingly from their own place in the world – is canceled. They are free to choose, in the sense that, in this new global dispensation, they can now select any cultural feature they desire. Of course, it can only be acquired through the market, and has to be paid for. This severely limits the scope and reach of this culture. It may be called freedom by its proponents, although it is a highly restricted kind of freedom, and is proportionate to the quantity of disposable income at the disposal of the individual. This is why poverty is such a painful experience in rich market economies: to confront the multitude of possibilities in the global market without the resources to acquire them is torment indeed. This perhaps helps to explain why the richest societies the world has ever known are also scarred by violence and crime. Dependency upon the market suggests new kinds of unfreedom, not known to the unselfconscious actors within the choiceless cultures of tradition. It is clear that the freedoms of this culture are ambiguous – they also entail great forfeits and losses. Participants in this culture are, paradoxically, both free and constrained.

In a way, market culture realizes an ancient dream: to stand outside, to be unencumbered with these or those cultural traits, to be liberated from superstition, irrational belief, antiquated or archaic custom. It offers a kind of secular transcendence, a range of possibilities to the individual, relieved of all the limiting features which have weighed her down in this or that location, bound her to particular customs and rituals. This has an enticing, even intoxicating, appeal.

But to exist without any of the features which have formed earlier generations, shaped their conduct and behavior from within ancient traditions, also represents a denudation, an impossibly perplexing absence. How are we to know who we are without the guidance of the gods, ancestors, practices, traditions of those who went before?

Well, these must now all be bought in. Market culture also embodies a unique and particular relationship to place; one which at least appears to be decreasingly anchored in the resource-base of the earth. Global culture also promises that human beings can overcome dependency on the very biosphere which is essential for the maintenance of life. It installs people in a free-floating technosphere insulated from the determining features of place. Those born into the global market are no longer defined by the past, by region, by kinship. It is not only another country, it is also a rebirth into another existence, one without qualities, a featureless landscape of perpetual emptiness, bound only by limitless horizons, against which we must struggle to define ourselves. The influences which determine identity are curiously disembodied, despite the intensely material power their brands exercise over our imagination.

No longer inheritors of a cluster of beliefs and values, we truly make ourselves, beginning with the state of existential nudity which we must clothe in the characteristics of our choice. No more ceremonies, rites of passage, practices marking the succeeding stages of life, rituals that reiterate and reassert continuity. We have shed all such obstacles. We are

No longer inheritors of a cluster of beliefs and values, we truly make ourselves

without defining qualities. It also brings epic forgettings. An elusive sense of exile and longing which is difficult even to articulate, let alone assuage, is a small part of the price to be paid for this version of liberation. This is why the word 'choice' is heard so frequently in the places of origin of this culture, the rich Western world. Freedom to choose becomes, not merely selection of a bewildering range of goods and services, but also the elective identity acquired in an existential hypermarket.

New generations are installed in an industrial life-support machine, apparently independent of the natural world, and which has all but blotted out its connectedness with the earth. They have undergone even more profound expungings of the onerous clutter of custom and tradition than the old countrypeople who for 200 years have been coming, with their waning rural convictions, from the impoverished countryside into the mysterious labyrinth of city slums. Of course, vestiges remain; we speak this or that language, our being reflects faint inflections of the localities which – by chance – saw our birth, but we are free of cultural constraints, that accumulation of the ages which used to provide us with a sense of who we are.

Market culture bestows new freedoms, in which it becomes our purpose to acquire for ourselves all the cultural characteristics needful for a full life. It is our unfree liberty to create ourselves through the market. For identity, meaning and purpose we must see what the shops have to offer. Granted nothing by birth, we must acquire everything in a market place so dense with possibilities that it almost overwhelms us. But we are blank spaces, on which we will carve our own inscriptions, the empty slate on which we shall write our destiny, the receptive vessel into which the products of the ransacked cultures of the world may be promiscuously poured.

Stripped of the features of culture which cling like barnacles to the identity of our elders, robbed of memory and rootedness, we have become remote from the culture of our place of broken belonging: we are all anthropologists of our own estrangement, archaeologists digging through the buried strata of our forgotten origins. We are our own begetters, the orphaned celebrants of freedoms undreamed-of. Life has whatever meaning we choose to invest it with. Our minimal being must be ornamented, decorated, transformed, but only from within the costly plenitude, the expensive luxury of a market become global.

How difficult it is to make sense of what has become of us, and what we have become! By the time we have come to terms with this bewildering form of socialization, the profits will have been made, the future raided, the world pillaged, its cultural diversity devastated for the sake of the infinite variety required by the market, in which we rummage for the signs of our own misplaced identity.

This, then, is the culture that promises to supersede all others, to absorb and process them, transform them into industrial commodities. It then offers them, packaged and prepared, for sale, in its eager generosity to restore us to wholeness.

1 IFDA dossier 6, April 1979 quoted in Buchanan, Anne, *Food, Poverty and Power*, 1982, Spokesman Books, Nottingham. 2 Bronislew Malinowski, *Magic, Science and Religion and other essays*, Waveland Press, 1992.

3 The colonizing of hearts and minds

'From the 1950s onward, the market economy has not only imperialized every aspect of conventional life, it has also dissolved the memory of the alternative life-ways that preceded it.'

Murray Bookchin[1]

Much of the criticism of a 'global culture' has been directed at its economic hegemony; most evidenced by the conspicuous symbols of an identical consumer market across the globe.

This has often focused on the logos and brand names, particularly of companies which have opened up everywhere in the world, and which have resulted in an extreme separation between producers and consumers. In the spaces thus created, inflated budgets devoted to advertising and publicity have purged the commodities they make of the blood and sweat that went into them, and have promoted these as cult symbols to the people of the rich world. These include providers of fast food, fashionable articles of clothing and footwear, accessories and goods which people carry with them. Patterns of consumption, among those who can buy in to this world, show a convergence which does not distinguish between the cultures of people from Peru to Bangladesh, from Nigeria to New Guinea.

Focus on these symbols has helped to demonstrate the immense power which (mostly) Western transnational entities have in shaping the spending patterns of the people of the world; although it is only the middle class – rarely more than 20 per cent of the population – in the countries of the South who can participate in the global market. This is not insignificant, for these have disproportionate influence and power in their own countries. Indeed, the middle classes are now seen in the West as the spokespersons and representatives of the culture of their countries; and there is nothing more flattering to the West than to see a confirmation that the choices and example of their people is faithfully mirrored in the minority of privileged in the South.

Corporations vs countries

The power, reach and size of global corporations now equals and even exceeds that of individual countries

- There are 63,000 transnational corporations worldwide, with 690,000 foreign affiliates
- Fifty-one of the world's top 100 economies are corporations (based on a comparison of corporate sales and country GDPs)
- The top 200 corporations' combined sales are bigger than the combined economies of all countries minus the biggest 10
- By this measure, WalMart is bigger than Indonesia. General Motors is roughly the same size as Ireland, New Zealand and Hungary combined
- The top 200 corporations' combined sales are 18 times the size of the combined annual income of the 1.2 billion people (24 percent of the total world population) living in 'severe' poverty
- While the sales of the top 200 are the equivalent of 27.5 percent of world economic activity, they employ only 0.78 percent of the world's workforce
- Three-quarters of all transnational corporations are based in North America, Western Europe and Japan
- US corporations dominate the top 200, with 82 slots (41 percent of the total). Japanese firms are second, with 41 slots.

Source www.corporatewatch.org

Communism and globalization

It is too easy to read off, as it were, symbols of Western or transnational power, as evidence that other people's cultures are being transformed. Commentators often refer to 'McDonaldization' or 'Disneyfication' of other cultures. Identical products in the shopping enclosures of the world's cities are sometimes cited as proof of an homogenizing convergence. But the mere presence of foreign fast-food outlets, or malls offering goods from Fabergé, Cerruti, Elizabeth Arden, Daniel Hechter, Kookai, Texas Pancake, or Kentucky Fried Chicken are only superficial signs of economic, though not necessarily of cultural, invasion.

All countries have had authoritarian or undemocratic regimes during industrialization

The alliance between China's ostensibly Communist system and a highly competitive market economy is less anomalous than it appears. All countries – ever since the industrial revolution in Britain – have had authoritarian or undemocratic regimes during the period of industrialization. This is because the experience is often violent and coercive; it compels people to abandon traditional patterns of living and sets up new kinds of communities for changed methods of production. The imposition of a market economy on peasant or customary practices is rarely untroubled. The so-called 'Asian tigers', from Japan, South Korea, Taiwan, Singapore, Malaysia, Thailand and Indonesia, whose economic success was much admired by the West in the 1970s and 1980s, were characterized by 'strong government', varying from controlled democracy to military dictatorship.

John Gittings, who reported from China for *The Guardian* for many years, described the agitation caused by the relationship between Chinese culture and the new free market economy when the first Starbucks arrived in

Beijing.[2] He spoke to Professor Ye Lang of Beijing University, who said: 'Huge quantities of culture from the developed world have been dumped on the developing world, with unpredictable negative impact.'

'Not everything will be commercialized', a Ministry of Culture official, Jin Jiwei, told the *People's Daily*, but the focus will be on 'culture-related products for the domestic and overseas market.' The policy has been approved by the Communist Party, and written into China's five-year plan. Chinese culture experts argue that their country must compete with the West at its own game.

Chen Sihe, of Fudan University in Shanghai, believes that 'China must compete in the international market, producing its own cultural products with Chinese characteristics.'

Art and the market

The Culture Ministry has set up more than 300 'cultural agencies' in the main cities to market domestic art and culture. The companies operate in a new environment in which politics no longer always comes first.

Wu Tonggwu of the Shanghai Performance Company says: 'Our audiences are growing all the time: this is a fruit of economic reforms.' While foreign 'classical' cultural ensembles – the New York Philharmonic and Kirov Ballet – have been welcomed in Shanghai, the Shanghai Art Biennale adopts a different approach. 'Here the artists don't have to cater to Westernized taste', the museum director said at the opening of the exhibition. 'They can display their latest works of their own will.'

In reality, most of the artists have moved away from the Chinese tradition and explore dimensions of pop, installation, and performance art which clearly reflect Western influence.

Shanghai is a long way ahead of Beijing, where the Ministry of Culture continues to stress the necessity of 'resisting those [cultural influences] which are unsuitable to Chinese conditions.' But as art and antiquities become ever bigger business, the balance is likely to tip further towards the market. More than 27,000 'culture-related business organizations' have already been set up, according to the Culture Ministry's statistics. The culture industry employs 1.2 million people and its total annual turnover last year was estimated at 80 billion Yuan ($10 billion). The Ministry says the potential market is more than seven times that size.

Capitalism as pure spirit

Naomi Klein, in *No Logo*, has analyzed with passionate clarity what we may call in the West the etherialization of capitalism: that is to say, the process of dismantling the sites of manufacture, where objects and articles of daily utility were produced. The vacuum has been filled with branding, the proliferation of signs and symbols of transnational companies, which take on a magical, semi-religious aura, and which expand to fill all public space. Behind this process of replacing products with brands, what Klein calls 'a marketing renaissance' took place, 'led by a new breed of companies that saw themselves as 'meaning brokers' instead of product producers... Branding, in its truest and most advanced incarnations, is about corporate transcendence.'

Behind this process of capitalism projecting itself as pure spirit, lies a more material reality – casualization of labor, the reduction of work to short-term contractual, part-time and unprotected jobs, which are also mobile and temporary, capable of a limitless migration to the places where the cheapest labor is to be found. The transcendent

Capitalism is, at the same time, oddly dematerialized and made tangible

iconography of the objects of global desire floats across the world, both vision and aspiration, not merely for the rich, but equally, and even more potently, for the poor, except possibly, for those at the end of concealed chains of sub-contracting, who actually manufacture the goods in the infernal sweatshops of Jakarta or Manila, Nairobi or Mexico.

Capitalism is, at the same time, oddly dematerialized and made tangible: the objects exist, framed in the marble and glass settings of shopping malls, but also exuding the mysterious aura of the brand which seeps into the imagination of people everywhere, become part of the air breathed by a new generation. Paradoxically, at the same time impalpable and conspicuous, this is the very materialization of ideology. As this is spread globally, it creates resistance, both among the disaffected of the rich world, and the victims of exploitation and impoverishment in the South. But equally, it inspires revulsion in people embedded in traditional cultures and sensibilities, who feel themselves under attack, but have no apparent way of striking back at either the objects them-selves, nor of the underpinning ideology which affronts their deepest sense of self.

It is not by chance that terrorism has been the most dramatic reaction of those who feel themselves beleaguered, their culture under attack, their values overtaken by immensely powerful influences from elsewhere. Indeed, the attack on the World Trade Center of 11 September 2001 was a shocking attempt to bring back into the realm of the material something which has been felt by many to be insidious, unspoken yet inescapable – the bid to take over the hearts and souls of the peoples of other cultures.

The events of 11 September represented a materialization of what had, until then, been seen largely as a cultural struggle: its irruption into the heart-land of the US transformed it into something far more grim and implacable.

The social consequences

It is not possible to import the positive sides of globalization and keep out the negative ones. The global market comes with its own social and cultural package. You cannot have the goods without the evils it also engenders. We are on a journey to the heart of an industrialization without end, and have no choice but continue the one-way voyage into the somber interior of globalism, no matter how unsafe and cruel a place it may prove to be.

This, then, is the shining culture of market freedoms, which its beneficiaries wish to bestow upon the whole world. Here is the way of life that accompanies an economic restructuring of the psyche and the heart. Notes Murray Bookchin:

'We are all anonymous buyers and sellers these days, even of the miseries that afflict us. We not only buy and sell our labor power in all its subtle forms, we buy and sell our own neuroses, anomie, loneliness, spiritual emptiness, integrity, lack of self-worth and emotions, such as they are, to gurus, specialists in mental and physical "well-being", psychoanalysts, clerics in all garbs, and ultimately, to the armies of corporate and governmental bureaucrats who have finally become the authentic sinews of what we euphemistically call "society".'

Unhappily, this restructuring carries with it consequences which are still appearing in the world; many of them far removed from the state of emancipation which its defenders have suggested it offers.

If global market culture has detached itself from any sense of place, this is only so that it may expand to fill the known universe. It becomes truly cosmos, just as the limited physical spaces of the Bushmen, the Zuni or the pygmies marked, for them, the limits of the knowable. In this sense, global market culture sharply differentiates itself from, yet remains identical with, the most so-called 'primitive' cultures.

Let us make a comparison. To the Zuni, in the arid land of New Mexico, 'fertility is above all else the blessing within the bestowal of the gods, and in the desert country of the Zuni plateau, rain is the prime requisite for the growth of crops. The retreats of the priests, the dances of the masked gods, even many of the activities of the medicine societies are judged by whether or not there has been rain. To 'bless with water' is the synonym of all blessing... The dead, too, come back in the rain-clouds, bringing the universal blessing. People say to the children when the summer afternoon rain clouds come up in the sky, 'Your grandfathers are coming', and the reference is not to individual dead relatives, but applies impersonally to all forbears. The masked gods are also the rain and when they dance they constrain their own being – rain – to descend upon the people'.[3]

Money matters

In market culture, the unique source of all blessing is money. This is why the process of 'wealth-creation' has been made sacred. Awe and reverence for extravagant sums of money are the closest we come to worship: six-figure salaries, multi-million dollar mansions, the billions spent on investment – these are the facts that silence us into wonder. But to ensure the continuity of the perpetual harvest of money, certain propitiatory rituals are necessary: no one must interfere with its workings, nor look too closely at how it functions. Above all, the State must stand back and permit individuals to follow their individual self-interest; and in this way, the 'hidden hand' will ensure the benefit of all. It is given to certain charismatic individuals, go-getters and entrepreneurs – to show the way; and they are known by the fruits of their spectacular endeavors. The wealth created in this way is of a highly particular kind: it is purely monetary. There is no consideration of all the other multiple forms of wealth that have been known to the world – the wealth of experience, the wealth of detail in a work of art, the natural wealth of the earth. All these must be melted down into its supreme manifestation, which becomes the equivalent of a kind of materialized divine grace, and distributed with the same random relationship to observable human worth or 'merit'.

> **In market culture, the unique source of all blessing is money**

This form of human culture is not an entity or a thing; nor is it static. It is itself evolving, in the process of becoming, and it unfolds according to the society with which it interacts. But its contours are unmistakable, as indeed, they have been ever since the early industrial era. Many people in the South today lament the way in which the market economy has usurped traditional ways of answering need, and with it, the festivals, ceremonies and practices which went with it. Even education is no exception.

Tragic invasions

One of the most tragic invasions by the global market of a self-reliant culture was chronicled by Helena Norberg-Hodge in Ladakh in Jammu and Kashmir, North India. She states: 'For generation after generation, Ladakhis grew up learning how to provide themselves with clothing and shelter; how to make shoes out of yak skin and robes from the wool of sheep; how to build houses out of mud and stone. Education was location-specific and nurtured an intimate relationship with the living world. None of that knowledge is provided in the modern school. School is a place to forget traditional skills, and worse, to look down on them.'[4]

Vandana Shiva records the long-term effects of this same process of enclosure and undermining of self-reliance, the removal of the people's capacity for self-provisioning; only she is looking at its outcome in the rural areas of India and Africa – some of the last places on earth to have been reached by the spread of the universal market, with its eagerness to transform everything into goods and services to be traded, rather than consumed by the grower and her dependants. She says: 'Traditional economies with a stable ecology have shared with industrially advanced affluent economies the ability to use natural resources to satisfy basic vital needs. The former differ from the latter in two essential ways: first, the same needs are satisfied in industrial societies through longer technological chains requiring higher energy and resource inputs and excluding large numbers without purchasing power; and second, affluence generates new and artificial needs requiring the increased production of industrial goods and services. Traditional economies are not advanced in the matter of non-vital needs satisfaction, but as far as the satisfaction of basic and vital needs is concerned, they are often what Marshall Sahlins has called "the original affluent society" The needs of the Amazonian tribes are more than satisfied by the rich rainforest; their poverty begins with its destruction. The story is the same for the Gonds of Bastar in India or the Penans of Sarawak in Malaysia.'[5]

The descriptions of Helena Norberg-Hodge or Vandana Shiva about the ruin of ancient sustainable cultures have direct echoes of what British writers and observers were saying in the 1820s. In his *Rural Rides*, British social commentator William Cobbett complained of how fairs and local markets were being replaced by shops, which he detested. 'Does not every one see, in a minute, how this exchanging of fairs and markets for shops created *idlers and traffickers*; creates those locusts, called middlemen, who create nothing, who add to the value of nothing, who improve nothing, but who live in idleness, and live well, too, out of the labor of the producer and the consumer.

Industrial society is not the first to have created wide-spread prosperity

The fair and the market, those wise institutions of our forefathers, and with regard to the management of which they were so scrupulously careful; the fair and the market bring the producer and the consumer in contact with each other.'

Cultures of plenty

Industrial society is not the first in human history to have created widespread prosperity. Of course, no pre-industrial society could match the factory system in the production of material goods. But many societies which remained within the bounds of their own resources were able to create, not only enough, but also an overabundance, which some of them squandered in ways that anticipate the prodigality of our own society.

The Northwest Pacific coast of the US was the home of a number of cultures which became extinguished in the latter half of the 19th century. Only that of Kwakiutl around Vancouver Island remained into the 20th century.

Ruth Benedict described them as people 'whose civilization was built upon an ample supply of goods, inexhaustible, and obtained without excessive expenditure of labor.'

The culture evoked by its dying remnants is like an idealized version of the 'innocence' which people in complex industrial societies have often sought – sometimes falsely – among simpler cultures. Benedict writes: 'The fish, upon which they depended for food, could be taken out of the sea in great hauls. Salmon, cod, halibut, seal and candlefish were dried for storage or tried out for oil. Stranded whales were always utilized, and the more southern tribes went whaling as well. Their life would have been impossible without the sea. The mountains abutted sharply upon their shore territory; they built upon the beaches…The sea life that haunts this region is proverbial. It is still the great spawning ground of the world, and the tribes of the Northwest Coast knew the calendar of the fish runs as other people have known the habits of bears or the season for putting seed in the earth.'

Benedict describes the culture as 'Dionysian'. In their religious rituals they sought ecstasy. Some dancers had to be tied down so they should not harm themselves in their trances. They sang of 'the gift of the spirit that destroys man's reason.'

One of the most significant aspects of the culture was that it enjoyed access to far more than anyone needed, and enshrined this superfluity, both in material things, but equally, in immaterial possessions, names, myths, songs and privileges which were the great boast of a man of wealth. 'Manipulation of wealth in this culture had gone far beyond any realistic transcription of economic needs and the filling of those needs. It involved ideas of capital, of interest, and of conspicuous waste. Wealth had become not merely economic goods, even goods put away in boxes for potlatches and never used except in exchange, but even more characteristically, prerogatives with no economic functions.' She continues: 'The manipulation of wealth on the Northwest Coast is clearly enough in many ways a parody of our own economic arrangements.'[6]

Needs and the market

The important issue here is not that industrial society 'generates new and artificial needs', so much as that it actually fails to answer some of the very basic needs of its people. It is this, rather than the artificial needs, that sets them on the long journey through an intensifying industrialism, seeking the answer to needs which simply cannot be answered in this way. Chilean economist Manfred Max-Neef recognized this, when he stated that the mode in which certain needs are answered within industrial society undermines the answering of others.[7]

Industrial society fails to answer some of the basic needs of its people

One of the most basic human urges is to provide for ourselves: industrial society, and the culture that accompanies it, ensures that every need becomes the object of a monetary exchange. The means by which the need is apparently answered, radically falsifies that answer. Unless human beings have the satisfaction of a sense of their own function in producing, creating, making or answering their own and other people's needs, they are being denied a fundamental necessity.

Thirty years ago, Ivan Illich identified this development. In *Tools for Conviviality*, he wrote: 'People have a native capacity for healing, consoling,

Increasing poverty

In 59 countries the situation of the poor has got worse, not better, during the 1990s

- Income poverty: high poverty rates increased in 37 of 67 countries with data
- Hunger: in 19 countries more than one person in four is going hungry, and the situation is failing to improve or getting worse. In 21 countries the hunger rate has increased
- Survival: in 14 countries under-five mortality rates increased and in 7 countries almost one in four children will not see their fifth birthday
- Water: in 9 countries more than one person in four does not have access to safe water, and the situation is failing to improve or getting worse
- Sanitation: in 15 countries more than one person in four does not have access to adequate sanitation and the situation is failing to improve or getting worse.

Source: *Human Development Report 2003*, UNDP

moving, learning, building their houses and burying their dead. Each of these capacities meets a need. The means for the satisfaction of these needs are abundant so long as they depend primarily on what people can do for themselves, with only marginal dependency on commodities.'

Critics of advanced industrialism say that where everything has to be paid for, bought in, both in response to material as well as cultural needs, this sets up strange pathologies, which are much harder to trace to their source than they are in societies of obvious insufficiency.

Global market culture, then, is a *process*. It encroaches at a variable pace upon older cultural formations; sometimes all but overwhelming them, sometimes inching slyly into the heart and imagination of the people. An example of the former might be the Gulf States, where dependency of a whole world upon oil brought a sudden flood of cash.

Dubai, for instance, has become a kind of technological mirage, rising out of the desert, capable of buying in everything to create a breathtaking human-made variety of goods and services. Indeed, Dubai airport has some of the most sought-after shopping facilities in the world; and the country has successfully marketed itself as a holiday destination for those looking for inspiration and stimulus in the spending of their money. The Saudi novelist Abdelrahman Munif described such places as: 'cities that offer no sustainable existence. When the waters come in, the first waves will dissolve the salt and reduce these great glass cities to dust.'[8]

This has not effaced the culture of the Gulf, but it has conspicuously overlaid it. The impact on the elites of such countries is twofold: most remain untroubled, and are content to accommodate the excesses of consumerism within a flexible form of traditional culture. Others find it an affront to the religious roots of culture, and they react violently.

The rickety shelter of poverty

Some cultures have been 'protected' from the colonizing thrust of market culture by their own poverty. A 'buy-in' culture is an impossibility for those with little or no money at their disposal. To some degree, this has been the case of poor rural societies in Africa and parts of Asia.

There are two major consequences of poverty. It both diminishes human life and also protects cultures from an invasive colonizing influence dependent on money. There is a powerful distinction in the contemporary world between global culture on the one hand, with its intensive market penetration, and cultures that derive from non-cash or limited-cash economies.

Traditional societies have been made poor by the violent disturbance caused by alien values, and by the erosion of their resources by the extractive project of imperialism. Perhaps it would be more accurate to say that what such societies had regarded as sufficiency came to appear inadequate in the blinding light of the global market. These external influences throw into disarray the cosmology of cultures, and equally, their means of answering their own needs from within their own resources, both material and human. They then cross a threshold into a 'poverty' that has been artificially created by others, and replaced their own abundance with penury and want.

Poverty certainly prevents people from participating in the global market, in the sense that they cannot afford to do so; but at a deeper level, their former sufficiency and traditional survival-mechanisms in lean times represented an independent self-reliance, which was first degraded, and then turned into the poverty of present-day Ethiopia, Honduras or Tanzania.

The impact of globalization is twofold: it attacks the cultural forms of the areas it invades, but more significantly, it also replaces the know-how people have developed to cope with their environment with a shining imagery of luxury. The assault is both external – on livelihood and survival in a particular environment – and internal – upon the social and spiritual purposes of other cultures.

1 Murray Bookchin *The Modern Crisis* Black Rose Books, Montreal, Canada, 1987.
2 John Gittings, 'New cultural revolution divides China', *The Guardian*, 6 December 2000. **3** Ruth Benedict, *Patterns of Culture*, Mentor Books 1951. **4** Helena Norberg-Hodge, *Ancient Futures: learning from Ladakh*, Sierra Club Books 1991. **5** Vandana Shiva, *Staying Alive*, Zed Books, 1988. **6** Ruth Benedict, *Patterns of Culture*, Mentor Books 1951. **7** Manfred Max-Neef *From the Outside Looking in: Experiences in Barefoot Economics*, Dag Hammarskjöld Foundation 1981. **8** Cited in Tariq Ali, *The Clash of Fundamentalisms*, Verso 2002.

4 When worlds collide

'Economic modernization and social change throughout the world are separating people from longstanding local identities...The great divisions among humankind and the dominating source of conflict will be cultural.'

Samuel Huntington[1]

The fact that virtually every country in the world now follows the orthodoxies of neo-liberalism suggests that the establishment of the global market and its ideology should be fairly effortless. Since the modern world promises wealth without end to societies haunted by poverty from time out of memory, there should be little problem for them to set aside customs and traditions which stand in the way of the creation of wealth.

In practice, it isn't quite so simple. Even when governments accept the economic principles by which, it is claimed, their countries will grow rich, old habits and practices prove more tenacious. It turns out that 'economic modernization' comes with some powerful conditionalities attached, and these strike at the base of ancient ways of life. Of course, some cultures that have been eroded by the long war of attrition of colonialism, or which were long ago conquered, yield more readily; but others develop strategies of resistance. But although cultures may not always give way without a struggle to the culture of globalism, neither do they remain intact.

All cultures are inflected by the global market, and all are inflected in the same way, although the rate and intensity of that process may vary. Broadly speaking, those elements of culture which can be turned into a commodity, service or experience that can be marketed, will move quickly in this direction. A spectacular example of this is the way that local musical traditions are taken up globally – a group from Senegal, a ceremonial dance from central Africa, a drama from Bangladesh, a singer from Morocco. Some of these will be incorporated into the reper-toire of global culture, moving from one capital city to another, from one continent to another. These will develop a following, which ensures their survival in the intensely competitive context of global entertainment. Of course, these cultural phenomena will

Elements of traditional cultures which find no place in the wider world simply lapse

have been taken out of their context – so that songs of harvest, laments of grief over lost land or fallen heroes, the celebration of initiation ceremonies, fall into oblivion. They become items of cultural consumption.

Those elements of traditional cultures which find no place in the wider world simply lapse. While certain artifacts may enjoy a fashionable moment in the rich world, particularly when these are brought back by tourists – bamboo furniture, fabrics, wallhangings, carpets, lamps, metal goods – they may lose their luster; and some of the more modest artifacts which adorned daily life in forest or farm have no appeal outside – wooden birdcages, perhaps, bamboo flutes, body ornaments fashioned out of seashells or stones without value – will occupy a declining local market; while many locally produced goods in daily use will be displaced by industrially made objects. Elegant objects of bamboo, wood and reeds give way to plastic buckets and bowls; plates made of leaves are ousted by metal, *neem* twigs used for tooth cleaning are displaced by Colgate, traditional soapberries yield to Lux, the fruits of the jungle are supplanted by the exotic confectionery of Cadbury or Hershey. The example of the work of Nestlé in the South is emblematic of the shocking potency of the market and its ability to penetrate the most intimate cultural practices; if it can replace mother's milk with industrialized formulae, what will remain proof against its invasive power?

Cecilia, a young Kenyan asylum seeker in Britain, notes how her home country has moved from being influenced by Britain to being 'Americanized'. 'It didn't feel too strange coming to Britain at first because there is so much British influence in Kenya. It is the language of education, of the law and the courts, even of business. For example, if people want to be accountants their papers are sent back to England for examination.

'But now American influence is coming – everything is becoming American. The shops are full of American stuff, the music is American R & B. We have American clothes, American entertainment and TV. We have a few British programmes – *Men Behaving Badly* and *Mr Bean* – but otherwise it is all American.

'Especially in Nairobi people can no longer speak their mother tongue but only English. This means that you are never sure who you really are, where you are from, the bottom line is this gives you your identity. A friend of mine recently quoted something to me in Swahili and then was shocked when I did not understand him – I speak Swahili, but this was a saying that I didn't under-stand and he said: "What are you going to teach your children?" I don't know what will happen with the next generation in Kenya... They may not know their own culture.'[2]

Violent assault

Cultures which still depend directly upon their resource base – forestpeople, fishing communities, nomads, subsistence farmers, *jhum* or swidden (slash-and -burn and shifting) cultivators – are under the most violent assault, since the very environment which has ensured their survival is enclosed by an omnivorous market. The sacred waters, earth and trees are transformed into industrial raw materials; and with the felling of each cluster of trees, a whole cosmos crashes into extinction. 'Land is our life and blood – without our forest we cannot survive,' says a Penan man from Sarawak in Malaysia.

Indian ecologist Vandana Shiva has analyzed the particular violence of this. In *Staying Alive*, she describes how 'economic development' strikes a radical blow at ancient conserving societies, particularly through the industrialization of agriculture. 'The very meaning of agriculture was transformed with the introduction of the Western Green Revolution paradigm… The shift from thinking in the context of nature's economy, to thinking exclusively in the context of the market economy, created the specificity of hybrid seeds, chemical fertilizers and pesticides, mechanization and large-scale irrigation. These technologies were responses to the need for maximizing profits from agriculture. They were aimed neither at protecting the soil and maintaining its fertility, nor at making food available to all as a basic human right or providing livelihoods in food production.'

It is not just indigenous cultures that are under attack. When the market economy was imposed as 'shock treatment', notably in the former Soviet Union and the countries emerging from its shadow, this was accompanied by a powerful punitive element. Those who had recanted the long and troubling heresy of Socialism were not to be allowed to escape scot-free. Socialism was heretical, because it suggested that industrial society might serve another purpose than private profit; it didn't question the industrial paradigm itself. The cultural impact of corruption, banditry, crime, alcoholism and despair, the loss of security, the devaluing of pensions and destruction of livelihood that went with the imposition of a florid and lawless version of capitalism – globalization – not merely as medicine, but as retribution.

The ruthlessness with which the old belief-system of socialism was dismantled had powerful echoes of earlier colonial violence against traditional cultures – the wiping out of 'barbaric' practices, the destruction of belief- and knowledge-systems labeled superstitious or primitive. Of course, the Soviet Union, unlike older cultures, had not grown organically out of traditional practices, but had been imposed, indeed, artificially created. But however bizarre and aberrant the ideology of Communism may have been, the rapidity and cruelty of its dissolution tore meaning from the lives of millions. People were evicted, like aboriginals and indigenous peoples from other ruined social systems. Just as the latter were 'liberated', and freed to mourn the passing of their life-ways on reservations, or in city slums, so the Russian people were left to re-enact the destruction of their world with the consolations of drugs and alcohol, which were mysteriously readily available through the conduits of globalization. In the first two years of the new policy in Russia, living standards declined by 50 per cent, the ruble fell to one six-hundredth of its value, inflation reached 2,500 per cent. Life expectancy fell. However impressive subsequent growth, one consequence is that the population of Russia is falling fast, is ageing, and the birth-rate has fallen far below what is required even to maintain the existing population.

Globalization, not merely as medicine, but as retribution

The death of socialism in Ethiopia

I was in Addis Ababa when the Mengistu regime was disintegrating in 1990. Dependent upon the Soviet Union, the government had embarked on a forced 'villagization' programme, which many people had escaped by seeking refuge in the capital city.

Outside the *kebele* (neighborhood) headquarters in one of the most wretched suburbs of Addis, the painted Amharic slogan still says: 'Scientific Socialism is Our Principle'. The secretary sits in a bare, dingy room, a portrait of Colonel Mengistu Haile Mariam above his head. He says: 'Do you have permission to be here?' He reaches for the phone to check with the Interior Ministry, but thinks better of it; a sign that the regime is losing its grip, as Mengistu's angry denunciation of the betrayers of socialism in Europe showed earlier in the year.

War, hunger, environmental degradation, a compulsory villagization programme, and the collapse of the Soviet Union negated all promises of liberation. The portraits of Marx and Lenin have been removed from the ceremonial arches of Africa Avenue, and few slogans remain on the archaically futuristic buildings of central Addis: incongruously, 'Peace, Solidarity and Friendship' still adorns the Hilton Hotel, but behind the monument to the martyrs or the revolution, redundant metal red stars and hammer-and-sickle emblems are falling into rusty decay.

In this *kebele* there are 1,300 huts housing 10,000 people. Stony lanes follow the contours of the hills, flanked by houses of Nile-green corrugated metal or wood-frame houses with mud walls. There are none of the plantains, conifers or eucalyptus that relieve the squalor of other parts of Addis: young girls of about 15 or 16 stand in the mid-afternoon sunshine, offering sex; they wear bright satin dresses and jewellery, gleaming against the shadowy rooms they rent by the hour.

Every part of the road is taken up with people selling something: bronze fowls in wooden cages, cheese wrapped in banana leaves, dried chilies, grain – maize, wheat or the Ethiopian staple *teff* – in sacks labeled: 'World Food Programme' or 'Gift of the Government of Canada'. People must be registered with the *kebele* to get their subsidized rations of *teff* and sugar. Many sell a portion of their ration to entrepreneurs who can market it in areas of shortage. With the money, they invest in some other commodity that will bring an income – vegetables, saffron, pepper or *chat*, the mildly intoxicating leaf chewed by the unemployed at the roadside.

Children as young as six or seven work shining shoes, collecting fares in the shared taxis, selling plastic carrier-bags, chewing gum or Indian incense-sticks. Men hammer pieces of shapeless metal in fume-filled workshops, skillfully working the panel of an abandoned car, an iron bed-frame, into utensils, lamps and tools. One man is cutting barbed wire taken by night from some military installation; another is straightening rusty nails; a shoe-repairer works at an incredibly derelict boot. A man embroiders a shirt with gold thread in an intricate traditional design. Women sell eucalyptus twigs for firewood. (In the early 20th century, Addis was threatened with ruin because of the lack of fuel wood: only the introduction of the exotic eucalyptus saved the city.) The uneven stone of the

An economic and social system on the verge of collapse

streets is shiny, scoured by swirling dust and bare feet. A boy trails the skin of a newly killed goat. Women are making dishes with dry cereal stalks, containers for the traditional *injera* (*teff* pancakes). A rusty tin on a stick indicates a home distillery, where *tela*, made from sorghum, is on sale. Half the two million people of Addis are under 20. Children greet us everywhere, shouting one of three English words: 'foreign', 'father' and 'money'.

My friends, university students, say: 'If socialism had achieved anything, it would have provided security to people like these. The sooner it goes, the better. There is nothing like a dose of socialism for raising people's consciousness, if only to let them know what they don't want.'

Here, an economic and social system on the verge of collapse; a sense of expectation and suppressed excitement at what will follow. That the people are about to be thrown into the tender embrace of globalization has yet to dawn upon them.

Moral and spiritual values

Under the assault of globalism, beliefs and values sometimes harden into dogma. They may become a caricature of themselves. This is especially true of powerful, regionally dominant cultures, especially those based upon a revealed faith or a language which have bequeathed to those that profess or speak them a strong sense of identity.

Economic transformation undermines not only the material survival of cultures, but also people's psychological and spiritual lives. Chandra Muzaffar, writing from Malaysia, states that economic globalization violates many of the most deeply held of human moral and spiritual values. In Asian societies, he maintains, rights cannot be separated from responsibilities, and he sees in the elevation of individual freedom as a cornerstone of globalization a denial of communitarian values which are a vital component of Asian societies: individualism does not remain confined to the limited sphere of economic activity, but corrodes other aspects of custom and tradition.

Economic global-ization violates many deeply held moral and spiritual values

For example, networks of friendship, mutuality and kinship which exist in some Asian countries, are attacked by the agents of the global economy as 'cronyism' and 'nepotism'. These relationships are felt to be an impediment to economic efficiency. That is to say, personal preferences and attachments must not take precedence over the majestic impersonality of market relationships.

In his book *Trust*, Francis Fukuyama writes trust in the system is likely to be more creative and innovative than one in which people stick together because they come from the same village, or they have obligations and duties of kinship. He says: 'The earlier social theorists who saw the strong family as an obstacle to development were not entirely wrong… In the West, many observers believe that family ties had to weaken if economic progress was to occur.'

But what of the resulting isolation of people in the West (where one in three households consists of a single person), the fear of strangers, the elderly people who will not open their door, the fear of crime, the women who dare not go out after dark?

Here is the heart of market culture: sentimental bondings between human beings must be swept away, so that 'pure' capitalism may govern all relationships between people. In south and southeast Asia, homo-affective relationships are a powerful cultural reality; forged in youth, they are, in part, a consequence of the *de facto* gender apartheid in Bangladesh, Pakistan and India. These friendships survive into adulthood, and it is regarded as only natural that people should use them to further their own interests. What appears to the outside world as 'cronyism' may be a redeeming of youthful promises, a keeping faith with lifelong friendships; attachments which their Western counterparts have doubt-less outgrown in their more mature appreciation of the necessary scheme of things. (Or perhaps not: the relationships between members of the Bush administration and the oil and power industries in the US, the allocation of contracts for the reconstruction of Iraq, suggests something other than the stainless economic relationships preached to a wider world.)

In Japan, some commentators have argued that its prolonged economic recession is a consequence of the Japanese being 'too Japanese.' The *Washington Post*[3] suggests that those traits for which Japan was so admired in the creation of its economic miracle after the Second World War – discipline, order and conformism – are no longer what Japan needs. A commission set up by a former Prime Minister of Japan to look at what Japan should do if it is successfully to face the 21st century, recommended that Japan should become more like America. The Japanese should become more tolerant of originality, less preoccupied with regimentation. They should adopt English as a second language, increase immigration and give more freedom to students to follow 'fun' subjects. This will release the creativity and vitality of people, and promote greater individualism.

Tadashi Yamamoto, director of the commission, said that the starting point was that: 'Something is basically wrong with society... We are really advocating a fundamental reorientation of society.'

When Japan was compelled to 'open up' by the US in the 19th century, and to 'reconstruct' after the Second World War, a spirit of collective endeavor was necessary. Now, says Tadashi Yamamoto, 'the 21st century will be the era of individuals. Individuals have become more important through globalization, the internet, networking.' He rejects the idea that these are 'American' values.

A significant response to this assault on cultural identity has been fundamentalism

He denies that dynamism is 'an American monopoly', and then adds, more obscurely, that 'democracy is a universal value.'

But not everyone would agree. Another significant response to this fundamental assault on cultural identity has been, unsurprisingly, fundamentalism – Islamic, Hindu, and indeed, Christian. Many Islamic countries prohibit dealings in commodities which the West regards as normal objects of commerce – alcohol, cosmetics, sex tourism. The profoundest elements of many religious teachings counsel restraint, self-control and modest use of resources – all of which run counter to the Western economic paradigm. Not only are religious fundamentalisms a response to Western economic fundamentalism, but they also replicate its economic intolerance in the arena of belief and society. The totalizing thrust of Western economic culture is quite clear.

The plurality of cultures

The proponents of globalization regard cultural obstacles to its further expansion as relatively minor impediments on the road to the universal rule of the market. The persistence of inconvenient cultural traits is nothing more than an irritant, so confident are they of sweeping all before them. In any case, they say, the criticism that globalization curtails local autonomy or undermines self-reliance is mistaken: cultures absorb and mediate market economics after their own fashion. Even after the most far-reaching of economic reforms, cultural continuity is not impaired. There is no leveling 'market culture', with its reductive convergences. When the market interacts with so many faiths, languages and traditions, it does not wipe these out. Do people stop speaking Wollo or Telugu? Do they cease their observances of Islam or stop being Hindu? Of course not. Tariq Ali points out that 'the world of Islam has not been monolithic for over a thousand years. The social and cultural differences between Senegalese, Chinese, Indonesian, Arab and Asian Muslims are far greater than the similarities they share with non-Muslim members of the same nationality.'[4]

The defenders of economic development cite the resilience of major religions and belief-systems. Samuel Huntington in his *Clash of Civilizations* cited eight, including the Western, Confucian, Islamic, Japanese, Hindu, Slav-Orthodox, Latin American and 'African.' There are some curious anomalies in his list – notably that Western civilization is not denominated by its religious underpinning, and that Africa is included as representing a single culture; and significantly, socialism has no place as a global culture, while the newly emerging internationalism of the anti-globalization movement is perhaps still considered to be not yet sufficiently developed to be called a 'civilization'.

Changing from within

In any case, all of those described by Huntington have one thing in common with that of the West: each dominates, or seeks to prevail in its own particular area of the world. In this way, we have to consider that globalization does not refer only to the spread of a single Western culture, but also that as a consequence, large-scale cultures (or civilizations) mimic it, in imposing themselves upon their own neighbors, while at the same time being changed by the dominant culture itself. This clearly does not mean that people stop speaking their mother-tongue or change their religion (although both these things are occurring on a wide scale). But it may suggest that cultures change from within.

Societies continue practices that no longer correspond to their original function

It is common for societies to continue practices and observances that no longer correspond to their original function. Outer forms of worship, for instance, may be prolonged, even when faith in the gods is failing. Or, to take a precise contemporary example, the British system of honors continues to offer orders and companions of the 'British Empire', long after that entity was formally dissolved. One of the most disturbing aspects of the effects of globalization on culture is that it can leave appearances intact, while damaging or altering the substance at its core.

Ancient celebrations may become highly commercial (is Christmas a religious festival or an economic ritual?); a Javanese village may be re-created as a photo-opportunity for tourists; an African song of harvest may become an item of consumption in the rich world.

New pathologies

Indeed, the fact that certain defenders of cultures sometimes have recourse to violence – self-immolation, terrorism or apparently wanton destruction, in the name of their values, says as much about the perceived threat to those values as to the intensity of the desire to protect them against the forces of disintegration and loss. Examples are at hand all over the world. During the failed talks at the World Trade Organization in Cancún in September 2003, a Korean farmer killed himself in protest against trade rules that had irreparably damaged the culture of poor farmers, not only in his own country, but all over the South. Kyung-hai Lee was a 56-year-old dairy farmer who lost his land in the early 1990s, when cheap imported milk began pouring into the country. He had planned to take his life in Cancún, as a statement about the plight of poor farmers.

His action became a symbolic martyrdom for millions of farmers around the world, whose livelihood and way of life is being undermined by a flood of cheap (sometimes heavily subsidized) imports from the US and Europe. Poor farmers suffer not only from loss of income, but also from the decline of the culture which sustained agricultural life.

There have been hundreds of reported suicides of farmers in India during the past decade. A significant proportion of these were in Karnataka, close to the high-tech capital of Bangalore – the most brutal contrast between what is promoted as the culture of deliverance and the reality of life for the 70 per cent of the Indian population dependent upon agriculture. The farmers who died were those who, abandoning subsistence, had taken up the growing of commercial crops – such as cotton – which require expensive inputs – seeds, fertilizers and pesticides. Since they had no access to formal credit, they borrowed from moneylenders, many of whom are also traders and suppliers of the inputs. The money was advanced on the promise of profits that would enable the farmer to back the loan and the interest, buy in enough food for the family and leave more for other expenses.

This is how people are lured out of self-reliance. When an unforeseen pest wipes out the crop, not only is the farmer resourceless, but the debt and the interest accumulate, so that she or he will never be able to pay off what is owed. Local traders push chemical pesticides, and in some cases, sell those which are ineffective against the pests that attack the particular crop. It is a savage irony that many of the farmers who have killed themselves have done so by consuming the very pesticides which failed to protect their crop.

These deaths figure only as a few lines in the press. Yet they are not isolated individual cases. They are the outcrop of a more widespread and insidious re-arrangement of social and cultural practice. While people absorb and internal-ize the damage to their way of life, it produces no scandal, no sustained outcry. These farmers are the lamentable sacrifices to progress, unfortunates who chose the wrong crop, or were at the mercy of the vagaries of climate. Against whom would they make their protest, from the arid, rocky places in Andhra Pradesh or Karnataka, what do they know of transnational companies that send out their sales personnel all over the world, seducing old subsistence ways of life with a promise of riches? As long as the consequences of this can be contained by self-immolation, the systemic origins of the sickness can be concealed. It is only when, in anger and grief, people strike out, however randomly, however destructively, at the perceived agents of loss, that the world takes notice. Then it is called extremism, or worse, terrorism; and the fact that it is reactive must at all costs be buried in the moralizing rhetoric of an amoral system.

This violence which saturates rural life all over the planet is driving people out of familiar environments, forcing them into urban areas, where over-crowding, squalor, drugs and crime set up new pathologies, strange new cultures of poverty and privation.

The malignancies of tradition
The critique of market culture does not imply that traditional cultures are superior: it is simply that globalization threatens to extinguish much that is

essential to human survival, especially precious lessons in conservation and sustainability. Older cultures also contained much that was damaging to some of their members. Indeed, contact with the new global culture does not automatically erase these malignant practices; sometimes, it can even exacerbate them. For instance, the dowry system in India has been much influenced by consumer culture; with the result that the families of many women are under pressure to provide an extravagant array of goods and money to the family of the groom.

Globalization threatens to extinguish much that is essential to human survival

To defend the right of people to live in accordance with their traditions is one thing; when these involve violence, mutilation and injustice, especially to women, it is impossible to acknowledge that such practices, even if they are an ancient and inseparable element of culture, should continue unscathed in the contemporary world.

One such example is that of so-called 'honor killings', which have been widely reported from rural, conservative parts of Turkey, including Kurdish areas. Such killings are also reported every year from Pakistan, Bangladesh, Egypt and Jordan.

It is estimated that there are about 200 'honor killings' in Turkey each year, some of them of girls as young as 12. Mehmet Farc, author of *Women in the Grip of Tribal Customs*, says: 'It's very important because all the signs are that honor killings are on the rise in Turkey. This is a problem that stems from a lack of education, a clash of lifestyles, poverty and very old mindsets.'

The source of these murders lies in the infringement of the 'modesty' of a woman. This reflects, in part, the idea that a woman's identity depends, for its fulfillment, on the man she marries, and the dowry she can bring with her. Any hint or rumor of immodesty casts a shadow over the family, and pressure is upon them to punish, and in extreme cases, to do away with her. Even if the young woman is molested or raped, she must die: the 'stain' is indelible. Murder then becomes an act of virtue and cleansing.

Such killings also occur in the West, where young women are torn between the world of school and college and the very different and more circumscribed world of the family. Indeed, the preservation of 'honor' may lead to an increase in violence as one world seeks to preserve itself from another. Such clashes illustrate clearly the difficulty of blending the best of the old with the best of the new. When worlds collide there is an intensification of tradition which can often be malignant rather than benign. And it is not as though the modern world has eliminated these elements from its own culture, as the incidence of violence against women shows – in Britain two women a week are killed by their partners; in the US a woman is beaten every 18 minutes and in Russia one woman in five is regularly beaten by her partner.

1 Samuel Huntington, *The Clash of Civilizations and the Remaking of World Order*, Simon and Schuster, 1996. **2** From interview with Nikki van der Gaag for *Our Clothes, our City*, Sunday Times Oxford Literary Festival 2004. **3** Doug Struck, 21 January 2000. **4** Tariq Ali, *The Clash of Fundamentalisms*, Verso 2002.

5 The haunted labyrinths of the heart

'Men are made of what is made,
The meat, the drink, the life, the corn,
Laid up by them, in them reborn,
And self-begotten cycles close
About our way; indigenous art
And simple spells make unafraid
The haunted labyrinths of the heart.'

Edwin Muir[1]

As a child, I absorbed from my mother and her 10 surviving brothers and sisters an account of the life of their family, scattered across the countryside of Northamptonshire. A central event in this narrative was the suicide of a distant patriarch, who had fathered a child with his own daughter, and then, tormented by remorse, had gone to the highest point in the neighborhood and cut his own throat. This occurred some time in the second half of the 18th century. Although a very public happening, it was transmitted through time as a secret; and the shame surrounding the story ensured that it would continue to be told.

As indeed it was. But this sad tale was not the main purpose of an oral tradition which came down through one family. We were part of a long collective memory which evoked a whole archaic rural culture, dominated by ancient superstitions and customs, signs and portents for human life read in the skies and the countryside, in the flowering of the fields and the behavior of birds and animals; herbal remedies and folk-medicine, and faith in a complex web of belief which fell into disuse during my mother's lifetime, and which is now forgotten beyond recall.

That I felt a keen desire to write all this down showed how distant it seemed to me; it was already memory, and it had no informing purpose in my own life. The tradition embodied in my family was already virtually extinct.

This was symbolized by the family of my grandmother, the eleven children born between 1880 and 1905, and who, in the next generation, managed to produce barely as many between them. This falling away was, in part, a reflection of the spread of birth control, but was also a symptom of a faltering culture. Of this, my generation, one committed suicide, one was severely anorexic (before the condition was named), one was

They used words known to Shakespeare, but lost to the standard tongue

killed in the Second World War, one was raped in a park when she was 13, which ruined her life. Five were childless. In these family histories, it is difficult to extricate the social from the personal; but it seems to me beyond doubt that the loss of faith in their values played a significant part in this dwindling cultural tradition.

They had preserved a raw local culture, another dialect, unique to the isolated market-town which Northampton then was. In their daily speech, they unselfconsciously used words known to Shakespeare and Chaucer, but already lost to the standard tongue. One of the great delights of my adolescence was the discovery of a Northamptonshire Glossary, in two volumes, compiled in the mid-19th century by a country clergyman's wife. I would sit with my mother hour after hour, asking her if she knew the meaning of this or that word, or was familiar with certain expressions; until exasperated, she demanded to know why I showed such a perverse interest in things she had tried to educate me out of.

It is now a familiar story: a local culture of home, limited and constricting, which an aspiring generation seeks to leave behind; only to find that those who come after are avid to re-acquire the heritage apparently squandered by its predecessor.

Ancient paganism and popular Christianity

The family story was enthralling. It encompassed a great network of kinsfolk, spread in time if not in place. Its recall re-affirmed an identity rooted in that locality, an identity which, if narrow, was nevertheless deep, in which daily trivia did not obscure the deeper meaning of existence. This ancient country lore was already far decayed in my mother's childhood; but something of its traces tugged at the memory of her and her sisters. I listened to my aunts as they talked together; some of the subjects of their conversation suggested a lingering faith in ancient beliefs not completely ousted by generations of teachings by their betters.

One day, speaking of the misfortunes of a woman who lived nearby, they wondered whether or not she had been 'ill-wished'. Two of her children had died, her husband was a philanderer and she was afflicted by a nervous tic. Although they didn't believe she was a victim of witchcraft, they reserved judgment. 'You never know'. They spoke of a woman frightened by a goat when she was pregnant whose child had never learned to speak but made bleating sounds. They said of wrongdoers, 'It'll find you out in the end.'

Their speech was a mixture of an ancient paganism and popular Christianity, which co-existed uneasily with a more rational interpretation of the world. They showed how diverse cultural influences persist. Much ancient superstition and belief sank below the surface, but never quite faded, lingering to be brought forth whenever they were faced by some bewildering event – the murder of a child, for instance, or what they saw as sexual malpractice. They didn't entirely disavow anything they had absorbed from their past. They offered instruction in the subterranean tenacity of cultures which are believed to have passed away. Elements of these remain in the consciousness of people and lie there, ready to be called back into life, if and when a time comes favorable for their return.

Shoemakers

Perhaps the particular circumstances of their lives helped to preserve certain traditions. Because of its closeness to the countryside – the fact that it depended upon hides and tree-bark for skins and tanning, the leather industry remained semi-rural. My grandfather had worked from home in his cottage in a village some 12 miles from town. He would walk to Northampton once or twice a week, to collect the 'uppers' and soles from 'shop', which he would stitch into shoes.

The trauma of leaving the countryside remained with my grandparents

When he was in his thirties, the income from this declined, and he migrated with his family to the growing industrial town. The shoe-making industry had remained a semi-domestic occupation until well into the nineteenth century. Cobblers were known to be independent, philosophical, sometimes self-taught intellectuals, who had time to reflect and think at their work. The mass production of shoes occurred later than the industrialization of most other goods; but by the 1890s, few independent shoemakers remained. The trauma of leaving the countryside for the straitened life of factory and street remained with my grandparents for the rest of their lives. He drank heavily, and treated his wife and children harshly. The significance of 'drink' in the working class culture was not simply that it represented the shortest way out of their situation, although there was no doubt truth in that. But alcohol also represented oblivion from profound losses in the abandonment of country life – control over the hours of work, belonging and a recognition of the kinship between human life and that of the natural world, were just a few of them. Although my grandfather was always in work, in the town, where factory wages no longer depended upon skill, but upon the cyclical rise and fall of trade, the family grew and became poorer.

All the children of my grandparents began work in the tanneries and boot and shoe factories of Northampton. The town was not large, and since you could still see, through the red-brick funnel of the streets, the hills and meadows that enclosed it, the courts, squares and alleys felt even more enclosed and claustrophobic. The industry responded, not only to fluctuations in the economy, but equally to the pulse of war and peace. In wartime there was always plenty of work from military contracts, which gave people a prosperity that was slightly shaming, based as it was on conflict and violence. When business was slack, they fell into a grudging and penny-pinching poverty.

A closed world

A new culture grew around the staple industry. This, of course, shared many characteristics with that of other industrial areas – textiles, shipbuilding, hosiery, steel and even pit-villages – but its rural background gave leather-workers a distinctive inflection. The people retained a rough, non-urban accent, and continued to resent the factories, which had transformed formerly semi-independent cobblers into 'operatives'. They were obstinate, taciturn, stingy, suspicious of outsiders. Their view of the world was pessimistic and somber. But they were also incorruptible. Northampton elected Charles Bradlaugh to Parliament in 1880. Freethinker and republican, he refused to take the oath in the House of Commons and his seat was declared vacant. He won three subsequent by-elections, and by 1895, gained the right for Members of Parliament to affirm rather than to take the traditional oath. He earned for the electors of Northampton an undeserved reputation for atheism. In fact, they were merely expressing their own sense of rectitude, their idea of justice, which often struck others as perverse or unnecessarily obstructive. They exhibited a surly egalitarianism, did not defer to the orthodoxies of the age, and scarcely acknowledged the existence of any social superiors.

It was a closed world. The population of the town remained below 100,000 until well into the 20th century; and the community was sufficiently limited for everyone in each of the small industrial suburbs to know one another – perhaps 15,000 families in all, divided into five or six areas. They followed each other's births and deaths through the local paper, observed and noted who had been in court for disturbing the peace, being drunk and disorderly, stealing or breaking and entering, fighting, who was granted a *decree nisi* and for what reason, who had stolen clothes from washing lines or had been arrested for importuning in public lavatories.

This knowledge was stored away in the long deep cavities of social memory. If they met the individuals involved, it would never be mentioned, but everybody knew that lives were transparent, secrets hard to maintain. Perhaps for this reason few tried to pretend to be something they weren't, to put on airs: they hated snobbery.

People ran into one another on the market square every Saturday, among the crude trestles with their piles of home-produced seasonal fruits and vegetables – misshapen apples, sour cherries, pink stalks of rhubarb, blue-green Savoy cabbages, plums covered with the sugary secretion of wasps. They never met by appointment, only by chance, but whenever they saw someone they hadn't seen for weeks, months or years, they stopped to hear first-hand news they were already familiar with from gossip; so that the simple chore of shopping might require half a day to get from on side of the square to the other, taking shelter under the dripping canvas when it rained, and the stories they told each other were interesting enough.

The bush fires of affluence

When I started to maintain a record of these things in the early 1960s, they had a double poignancy: the industrial culture which had overlaid its rural forerunner was itself already close to dissolution. The fabric of the town, the redbrick streets which had grown up around the older sandstone buildings of the center, seemed to us to have been there for ever, although few had been there more than a century.

It was oppressive, the sameness of the streets and the social conformity they seemed to impose. The town appeared as immutable as the censorious sensibility of the people, which was always on the lookout for those who strayed from the pathways of moral propriety, socially extremely conservative, even if still tinged with a fading political radicalism. Growing up in the early 1950s, it looked as though it would go on for ever. This was an illusion.

The bush fires of affluence were sweeping through the old industrial areas

Already the bush-fires of affluence (the forerunner of consumerism) were sweeping through the old industrial areas of Britain, reshaping the people to another destiny than that of a lifetime of labor at factory bench; just as two or three generations earlier, people had been compelled to forsake the rhythms of the countryside and its seasons for the harsher tempo of wage-labor. The customs and values of the rural life that had so powerfully marked my mother's generation had long been buried by an industrial culture which was itself already about to disappear.

In every town and city in the country, the old streets were crashing to extinction in a powder of red dust, and the sour earth which had held the foundations of slums and courtyards was being turned for the first time in over 100 years. Old women stood on the carefully scrubbed doorsteps of their houses, in the pinafores and felt hats they always wore indoors, and looked anxiously as the bulldozers and cranes that appeared over the rooftops, as the material structure of the town was being remade. The men turned over in their scarred hands the compulsory purchase notices that would divest them of the allotments, the small patches of ground where they had grown onions, runner beans, dahlias and the pungent bunches of dusty blackcurrants, where new civic buildings would arise to house functionaries of the welfare state.

New compulsions would shape the next generation. They would be absorbed by the necessities of an intensifying market culture, as it penetrated the old defensive, in-turned working class communities – the very places in which the evictees from a former country life had sought a kind of refuge.

Losing faith

As the industrial towns and cities of Britain were transformed, the testimonies that came out of the mining communities, mill-towns, manufacturing districts and single-industry towns showed a remarkable similarity. It seemed that what we had regarded as the distinctive features of our town were less unique than we had believed. The poverty was the same, the sense of insecurity, the fear of ending their days in the workhouse or the casual ward, the long shadow of unemployment, second-hand clothing, boots perforated with the initials of some charitable concern to prevent them from being sold, the presence of representatives of the Board of Guardians at cinema matinees to see who could afford to go to the pictures when he or she was unemployed, the necessity of selling a last treasure – a wedding ring or a small family heirloom – before people would be entitled to receive any relief. Even their recreations were similar: they took their own food for a week's holiday to Blackpool, with their name written on each egg in indelible pencil so they should not be palmed off with somebody else's stale stuff, the Sunday night in the Park, where the brass band played selections from the *Merry Widow*; the women sat in the Snug on a Saturday night swaying to the tune of the *Barcarole*. The only real distinction was the labor around which each locality had grown. The survival of country lore and the regional accent remained our chief characteristics after the transformation that had turned a wasting peasantry into industrial workers.

I was accused of being romantic, nostalgic, setting my face against progress

However similar the life of our town had been to that of other industrial areas, its breakdown and the loss of the values that had accompanied it created new disturbances in people's lives. There are few experiences more disruptive and traumatic to human beings than to lose faith in the values and beliefs by which they have interpreted the world, and which have given them meaning.

When I tried to express the disorientation and sense of loss (a feeling of grief similar to that chronicled by William Cobbett, who traveled on his 'rural rides' in the England of the 1820s, recording the condition of the agricultural laborers), it was ridiculed. I was accused of being romantic, nostalgic, setting my face against progress, showing myself to be a lover of poverty, and of selfishness, kicking away the ladder which had permitted my own rise in the world. And it proved almost impossible to make the more subtle point that the issue was the decay of a system of belief that led to social dislocation and breakdown; not whether those beliefs might be worthy or without merit, not even whether they might not evolve into something altogether more positive and enhancing. The decay of faith in a sustaining way of life has been the story of the modern world; and few who have lived through that loss can remain unmoved by its passing.

That all this was happening at a time when people were becoming better off than they had ever been did not lessen the confusion and anxiety of generations raised to work and want. Confusion, because what they had wanted above all, both in the earlier rural society, and in the industrial life into which they had been driven, was an assured sufficiency, security and a moment of peace in which to bring up a new generation. The volume and variety of goods which were suddenly brought into the reach of people schooled to frugality and restraint proved overpowering. Who was going to distinguish between the answering of basic needs and a consumerism which appeared to be able to perform this long desired achievement a hundredfold?

The remaking of the psyche

Indeed, the abundance of the mid-century served many purposes other than bringing relief to people who had always labored in penury for a grudging sustenance. First of all, it submerged the pain associated with the breaking of a culture, the remaking of the psyche and sensibility of the people. It also concealed the possibility that other, less tangible, but no less vital human needs might have been by-passed (among them, the need for social purpose and useful function in the world, the need for meaning and for the life of the spirit). Further, consumerism disguised the fact that an economic necessity which had overtaken human need was itself a form of colonization. At the same time, it scarcely seemed possible that there could be any cost involved in these

There might have been more just and more joyful ways out of poverty

improvements other than the cover-price, the knock-down bargain, the rewards, prizes and free gifts that were so conspicuously advertised in the promised new life.

This version of plenty bore only an incidental relationship to what people had striven for, to the effort and pain of the defenses built up over the years by the labor and trade union movements. That this appeared the only pathway out of poverty was not questioned by people who had above all, wanted a way out of the sparing, ungenerous subsistence which had always been their fate. It occurred to few that there might have been more just and more joyful ways out of poverty. People were not disposed to consider whether the full cost might appear only later, that the point of consumption was only the beginning of a long journey into dependency and debt; and that the price to be paid socially – as opposed to economically – might one day become almost unbearable.

The dust set up by the altered environment, the dazzling light let in by the demolition of hated sites of exploitation and overwork, the sound of hammering, beating and re-assembling of the new décor, made us unaware of its true nature. Only now can we begin to take account of the costs of the better world of which we are now the long-term inheritors.

Macabre attendants

It is not that people didn't desperately need relief from poverty. What they didn't ask for was the macabre attendants of that relief – the multiple addictions generated by market-dependency, crime and violence, fear of strangers and estrangement from our familiars, insecurity, the breakdown of old associations of kin and neighborhood. That these brutal things are attributed by the defenders of this version of wealth to human nature has been the facile explanation for the nature of capitalist plenty. Instead of prosperity we got consumerism, instead of security an unquiet dependency on the market, instead of plenty, more shopping facilities, instead of peace, a driven, relentless competitiveness.

This required the sudden discarding of habits of frugality, prudence, making and mending, conserving, creative improvisation, thrift and reliance upon the home-grown and the locally made. All the principles and precepts for living, stored up over generations – sometimes, it is true, under the most unfavorable circumstances – were devalued. The odious conditions of poverty were easily confused with the humane response these had generated.

People had to learn how to want in a new way: a culture of want became a culture of wanting. They were required to discover new kinds of poverty that had nothing to do with insufficiency. The precious lessons in a sparing use of things, and the most careful tending of resources were despised, and replaced by the multiple dissipations and wastings of what proved to be, after all, only a version of affluence.

Spoiled fruit

By the last years of the 20th century, the shape and purpose of the restructuring of the popular sensibility had become clear. Our rural origins have been so far forgotten that we have become estranged from the resource-base that sustains us; and we have become so estranged from the defensive industrial culture that it seems we no longer see the value of collective resistance, solidarity and the recognition of a common predicament.

By mid-October in the suburbanized villages, the ripe plums have exploded on the grass, and wasps weave the invisible skeins of their flight over the decaying fruit. The pears, too, brown and rotted by the rain, return their uneaten flesh to the earth. Apples do not fall so quickly; among the fading leaves, they form red, green and gold globes of light in the late sunshine. Some linger on the branches after the leaves have fallen to ornament the approaching winter. Blackberries have become mildewed, the black beads of elderberries shriveled, while the coarse shells of sweet chestnuts and the squat umbrellas of field mushrooms remain untouched.

This annual wasted harvest of resources goes uncommented. Like the gleaners who followed the cutting of the corn, the hunters of rabbits displaced by reapers, the collection of fruit from gnarled trees and abandoned orchards are archaic activities, not to be taken seriously, like the sour wild damsons, crab-apples and hazelnuts, no longer even noticed, part of the 'scenery' which has become another item of urban consumption.

As fruit rots on the trees, you can buy perfect apples in the super-markets

It is not that such things have been eliminated from our diet. As fruit rots on the trees, you can buy perfect apples in the supermarkets, luscious clusters of blackberries, snow-white mushrooms, yellow pears packed in snug individual nests, outsize plums from Spain.

The forlorn harvests of the British countryside are a metaphor for the market economy: things freely available which do not figure in any economic accounting-system are rejected. The economic system itself sanctifies the commodities it blesses with its pricing system.

It isn't only the modest waste represented by indifference to the natural bounty of free harvests: our human resources, too, must also be turned into products before they are acknowledged. Companies, government bureaucracies now, curiously, have departments of Human Resources, which have nothing to do with the resourcefulness of people. These are a means of processing our abilities, of enclosing the free gifts of our competence and power to look after each other, to bear one another up and give comfort at times of adversity, and transforming them into market-determined pseudo-professions and mock-skills. Gazing passively at a mugging in the street, imagining it to be part of a TV film, not knowing what to do in an emergency, unable to hear the screams through the paper-thin walls, incapable of recognizing the cries for help of the strange and eccentric to monitor the silent deaths in closed flats until the smell of decay prompts a call to the police – the neglect of the human harvests mimics the ungarnered riches of the natural world.

We don't even notice the spoiled fruit – items that were the object of such careful husbanding and conservation, when every autumn fruit was preserved, jam was made, pickles and preserves stored up the nutrients of summer; but are drawn instead to the Christmas displays of wanton and redundant abundance in the shopping malls. And the granaries and storehouses of our human wisdom are left to rats and pests, in the same way that the fruits of the earth are abandoned to the wasps and worms on the overgrown orchard floor.

Long-lost values

The values of a rural past have long been lost; but those of the working class have melted away even more swiftly. Collective resistance, sharing of inadequate resources, the work of being present at the time of birth, comforting the sick, laying out the dead, the daily recognition of a common destiny in a thousand acts of freely given mercy and humanity – all this fell rapidly into decay under the impulse of a combination of institutionalized welfare and individualistic consumption. That these values grew in response to exploitative labor, to the suppression of individual needs, especially of women, to the inability of intelligence to flower and under the rigorous disciplines of a self-policing community, does not make them worthless. It is a story of ways of life to which people stuck and in which they believed. It is a story of the perpetual reshaping of the human material into

> **It is a story, not of progress or development, but of how everything must change**

whatever new form is required for profit. It is a story, not of progress or development, but of how everything must change in order to maintain the one lasting, enduring element in two and a half centuries of industrialization – the maintenance of wealth and power where these are already concentrated.

When I was growing up, I was aware that there was no longer any place for the melancholy but dignified application of my mother's half-peasant heritage. I learned quickly that the working-class life of the streets was not going to be mine, the predetermined pattern of labor and penury. I would never know the journey to work on an old bone-shaker of a bicycle every day for 45 years, the pursed mouths and twisted smiles of the shotgun wedding, the parlor opened only for Christmas and funerals, the regimented tread of boots on the pavement in the early morning, the cold houses where the ice-flowers bloomed overnight on the inside of the windowpanes, the outside lavatory and the wind blowing the sooty smoke back down the chimney, the plain food and modest diversions of cribbage and darts, sour beer and dour philosophy, the miserable conviction that nothing was done without trouble except letting the fire go out, that it would all be worse before it was better, that if you wanted to know how lucky you were, you had to go only as far as the nearest churchyard with its sooty gravestones recording the deaths of children: 'also Eliza, relict of the above…'

Estrangement

We, who were to fulfill our parents' failed hopes of becoming educated, were destined for another fate. Penetrated by a sense of our own worth, we were, without knowing it, the pioneers of meritocracy. Our true value was being recognized by a system which had failed to perceive the sensitivity and intelligence of our forbears, the women filling their aprons with crab apples and their bellies with babies, the men kicking their boots against the flinty pavements and carrying with them the feral smell of leather that pervaded almost every house in the town. We were already being formed for yet another culture, of mysterious limitless horizons, where we might enter the professions and stride bravely down the broad avenues of mobility that had suddenly opened up where the narrow streets and cramped yards of our future once seemed to lie.

My friends and I were estranged from this raw shoemaking culture, with its suspiciousness and distrust, the certainty that everybody's arse hung in the same place, that getting above yourself was the worst of social crimes, that life was a tale of woe and want, and the best you could look forward to was the day when we'd all be put to bed with a bloody shovel.

What exasperation and amusement we felt over the narrowness of their view of the world; my mother's stern declaration that anyone out after nine thirty at night was either thieving or whore-hopping, or that bad luck would ensue if anyone brought may-blossom into the house.

How absurd seemed to us the gloomy serious-ness of their lives

We knew by heart the lore and the repertoire of the stories they told at family gatherings, the young women who had gone into service and had had to forfeit their given name for a more suitable servant-name – Ada or Nellie rather than Charlotte or Maria; the trade union workers dismissed and told they would never work in this town again; the sorrowful partings of relatives to Canada or Australia, and the better life they had sought there, the photographs that came back of smiling sun-weathered faces in settings of bungalows, strange vegetation and sunshine. They also spoke of more solemn things: was it Meant that their mother should fall in the garden that September day and break the thigh that eventually killed her? Had they done what they were Put Here (on earth) to do? They spoke of their pride that they had never owed anybody a halfpenny and could look anyone in the eye, even, blasphemously, in their fierce pride, their Maker, and say they had lived what they called 'clean' lives, which meant they had avoided extra-marital sex, however miserable and unsatisfactory its intra-marital version had been. How absurd seemed to us the gloomy seriousness of their lives. We could not wait to get away from it, into a vast future, which promised us the world. We were eager to embark onto the journey into the heart of what was to become the adventure of globalism.

Fragile cultures and arbitrary certainties

We had no wish to join the stratum of society immediately above us. It required only the most superficial contact with school, and the people who came from detached houses, hydrangeas in front gardens, stained glass in their doors, book-cases in the front rooms, white-collar work and tortured vowels which suggested efforts to distance themselves from the local accent, three-tier cake-stands and doilies on the backs of chairs – to learn that this, too, was no object of desire. Something beyond, leap-frogging, as it were, the ordinary progress of class mobility, beckoned to us from beyond the confines of the known world of the provincial town.

These experiences made it easy to understand how fragile cultures are (but not, at the time, their tenacity), the mutability of values, the provisional nature of social customs and conventions by which people lead their lives and are led by them. How arbitrary it all seemed, the certainties which could be swept away in an instant, the rigid responses and fixed ideas, versions of right and wrong, observances and rituals that proved to be so thin and insubstantial when tested against the superior wisdom of those who, for whatever reason, had become estranged from them.

Estranged, because these values were already dying. We peered into the lives of our loved ones like anthropologists investigating the strange practices of a dying tribe in a remote forest. That is how far we felt we had traveled. But we made a serious mistake. They, too, were changing. If they vehemently expressed their adherence to immutable certainties, this was because they sensed these were in a state of decline, of which our own removal was only a symptom. And indeed, within another generation, the working-class, made, as E P Thompson described,[2] in such pain and struggle against oppression and exploitation, had been un-made, this time effortlessly, under the seductions, not of work and want, but of the freedom and plenty as defined by capital. And their own definitions of need – sustenance, security and a modest sufficiency – were easily drowned by the rising tide of affluence, just as ancient villages are drowned by the dam-waters of some developmental mega-project.

It isn't the values of the culture that matters; only that they are believed in

It was this experience that gave me an unbidden insight into the arbitrary and shifting nature of cultures and the system of faith that underpins them. How easily they could be undermined, replaced by others; yet at the same time, how vital they are to the psychic wellbeing and health of those whose lives they sustain!

It isn't the set of values of the culture that matters; only that they are believed in. What counts is their role in the lives of those they animate. It is very difficult to describe the pain of their passing away, as people move from one culture into another. This is why the arguments about whether the old working-class culture was oppressive to women, exploitative of men, controlling of children – all the value-judgments brought into play to explain why we were entering a better tomorrow – are less important than the function they had served in the lives of people. It now seems that the coming of consumerism was less than the total liberation it was at that time represented to be. It was simply another form of colonization, just as the processes of industrialization had been. Nobody believed that early industrial society was liberating; but few doubted that capitalism's realm of freedom was precisely that. The people were being refashioned once more, and the emancipatory appearances concealed the fact that the changes were determined, not by the modest needs and desires they had formulated in pain and want, but by circumstances that would continue to benefit power and privilege – the only object of true conservation in a wasting and wasteful world.

These insights made it easier to understand what happens to the psychic structures, the inner landscapes of peoples all over the world, whose lives have been transformed by modernization, the better life, progress, the market economy.

A question of degree

The experience of the peoples of the world echoes and parallels that of people in Britain. It is a question of degree: elsewhere the uprooting of ancient cultures is far more intense and brutal. Indigenous peoples everywhere, tribal people (*adivasis*) of India, the forest-dwellers, coastal and riverine communities, subsistence farmers, nomads, slash-and-burn cultivators, have seen their lives broken, first of all by colonial interference in patterns of life that had subsisted for millennia, and later by a globalization in which the universal market makes its superior claim to their lands, wood, water, forest, the minerals that lie beneath the earth they occupy.

When my generation was reacting with scorn, mockery and defiance to the dour culture of the shoemaking community of our home town, we didn't realize that we were released from the compulsions of its labor by the fact that it was on the verge of being dismantled. Even less were we aware that the manufacturing society which had been imposed upon our people with such violence during the early industrial era was being forced upon the same innocents we had once been in other parts of the world, the children tending cattle, the laborers on farms, the women ankle-deep in the water of rice-fields, about to be summoned into the mills and manufactories which had been dismantled and displaced from the industrial West. The same migrations of fear and hope were to take place that had convulsed the social and physical land-scapes of Britain only a century and a half earlier. At the time, who could have foreseen our relationship with them, the connection between the 'liberation' of the people of the West and the new forms of servitude into which tens of millions of peasants all over the world were being summoned!

The story of the extinction of the industrial base of Britain is now familiar; and it occurred in a very short period of time: for the most part, between the early 1960s and late 1980s. It culminated in the coal-miners' strike of the mid-eighties, which was a battle for cultural survival rather than an industrial dispute. It marked a time when the division of labor within Britain, set up at the time of early industrialism, was being dissolved. The association of almost every town and city in the land with a distinctive function made the world intelligible – cutlery in Sheffield, cotton in Bolton and Blackburn, woolens in Leeds, china in Stoke-on-Trent, coal in Yorkshire and South Wales, ships on the Clyde and Tyne, fish in Grimsby and Aberdeen, lace and hosiery in Nottingham, leather in Leicester and Northampton, imported raw materials with the great seaports; while some places served as holiday resorts for workers – Blackpool, Great Yarmouth; while yet other places served a different, more genteel population – Cheltenham or Harrogate receiving the pensioners of empire.

It was not that shoes or curtains or clothing or chairs or cutlery or glass had been eliminated from the lives of the people. This was the beginning of global-ism, as this formerly national division of labor was being redistributed world-wide. In our town, it appeared as the closing down of the boot and shoe facto-ries; first of all, the small-scale companies on the street corner, then, later, the enterprises who, we were told as children, had shod the barefoot of the world, encasing the splayed and scarred feet of the natives of empire in a stout piece of Northampton shoeleather; our local modest contribution to the great civilizing mission of which we were made to feel part. This coincided with the import of footwear, first from Italy and Portugal, later from Taiwan and Brazil; many of these bore the names of manufacturers in whose factories our townspeople had, until recently, labored. Skilled workers picked up pieces of what they regarded as inferior produce and slapped them contemptuously on dusty benches, saying they would not last five minutes compared with the objects they had produced, which outwalked the lifetime of the people who bought them. They didn't understand that this was the point: they were not intended to last. Fashion now had little to do with function, either of the worker or the wearer.

In this way, when I first saw the sweatshops of Mumbai and Dhaka, the garment factories of Bangkok and Jakarta, the slums of Sao Paulo and Manila, full of migrants from a wasting and impoverished hinterland, these did not appear to be the representatives of alien cultures. The child-workers scavenging among the rubbish, the injuries to children in metal workshops and welding-shops; the young girls cutting threads beneath the factory benches of clothing factories, reminded me of the early life of my mother and her sisters, who sat beside the workbenches, cutting the threads and tying knots in the ends of machine-stitched shoes. The little

The sweatshops of Dhaka did not appear to be the representatives of alien cultures

maidservants in the middle-class compounds in Delhi and Dhaka recalled the journeys of my grandmother's sisters more than 100 years earlier, setting off from their village for a place in a London square, a small shared dormitory under the eaves, from which they would rise before dawn, to say their prayers, splash cold water on their faces, empty the grate, prepare breakfast before the family they served began to stir.

What we had known under the drizzle of grey skies and grey smoke above grey slate roofs is repeated, indeed, springs back into vibrant life under the sun of Calcutta and the towering clouds over Manila, as disoriented and uprooted country people depart on epic migrations from familiar paddy-fields and homesteads, from degraded villages and exhausted lands everywhere. This is the meaning of 'globalization' – the universalizing of the experience of the industrial West. We may be distracted by other skies or the color of other skins, other forms of worship and belief. But they

Development bears the promise that the people of the South can 'become like us'

are now passing through the same experiences. And they, too, will, in due course, get supermarkets instead of food security, consumerism in place of prosperity, Coca Cola or Fanta instead of safe drinking water, the precarious life of city slums instead of a safe place to protect and raise their children.

Development is the treacherous word which bears the promise that the people of the South can 'become like us', if only they will follow the pathways indicated by Western financial institutions to perpetual growth and expansion.

To become like us. Anyone who criticized the version of improvement brought to the West in the 1960s and 1970s was accused of being a lover of poverty, a reactionary, determined to keep the good things of life from the people; and under the weight of such accusations, critics were easily silenced. Similarly, today, the defenders of globalization declare that those who speak of controlling the onward march of the market wish to keep the poor of the earth from the benefits of the 21st century.

Under whatever threats the cultures of the world now live, we have been here before. There is no aspect of colonialism visited upon the world that was not tried and tested in the imperial heartlands of Britain, from child labor to the enclosing of common resources, from the discarding of conserving values to the spread of city slums, from the breaking and re-making of cultures, to the most ruthless punishment of dissenters.

We know this, not in theory, not as an academic exercise. It is part of the remembered historical experience. The great caravans of hope that are moving from farm and village to town, from small town to city, from city to metropolis, reflect a whole world set in movement shifts, not only of the places where people live, but the people themselves, the inner sites where sensibility and feelings are formed. People are being refashioned in the image of the global market, whose dependants it is proposed they should become – just as happened with us. People who have lived in symbiosis with the earth for generations must now go and squat in slums and shanties, where they will find the tainted consolations of alcohol and drugs, and where they will fall into a grieving without end for ways of life that can no longer sustain them.

A full belly and a quiet conscience

But there are other elements in our historical experience. If we have been victims of efforts to erase the past, to urge us to forget, in order to immerse ourselves in the waters of Lethe of the ever-present, this is because the remnants of older, tenacious cultures live on within us. The urgencies and excitements of consumerism have sought to enter and occupy the territory of the heart and the imagination. But cultures are not so easily annihilated. They cannot be extinguished, but go underground, as a river takes a subterranean course when it comes to terrain it cannot cross and it comes to the surface with greater vigor. The roots of a conserving radicalism go deep, far deeper than the shallow belief in money, sex and fun. In response to the wasteful and heedless using up of the earth, in face of the seductive, hedonistic nihilism of enjoyment and self-indulgence without consequences, the old local practices and beliefs bring the force of their skepticism and common-sense, ethics and wisdom; and out of them is forged resistance to a globalism that had appeared to sweep all before it, before whose unstoppable imperatives everything seems to go down.

The power of old local cultures lives on everywhere where people refuse the showy conformism and the pitiless orthodoxies of the age. Self-reliance, saving and husbanding resources, a frugality that is not joyless, a pride in leaving the world not strewn with the debris of what we have consumed, but as little damaged by our passage through it as possible – ideas that survive from the vanished countryside – animate a new generation, sometimes without their becoming aware of it. In the same way, the old shoemaking people, who refused to bend the knee to their superiors, their tenacity and endurance, their revulsion at extravagance and their sometimes austere virtues – these are the gifts of the vanquished to the future. Whether we know it or not, they inspire with their defeated wisdom, they breathe the life of their extinguished hopes, they provide the energy of their spirit in spite of the obituaries pronounced sonorously through time over the death of the peasantry and the funeral of the working class.

It is with a kind of wonder that I am still here to recognize the sagacity and judgment of what I could not wait to get away from when I was young! The aunts, scandalized by any kind of waste, who thought wasted food nourished the Devil, who carefully captured the sunshine of summer's fruits in the jars of plums and the purple blackcurrant jam which they stored on the cellar steps, who patched and darned and made and mended, and expressed their pride in how much they could with next to nothing – what dignity there was in the despised acuity, the superseded small wisdom! The working men, too, with their leveling temper, their understated generosity, the distribution among neighbors of bitter rhubarb and stringy beans from the allotment, their refusal to admit that anybody required more than enough for their sustenance, their obstreperous disbelief in the virtue of wealth, as they wondered what more anyone could ask of life than a full belly and a quiet conscience.

An old sadness

Perhaps it is the fate of all cultures to die before they are re-discovered, to pass away before they become the object of a sustained rescue-mission. I feel shame when I think of the heartless dismissiveness when I heard the raw, still semi-rural rasp of their voices, and that I was not able to tell them that I recognize that they live on within me. I have rediscovered their voices long after, as they would have said, they had their mouth stopped with mold. It is an old sadness, this recognition that always appears to come too late; but which nonetheless continues to do its work in the world in the face of all the fashionable ortho-doxies and transient certitudes of those who claim to have outlived ancient truths, and to believe in a life which can transcend the limitations of the ages, and can gain something more than its uncertain joys, modest affections and inevitable loss.

Cultures do die. Practices and customs may fall into disuse, but the animat-ing principles live on, waiting for their time once more. Of course, it is tragic to see how dependent people become on the traditions and rituals of their cultures and civilizations, and their disorientation when these are ridiculed and declared worthless, outdated, futile. But cultures are not so easily banished. They mutate and metamorphose; they take on new shapes, they remain, buried civilizations, or they assume a cunning new aspect to astonish with their novelty the old wisdom they represent.

And these quiet, conserving cultures are to be found, in one form or another, all over the world. They are not foreign or alien; they embody the familiar and the homely and the everyday – the things perpetually waiting to be rediscovered by those who think they have outgrown them, forsaken them for ever.

1 Edwin Muir, 'The Island', *Selected Poems*, Faber, London 1965. 2 EP Thompson, *The Making of the English Working Class*, Penguin Books, 1991.

PART 2

Consuming
Cultures

Globalization
as imperialism

Globaliza
and Local
Lives

6 A history of global culture

'Samoa knows but one way of life and teaches it to her children.
Will we, who have the knowledge of many ways, leave our children
free to choose among them?'

Margaret Mead[1]

The line of descent of the dominant Western ideology is a long one. Although this is now formally gift-wrapped in a package labeled 'economic progress', the informing values that animated the pioneers of imperialism have never deserted them. They have simply moved from one official ideology to another – from military might to religious conversions to superior race, to civilizing mission, to power of production, to economic pre-eminence. Whatever guise, or alias, these have assumed, military supremacy has always hovered menacingly over the shifting orthodoxies of the age.

1992 saw the commemoration of Christopher Columbus's journey to the Americas which had marked the beginning of 500 years of European imperialism. In fact, this had begun earlier. In 1336, the Spanish had occupied the northern Canary Islands. The native Guanches were massacred and had become extinct by the end of the century.

In October 1492, Columbus reached the island of Guanahani in the Caribbean. Although the Guanahinis welcomed the strangers, Columbus claimed the land for the Spanish king. An official of the Spanish court accompanied Columbus to ensure that the 'prescribed rites of annexation' were performed.

In their first encounters with groups of indigenous people, the Spaniards read them a statement in Spanish, informing them of the truth of Christianity, and demanding that they swear immediate allegiance to the Pope and the Crown. To the bewildered inhabitants, they went on:

The saving of souls and the salvage of gold were intertwined

'I certify to you that with the help of God, we shall powerfully enter into your country and shall make war against you in all ways and manners that we can and shall subject you to the yoke and obedience of the Church and their Highnesses. We shall take you and your wives and your children and shall make slaves of them… and we shall take your goods and do to you all the mischief and damage we can.'[2]

Of the estimated 75 – 100 million people inhabiting the Americas at the end of the 15th century, 90 per cent were wiped out within 150 years.

The saving of souls and the salvage of gold were clearly intertwined from the beginning. Imperial conquest requires the demonstration of both material and spiritual superiority. The second is usually taken for granted: in the encounter with the people of the Americas, there was no sense of a negotiation: the values of the Europeans were expected to 'prevail' (a word widely used by US President George W Bush during the Iraq War). If there was any moral discomfort in the seizures and annexations of land, the colonists managed to dispel them by claiming that the land they took possession of was 'waste', 'unused', 'empty', or 'unproductive.' Where this was manifestly untrue, they soon made it so.

The conquest of India

In India, Alfonso de Albuquerque, the Portuguese admiral who conquered Goa in 1510, wrote to King Manuel I: 'I set fire to the city and put them all to the sword, and for four whole days your soldiers caused carnage among them; no Moor was left alive wherever he happened to be found; the mosques were filled with them and set fire to.'

The British, who claimed that they had merely come to India for purposes of trade, embodied their virtuous intention in the charter to the East India Company granted by Elizabeth I. Whenever great powers express their dedication to 'trade' (which they subsequently prefaced by the word 'free') promises of universal wealth were never far behind. Evidence of the one-sided nature of this transaction may be seen today in the British Museum, 'the largest repository of stolen goods in the world', according to Indian writer Winin Pereira.

The occupied lands of India were soon regarded as the real estate of the colonial power, to be disposed of as the new owners saw fit. As part of the dowry of Catherine of Braganza to Charles II of England, Portugal 'gave' to the 'King of Great Britain, his heirs and successors for ever, the Port and Island of Bombay in the East Indies with all its rights, profits, territories and appurtenances whatsoever thereunto belonging, and together with all income and revenue, as also the direct and absolute Dominion and Sovereignty of the said Port and Island of Bombay and premises with all their royalties, freely, fully, entirely and absolutely.' Pereira observes that this marriage could be held responsible for the largest number of 'dowry deaths' ever recorded in India.

The Company progressed from being a trading venture to a ruling enterprise. Its shifting purpose illustrates the dynamism and fluidity of cultures, and their power to improvise and change, their essential opportunism, before they coalesce into what come to seem, to later generations, unalterable principles. The plunder of Bengal by the Company's servants brought the province to a state of dereliction: in the famine of 1769 – 70 almost a third of the population perished. Lord North's Regulating Act of 1773 brought the Company under greater government control and placed India under the rule of a Governor-General. Here is a great historical irony – the power of the East

India Company was considered to be too great in those innocent times, and was 'nationalized.'

Two hundred years later, the orthodoxy has been reversed: it is governments whose power must be curbed, and enterprises 'set free'. In this sense, the growth and development of the East India Company was a (premature) fore-runner of the multinational companies of today. The interlude of government control proved brief; just as the same attempt to curtail the play of free markets under socialist ideology was so swiftly vanquished. The orthodoxy has reverted to that of 'wealth-creation', in the way of which no other powers or interest should be allowed to stand.

> **The creation of wealth has been linked to 'culture' as an expression of power**

The uses of culture

The creation of wealth, however, has always been linked to the promotion of 'culture' as an expression of power. It accompanied the French, Portuguese and British empires, which did their best to stamp their languages, religion, admin-istration and infrastructure, their penal code, their system of education, their manners and customs on the places they had occupied.

If the politicians of Britain today seek to ally themselves with the US, as America diffuses its ideas and values across the world, this is because they recognize in this the ghost of their own former triumphal progression, and see there the fleeting shadows of their own brief supremacy. In their day, they too expressed themselves with a fervor and conviction shown by their American counterparts today.

Thomas Babington Macaulay, historian, writer and parliamentarian, was a member of the supreme council of the East India Company from 1834 – 1838. He published his famous *Minute on Indian Education* in 1835, as a rebuttal of members of the council who thought that Indian students should continue to be educated in Sanskrit and Arabic as well as English.

'All parties seem to be agreed on one point, that the dialects commonly spoken among the natives... contain neither literary nor scientific information, and are, moreover, so poor and rude that, until they are enriched from some other quarter, it will not be easy to translate any valuable work into them.' He dismisses the prospects of Sanskrit and Arabic, of which he admits he has no knowledge; but notes 'I am quite ready to take the Oriental learning at the valuation of the Orientalists themselves. I have never found one among them who could deny that a single shelf of a good European library was worth the whole native literature of India and Arabia.'

The way forward was clear: 'We have to educate a people who cannot at present be educated by means of their mother-tongue. We must teach them some foreign language. The claims of our own language it is hardly necessary to recapitulate. It stands pre-eminent even among the languages of the West. It abounds with works of imagination not inferior to the noblest which Greece has bequeathed to us; with models of every species of eloquence; with historical compositions... with just and lively representations of human life and human nature; with the most profound speculations on metaphysics, morals, government, jurisprudence and trade... It may safely be said, that the literature now extant in that language is of far greater value than all the literature which 300 years ago was extant in all the languages of the world together.

'It is impossible for us, with our limited means, to attempt to educate the body of the people. We must at present do our best to form a class who may be interpreters between us and the millions whom we govern; a class of persons, Indian in blood and color, but English in taste, in opinions, in morals and in intellect.'

I was reminded of this late in 2003, when controversy arose about the 'export' of British and American jobs to call-centers in India. Young Indian graduates were being engaged to undertake customer care for telephone, car hire, insurance, public utility and information services in the West. They were being 'educated' in the popular culture of the US and Britain, their ears trained to dialects. They underwent strenuous training in popular culture – soap-operas and TV shows, popular music and entertainment. They were instructed in quirks of pronunciation, geographical landmarks and subjects that were the topics of daily life in Britain. In some cases, they were expected to be familiar with the administrative machinery of the country from which the work was being 'out-sourced'.

The young Indians being trained to mimic their British masters in the early 19th century have their counterparts in young Indians who, already inheritors of the imperial language, were being trained to serve foreign companies. The 'multiculturalism' they were acquiring was to be deployed solely for private profit.

The candor of Macaulay deserted his more disingenuous successors, but his words foreshadow much of the aggrieved innocence with which Americans repudiate any bad faith in wishing the best of themselves upon the recalcitrant peoples it sweeps up in the radiance of its own enlightenment. The univer-salizing pretensions are the same, and the protest that there is no desire to interfere in the religious practices of others has not

The desire to 'help them help them-selves' masks more aggressive designs

changed. But at the same time, the values they are being encouraged to pursue also undermine some of the basic elements of their faith. 'Education' replaces superstition, just as economic 'progress' undermines older forms of satisfying basic needs. The desire to 'help them help themselves' masks more aggressive designs. The ostensibly practical nature of the intervention claims a restricted arena of operations, even though it has repercussions in the profoundest areas of faith and culture.

Edward Said states: 'Each great metropolitan centre that aspired to global dominance has said, and alas, done, many of the same things. There is always the appeal to power and national interest in running the affairs of lesser peoples; there is the same destructive zeal when the going gets a little rough, or when the natives rise up and reject a compliant and unpopular ruler who was ensnared and kept there by the imperial power; there is the horrifically predictable disclaimer that "we" are exceptional, not imperial, not about to repeat the mistake of earlier powers, a disclaimer that has been routinely followed by making the mistake, as witness the Vietnam and Gulf Wars.'[3]

The US: inoculated against imperialism?

The example of the British in India is well known. But the US, too, has been equally transparent in its use of culture in pursuit of its imperial adventures. The US protects itself from accusations of imperialism because the country itself was defined against British control. It is as though they had been inoculated against imperialism by their very origins; and in consequence, nothing they do in the world can be in any way be tainted by that from which they freed themselves for all time.

In the mid 1890s, Cuban rebels against the colonial power of Spain sought to enlist the sympathy of the US. The US sent a cruiser, *The Maine*, to Havana harbor. An explosion on board killed 254 men; and although this was subsequently reported to have been an accident, the disaster was attributed to Spain. Clamor for war in the US grew irresistible. The *Washington Post* summed up the new national mood:

'A new consciousness seems to have come upon us – the consciousness of strength – and with it a new appetite for yearning to show our ambition, interest, land hunger, pride, the mere joy of fighting, whatever it may be, we are animated by a new sensation… The taste of empire is in the mouth of the people even as the taste of blood in the jungle. It means an imperial policy.'

The war against Spain, when it came, started half a world away from Cuba. The Spanish fleet in Manila Bay was sunk in April 1898, intensifying Filipino insurgency against the Spanish colonial power.

At the beginning, it was not clear whether the US intervention, with the aim of bringing security to the islands under a US 'possession' was to be temporary or permanent. In this way, the US annexation of the Philippines was no clearly articulated imperial undertaking. The only clear policy was to secure the evacuation of Cuba by Spain. A senator from Indiana, Albert Jeremiah Beveridge, cried presciently: 'We are a conquering race… American law, American order, American civilization and the American flag will plant themselves on shores hitherto bloody and benighted, but by those agencies of God henceforth to be made beautiful and bright.'

In September 1898, President McKinley said to a group of Methodist missionaries that the Philippines could not be 'abandoned to the natives, who were unfit for self-government and would soon have anarchy and misrule.' His only choice, therefore, was to take the archipelago and 'to educate the Filipinos, and uplift and Christianize them, and by God's grace, do the very best we could by them, as our fellow men, for whom Christ died.' At the end of the year, an agreement was reached with Spain, offering $290 million. Cuba was granted independence, while Guam, Puerto Rico and the Philippines became US possessions.

Early in 1899, fighting broke out between US forces and the Filipinos under Aguinaldo; a fierce and bloody war, which lasted until Roosevelt, then president, declared victory in 1902. Around 200,000 Filipinos died. The brutality of the conflict was equal to that in many other colonial wars; but once over, the Americans believed it to be their responsibility to bestow the material and spiritual blessings of their exceptional society on their new possession – as though providence had anointed them to be its savior. During its half-century in the archipelago, the US refused to be labeled a colonial power, and even expunged the word colonial from its official vocabulary. Instead of establishing a colonial office, as the British did to govern their territories overseas, President McKinley consigned the Philippines to the Bureau of Insular Affairs, an agency of the War Department. Nor did Americans who were sent out to supervise the islands call themselves colonial civil servants, a term that evoked an image of white despots in topees, brandishing swagger sticks at cringing brown natives. In their own eyes, they were missionaries, not masters.

Having conquered the territory, the Americans proceeded to institute programs that would demonstrate their good will. They redistributed estates owned by the Catholic friars, which had inflamed Filipino sentiment against Spain. They constructed dams and irrigation schemes, developed mining and timber concessions, built roads, railways and ports. They initiated legal reforms, and spent generously on health, while the school system increased literacy from 20 to 50 per cent in a generation.

'Filipinos readily accepted American styles and institutions'

But America encouraged the elite and neglected the peasants, thereby prolonging a feudal oligarchy, which widened the gap between rich and poor. They created economic and trade dependency upon the US, and there was no limit on exports to the US from the Philippines.

'Filipinos readily accepted American styles and institutions. They learned to behave and dress and eat like Americans, sing American songs and speak Americanized English. Their lawyers familiarized themselves with American jurisprudence, and their politicians absorbed American democratic practices.

But they never became the Americans that the Americans tried to make them. To this day, they are trying to define their national identity'.[4] This experience served as a prototype for the cultural saturation of other countries and cultures. The long-term colonial humiliation of the Philippines has created (largely powerless) resistance to the country's further penetration by global culture. Its 'dependent independence' effectively bridged the transition from colonialism to globalization.

Intellectuals speak derisively of having been subjected to '300 years of Spain and 50 years of Hollywood'; but what remains is economic dependency, indebtedness and impoverishment; conditions exacerbated by the Marcos dictatorship, and scarcely alleviated by the coming of 'people power' and the return to democracy. The ruling castes, the old *ilustrados*, continue to enjoy privilege, and they have been joined by other groups in recent decades – business tycoons, show business and sporting stars, the beneficiaries

An older sens-ibility remains, preserved in the smaller islands, and in the slums

of the particular relationship with the US, and all the luminaries of globalization who operate both within and outside the country.

The impression today is of an intensely Americanized country, whose patterns of fast-food, entertainment, shopping malls appear familiar: even the local fast-food chains mimic the US model. But an older sensibility remains, preserved in some of the smaller islands, and equally, in the slums of Manila and Cebu: a raucous street-life persists, with its cock-fights, card-games, its vendors of *belote* (fertilized eggs cooked with the embryo of the bird inside), its disputatiousness, its gangs and family loyalties, the vigorous survival of Tagalog and scores of other languages. Even the most careful crafting of a modernized and American appearance has no more banished indigenous identity than the three centuries of Christianity did.

The E-word

Since the war in Iraq in particular, there has been much discussion on the extent to which the US can be seen as an imperial power. The comparison, as with the British, is with the Roman empire. This question arouses vehement passions, both for and against. A new generation on the Right in America are pleased to resuscitate what they call the 'E-word', and to proclaim their imperial intention, namely the global spread of the universal values of which they are the supreme bearers. British journalist Jonathan Freedland[5] quotes Charles Krauthammer, the conservative US commentator, who stated that 'no country has been as dominant culturally, economically, technologically and militarily in the history of the world since the Roman empire.'

Freedland examines the similarities – the overwhelming military strength, the history of colonizing and taking over the lands of the Cherokee, the Sioux and the Iroquois, the use of slaves, the global reach (the US has a military presence in over 130 of the 190 member states of the United Nations). The global spectacle of America inspires the mixture of admiration and fear: information superhighway is, perhaps, the equivalent of the straight Roman roads that served to convey their soldiery expeditiously to the remotest parts of empire. English is the new Latin. There is a mixture of both 'hard' and 'soft' imperialism: where necessary (Iraq), the military machine is deployed ruthlessly, but for the most part, the strategy has been in the seduction of peoples with technologically advanced material inducements: if the British liked togas, baths and central heating, the peoples of the world are drawn to Starbucks, Coca-Cola and the rest of it. There were rebellions against the Roman empire, sometimes of those who desperately wanted to participate more fully in it – much as is the case with the contemporary US. The sense of destiny is also present – the mythic founding of Rome and the heroic myth of the US past.

One of the few conspicuous differences, according to Freedland, is that the Romans proclaimed their mastery of the 'known' world, whereas the US, born of anti-imperial myth, prefers to deny its overlordship.

Perhaps these are characteristics of all imperial formations. But empires, like the cultures over which they exercise their supremacy, are organic. They rise, mature, decline and die.

However that may be, many Americans vehemently deny any imperial motivation. 'We're not a colonial power. We've never been a colonial power,' Defense Secretary Donald Rumsfeld said to the Al-Jazeera network. General Barry McCaffrey says: 'I would reject categorically the use of the word empire. I think it's silly… The last thing we're doing is empire, for God's sakes. If we were after empire, we ought to seize Cancún!'

Don Kagan, professor at Yale University, says: 'They better come up with a word that's different from the one that includes the Romans and Assyrians.' Being an empire, according to Kagan, means telling your 'subjects' what to do, 'knowing they will do it, with the certainty that if they don't do it, you will compel them to do it… take away lands, force them to pay taxes, to submit to military service. Nothing like that exists in connection with the United States.' He adds: 'We have the opportunity of being much more effective than the British Empire. We'll do it better if we don't try to be their bosses, but merely to lead.'[6]

Those who see elements of imperialism in the US often say that its great influence and power has accrued inadvertently, and that domination (or leadership) has been 'thrust upon them'. But most imperialists have been 'reluctant' – the British said they only went to India to trade; victims, no doubt, of the same circumstances of the unparalleled power which they possessed and could scarcely forbear to use. The imperial historian J R Seeley notes that: 'Our acquisition of India was made blindly. Nothing great that has been done by Englishmen was done as unintentionally, or accidentally, as the conquest of India'.[7]

Whatever the similarities between imperial formations through time, all have a dynamic life, birth and growth, reaching a zenith, maintaining this for a spell and then falling into decline. Each one thinks of itself as durable, representing unique and often universal values. Whether the US and its influence has already reached its peak, whether it is still in the ascendant, or whether already threatened by 'overstretch', is a matter for debate.

1 Margaret Mead, *Coming of Age in Samoa*, (1928), Penguin Books 1965. **2** David E Stannard, *American Holocaust, the Conquest of the New World*, OUP, 1993. **3** Edward Said, *Culture and Imperialism*, Vintage, 1993. **4** Stanley Karnow, *In Our Image*, Random House, New York, 1989. **5** *The Guardian*, 18 February 2002. **6** Craig Gilbert, *Milwaukee Sentinel*, 10 May 2002. **5** J R Seeley, *The Expansion of England* Macmillan, 1883.

7 Globalization as imperialism

'Development requires the removal of major sources of unfreedom; poverty as well as tyranny; poor economic opportunities as well as systematic social deprivation; neglect of public facilities as well as intolerance or overactivity of repressive states. Despite unprecedented increases in overall opulence, the contemporary world denies elementary freedoms to vast numbers – perhaps even the majority – of people.'

Amartya Sen[1]

The promise of 'development' was the export model of the 'progress' which the West promised – and indeed, in the post-War period, delivered – to its own peoples. It held out the offer to the impoverished countries of former empires that they could 'become like us', in opposition to the austere compulsions of nations that called themselves socialist. The metamorphosis of superiority now engaged itself in a new struggle for the soul of the poor and black majority in the world. In this noble venture, all mention of racism had to be suspended.

As evidence of the profound change of heart this seemed to suggest, the West adopted a certain humility in the presence of the diversity of culture emerging from imperial tutelage. Yesterday's terrorists became 'statesmen'. Freedom fighters were transformed into eminent leaders. Those referred to in the popular press as the 'butchers' of Malaya or Kenya, were transformed into honoured guests, received by the British Queen at Buckingham Palace. To complete their metamorphosis, they often arrived in military uniform, some-times modelled on that of the departed colonial power, whose laws against terrorism and subversion they saw no reason to abrogate. All too often, they turned these instead upon their own political opponents and enemies within.

The seductive proposition that they could become 'like us' rather than like the 'them' of the Communist world proved a potent appeal to many leaders of the newly freed countries. Personally fêted by the Western powers, they experienced luxury beyond anything they had ever dreamed of. If they accepted first-class treatment for themselves, this did not necessarily mean they were corrupt: this would eventually be extended to all the people languishing in poverty in the impoverished villages and broken farmsteads of their homeland. For whatever the Communists offered, this never included the conspicuous consumption of the West: communism promised struggle and a bare sufficiency, not the garden of earthly delights.

The 'competition' between capitalism and communism was the definitive struggle of the age. There was, it appeared, nothing else. The State or the Market would rule, each to some degree modified by the other. 'Non-align-ment', a position taken by many former colonial countries, never formulated a genuine alternative, squeezed, as they were, between the two aspects of industrial society represented by capitalism and socialism.

Long before the disintegration of the Soviet Union, it became clear that, economically and culturally, capitalism had won. The market had triumphed. Socialism, which had grown precisely in response to the cruelties of the free market, had been swallowed up by it, first of all within the Western heartlands themselves, and subsequently in the rest of the world. It was this capacity for absorption of the Western ideology, its flexibility, even while remaining true to itself, that the key to its survival lies. Its persistence was borne, at one time by a crusading religious zeal, at another by racism, in yet another era by its cultural superiority. It found a new incarnation for its distinctive claim on global domi-nance – through its economic system, renamed 'development', not capitalism.

The cunning of ideology

But the language in which this noble ideal is expressed betrays its continuity with an older project. The ideology of supremacy, resourceful as ever, flushed out of its old habitations of open racism and religious dogma, finds a new place to dwell. For what is the promise of 'economic development', if not a promise of progress to countries which are 'backward', 'primitive' 'underdeveloped', poor or stunted? Their 'less developed' status, in which Victorian anthropologists discovered them to be languishing, echoes the status of children. What is 'growth', if not directly related to the human organism itself? Western societies are 'advanced', the embodiment of 'mature' democracies. The very idea of development is only a transposition of Darwin's evolutionary principle. Where the Western institutions influence the economies of the South, they do so as instructors or healers; the teachers and doctors required by the dark places of the world in order to set them on the golden pathway towards 'development'.

The language of this noble ideal betrays its continuity with an older project

No question of racism in any of this; no declarations of the inferiority of blacks, of savage races, Asian tyranny, barbarism. There is no longer any talk of converting the heathen, bringing enlightenment to the ignorant, leading peoples from superstition. Now, it is all hyperactive 'missions' and conferences, experts dispatched to the remote corners of earth, seminars in five-star hotels, position papers, blueprints for structural adjustment or poverty-reduction papers, conclaves of highly qualified technical personnel. The objective is no longer the annexation of lands, the physical coercion of peoples, the violent seizure of resources, treasures and cultural artifacts. If these things are still required, they must be handed over under the auspices of the inviolable economic laws. The tribute remains, only it is exacted in a way more in keeping with the refinement of the age.

The real difference between the missionaries who preached religious cultural gospels and the bringers of the good-news tidings borne in the opaque language of the World Trade Organization (WTO), the World Bank and International Monetary Fund (IMF), is that the former were concerned ostensibly with the world to come (while divesting the natives of mere worldly things), whereas today they are firmly anchored in promises of wealth, if not tomorrow, then surely the day after, or next week at the latest.

It is not that the ideology has changed: it has simply conferred the role of messenger upon a different personnel. The scenario remains the same – only the cast has changed.

It is disingenuous to claim that the development paradigm is 'only economics.' The cultural humility expressed by the West in relation to the richness and diversity of other cultures is simply a modernized version of an older hypocrisy. For the global market generates its own culture, which absorbs the diversity of the world into its own mechanisms, processing cultural forms which it then reproduces as 'products', ready to take their place among the rest of the goods and services in the marketplace. As a result, cultures cease to flourish as organic celebrations of the life-ways out of which they grew, but in the new form: objects for sale. This is a more effective way of reducing them to ashes than by the plunder and violence of conquistadors, by the forced conversions of missionaries or by the military will of archaic imperialisms.

Global integration

The Western model of development – from which scarcely any country in the world now demurs – involves the global integration of all economies and peoples into a single entity.

That model is imposed at two levels; one is on the truly transnational frontierless open economy. This is then reinforced by the governments of nation states, whose members are in receipt of such profuse and insistent instruction from the international institutions on how to grow rich.

That model, which was constructed on the mercantile, industrial and colonial wealth of European empires, remains an imperial economy. That the vast majority of countries in the world which are now learning how to implement programmes for their enrichment have no territories to invade, exploit or 'open up' is a mere oversight in the blueprints and programmes issuing from the IMF, World Bank and other agencies of continuing dominion.

That is not strictly true. What many of them do have is 'peripheries', remote areas, many of which have sheltered traditional peoples for millennia. Governments are compelled, by the logic of wealth-creation, to place pressure upon such people, and more significantly, on the land they occupy, for resources, including tropical woods, crops, coal, minerals and precious metals. What we see is governments made up of dominant groups moving into the areas to be exploited, sending entrepreneurs, bureaucrats, economists and administrators into these areas, where their work faithfully mimics and replicates that of the old colonial order when it was first established in what have become the 'metropolitan' areas of the recently-emancipated colonies themselves. The logic of governments in Jakarta, Brasilia, or Lagos is essentially that of the former imperial rulers, who are under the compulsion to extract from their margins all the wealth they can in order to feed the economic growth, both of their nation, and the wider interests in the world – repayment of debt, exports to earn foreign exchange to finance the imports on which elites now depend.

Governments are compelled to place pressure upon people and on the land they occupy

There are two overlapping movements here. One is the reforming within the nation state of the mindset of the former occupying power; and the other is the transmission of this through contemporary instruments of global power and dominance.

A double pressure is exerted on the peoples whose misfortune it has been to survive in the forests and coasts and hills and undisturbed croplands. For these must be evicted, just as whole continents were evicted from sustainable subsistence in the early colonial era. What occurred then – and of course, even more destructively of indigenous cultures in Australia and North America – is repeating itself in the present day. It is undertaken less overtly by those with whom the policy originated, but they have already transmitted such ideas to their pupils and imitators all over the world, and even more importantly, to the global agencies of economic dominance which these same actors control.

The most extreme examples may be found in small-scale cultures, particularly those still dependent upon a resource-base that has remained relatively untouched by the world (of which few remain): those like the Sentinelese, who number only between 50 and 200 people, live on a small island (47 square kilometers) among the Andaman Islands, and have had no friendly contact with outsiders. They have attacked anyone who approaches their land. The Indian government has made a number of unsuccessful attempts to reach them, but at present no contact is being made.

They may well be right to attempt to stay in isolation. Of the Great Andamanese, whose population was 5,000 at the time of British contact 150 years ago, only 41 remain. Similarly, the number of the Onge people are reduced to about 99. The encroachment by poachers and entrepreneurs on lands which provided the people with sustenance and meaning (the two essential aspects of culture), also brought disease to which they have no immunity. Whole peoples can be wiped out by a single contact.

That the spectacular promise of wealth should be part of the accompanying cultural iconography of this process, should not be permitted to divert us from the sameness of outcome for the vulnerable in the world – extinction. In some cases this is such a severe reduction of the culture that it becomes deformed, embittered or misshaped in a way that will ensure the survival of at least an appearance, a simulacrum, an outer shell, of the original through the vicissitudes of globalization. It is of small use to talk of bringing the benefits of civilization, when that civilization spells the extinction of a people.

New forms of domination?

Whether such development differs from other forms of historic domination is debatable. It may be that efforts to impose the will, values or culture of victors upon the vanquished are always similar. Only the effectiveness of this has varied over time; it is not predictable, and, in any case, cultures are formed, grow and develop, sometimes around the most unforeseen stories, myths and legends. Why, for instance, did the Christian story take root in the Roman Empire, why did Buddhism retreat from India, why did Islam seize the imagination of the peoples of Arabia? Into what kind of context did the cargo cults emerge in the South Seas, what

What are the benefits when civilization spells the extinction of a people?

gave rise to the aetiological myths of tribal peoples? There is no schematic or simple way of formulating the answers to such things. The beliefs and faiths that underpin human cultures are not biddable, but may entwine themselves around the most random and adventitious story. Later, they are elaborated and expand, institutionalised and made official; orthodoxies arise, and these, in their turn, falter and decay, are overtaken by some new form of 'enlighten-ment' or revelation. Sometimes, elements in human experience that have been suppressed in one culture become prominent in its successor – sexual repression may be followed by sexual freedom, as has occurred in Western society in the past two generations, as industrial culture evolved into market culture.

The major differences which globalization brings to cultural interactions of major and lesser cultures in the past are obvious: the range of its means of propagation is vast. It is animated by an industrialized single-mindedness which endows it with great power. It also promises an end to material and secular woes of humanity – an end to material poverty. It does not depend upon religious observances and rituals, although it does demand behavior in conformity with certain values, which will earn individual participants a form of secular salvation. This alone gives it immense advantages over earlier new cultures which urged people to store up treasures above, to think of their immortal soul, to dwell upon eternity rather than the transient ills of this life. Religious cultures have always been haunted by the topography of elsewhere. The culture of the global market has a more specific geography – this world; a world which, paradoxically, it is in the process of undermining, staining and polluting, perhaps irreversibly. It would be an epic (cultural) irony that the establishment of the earthly paradise entails the calling into existence of a possibly terminal planetary dystopia.

However this may be, despite the enormous, even unparalleled advantages which the transmission and spread of this culture enjoy, there can be no foreseeably certain outcome. Its fate is unlikely to be any different from that of other cultures that have preceded it; whether or not it has reached its zenith, it must with time decay and perish; although we may wonder whether its capacity for lasting damage to the resource-base of earth may be unequalled by even the most ecologically destructive of all the cultures that went before.

The Amungme and the Kamoro in Papua

The Grasberg mine in the south-central highlands is the largest copper and gold mine in the world. It has had a devastating impact on both the Highland

Amungme people, on whose land it is situated, and the lowland Kamoro, who suffer from the effects of the waste from the mine. In the last 35 years, the Amungme have seen their sacred mountains destroyed by the mine, and watched as their relatives are killed by Indonesian soldiers 'defending' it, while the Kamoro have more than 200,000 tons of waste pumped into their rivers each day. Neither tribe has had its rights recognized or received proper compensation.

Grasberg makes a profit of over a million dollars a day. The US company Freeport McMoRan owns over 80 per cent of Grasberg; the Indonesian government and the British company Rio Tinto also have financial interests.

Freeport has been working in the area for the past 35 years. Many Amungme have been relocated to lowland villages, where they are prone to diseases unknown in the Highlands. Kamoro have also been moved because of pollution which has killed both the sago trees and the fish on which they depend for food. The current expansion of the mine with the help of $750 million from British company Rio Tinto can only compound the disaster. The government of Indonesia provides soldiers to protect it. This is now one of the most militarized areas in Indonesia. Killings, torture and disappearances have been common.

Freeport is currently exploring the whole mountain range, with the risk that the way of life of other tribes will be undermined. Proposed logging, palm-oil plantations, a road across the province and hydroelectric power stations also threaten the land and livelihood of the Papuans.

Resistance from Papuans, supported by Survival International, halted a Scott Paper pulp project which would have devastated the environment of the Ayuu people. The World Bank, under pressure, also ceased funding the transmigration programme. The tribal peoples are also organizing themselves: in Papua tribal leaders from all over the country formed the 'Presidium Council', demanding the right to decide their own future, to be independent from Indonesia and to retain the traditional, peaceful occupation of their own lands.[2]

Indonesia has been operating a policy of 'transmigration' for many years. This has involved moving people from the densely populated parts of Java and Sumatra to the outer islands, including Papua. The 'empty' land which the settlers have been given is actually the home and source of livelihood to the tribal peoples. The program is also intended to 'Indonesianize' the tribal peoples. Government officials have spoken of breeding the Papuans out of existence. A governor of Papua said: '[Intermarriage] will give birth to a new generation of people without curly hair, sowing the seeds for greater beauty.'

Although the official programme has slowed in recent years, economic migration continues to pose a grave threat to the survival of the people of Papua.

Cultural ruin

We are here at the edge of cultural ruin as a consequence of 'developmental' projects. The Amungme and Kamoro are the human sacrifice to this particular form of an industrial superstitious faith in wealth.

The story of the Amungme, the Kamoro, and thousands of other small cultures in the world, interrogates the values of the dominant powers which challenge their very existence. For these powers constantly express their commitment to diversity and pluralism. Not only this. They ritually express penitence over the extinction of indigenous and tribal cultures in the past. The sincerity of this regret has to be set against the determination of the world – and of its leading actors – to prevent a continuing passive extermination in the present; to allow traditional cultures to wither as

> **We are at the edge of cultural ruin as a consequence of 'development'**

a consequence of economic imperatives. This is the test of the commitment of a 'global community': will it permit cultures that have subsisted outside the global economy for centuries to remain there?

This has clearly not been the case with Tibet.

The Chinese in Tibet have behaved with systematic brutality in their efforts to demolish Tibetan culture and identity, and to ensure its permanent dilution by Han Chinese immigration.

Chinese occupation of Tibet has been characterized by efforts to eliminate the identity of the country. This has been accomplished by the classic features of colonialism – repressive rule and large-scale immigration. Article 49 of the Geneva Convention aims to prevent any movement of population by an occupying power from threatening the identity, culture and livelihood of the majority group in the area into which non-native populations are transferred.

It is estimated than on any given day, almost 100 million people are on the move across China in search of a livelihood. It takes only a small fraction of this number to have a significant impact on the culture, religion and identity of five million Tibetans. China's decision in the 1980s to 'integrate' Tibet into the economy and social structure of China has resulted in the arrival of scores of thousands of Han Chinese farmers, peasants and traders looking for employment. In 1994, this strategy was extended 'to open wide the doors of Tibet to inner parts of the country and to encourage traders, investment, economic units and individuals from China to Central Tibet to run different sorts of enterprises.'

According to the Government of Tibet in Exile, the country is almost 70 per cent grassland, and the animal population of 70 million supports almost a million nomadic herdspeople.[3] The fragile grasslands have been preserved and tended for generations, but the pasturelands have become increasingly degraded, as Chinese settlers moved in and converted land to agriculture. This has resulted in extensive desertification, so that the terrain has become unsuitable for both agriculture and grazing. Land has been extensively enclosed, and this has disrupted traditional migration practices of nomadic peoples. The traditional staple of barley has been replaced by wheat to feed rising numbers of Chinese military personnel and settlers. The introduction of hybrid wheat seeds, with their need for pesticides and chemical fertilizer, has been necessary to feed the incomers. Disease regularly affects new wheat varieties and occasionally wipes out the whole crop.

Cultural expansionism is no new thing in the world. Whether the current pursuit of cultural colonization by significant regional powers is in imitation of the globalizing thrust of the West, or whether this is an inherent feature of all civilizations that are in a position to extend themselves, may be disputed. The colonizing thrust of this is usually interpreted by the strong as a humane desire to bring enlightenment and order to the backward and incompetent of the world.

The rights of minorities

Most governments now regularly acknowledge the rights of their minorities. Many have ministers and bureaucratic structures dedicated to the welfare of marginalised ethnic or tribal peoples. Politicians now speak a language of inclusivism. They express a desire to bring to such people all the benefits of the modern world. In fact, this altruistic expression of wishing to include them is yet another means of undermining their threatened autonomy. Cultural extinction cannot be addressed by

Small tribal cultures cannot be 'integrated' without total loss of their identity

a desire to 'deliver' justice to people within the global system. Small tribal cultures cannot by their nature be 'integrated' without total loss or sacrifice of

Decline of indigenous peoples

The loss of their land is one of the main reason for the decline of indigenous peoples today

- Wealthy ranchers have taken lands belonging to the Awa in Brazil and the Enxet in Paraguay, while commercial oil-palm plantations threaten Awa and Chachi forest territories in Ecuador
- Uranium mining and nuclear testing have destroyed Aboriginal lands in Australia
- A World Bank-funded road virtually wiped out Nambiquara people in Brazil
- Gana and Gwi (San) people in the Kalahari have seen their houses razed, families trucked to bleak resettlement camps and water supplies cut off in a long-running attempt by Botswana's government to drive them off their lands
- Bagyeli 'pygmy' peoples in Cameroon have lost access to natural resources as a result of a World Bank-funded pipeline cutting their access to their lands
- Copper and gold mining has wrecked indigenous lands in West Papua
- Logging has decimated forest used by Dayaks in Malaysia
- *Adivasi* (tribal) communities in India have been forced off their lands in the Nagarhole National Park to make way for an eco-development project
- Oil and gas drilling companies and loggers have threatened to drive the Khanty and Udege people of Siberia off their lands
- Loggers and settlers have invaded and desertified the lands of the Wichi people of Argentina
- Lands belonging to Mapuche communities in Chile have been fragmented and taken over by industrial forestry plantations
- The Innu of Labrador and eastern Quebec have lost land to mining concessions.

Source: Survival International, reported in the *No-nonsense Guide to Indigenous Peoples* Lotte Hughes, Verso/New Internationalist 2003

their identity. The benefits of civilization which well-wishers are anxious to bring them also spell their doom, for it means their enclosure within a system of values which is the very opposite of that which gives meaning to their way of life.

When the government of Botswana, for instance, inaugurates a program for relocating the Bushmen for the sake of 'development', it compels them to settle in villages so they will be close to clinics and schools. Since mobility has been their principal cultural characteristic, it requires little imagination to perceive the damage this is likely to do. To Survival International it is uncomfortably reminiscent of what the US government had done for, and on behalf of, its indigenous people a century ago, when all-out war against them was replaced by their 'settlement' within areas designated by others, in order to place them within reach of the amenities of the modern world. These included alcohol, unemployment and despair – those meager consolations for the ruin of their cosmos.

Arguments are often advanced in the West that the environments of indigenous peoples should be preserved, since these may contain plants, herbs and shrubs as yet unclassified, and whose medicinal properties are unknown. These may be synthesised to help 'us' combat disease. This is not at all the same as saying that these environments should be saved for the sake of the peoples they sustain: it is a question of the rights of the 150 million indigenous peoples worldwide. They may indeed be custodians of a storehouse of biodiversity which could advantage all humankind, but this is not the main reason why they should be protected.

The crucial element in the wellbeing of indigenous peoples is the maintenance of their rights (not ownership) to the use of the land out of which their culture has grown.

Jonathan Mazower, of Survival International, says: 'It isn't simply contact with the outside world which destroys peoples – it is the nature of that contact. Where outsiders come as colonizers, settlers or usurpers of their land, the people are more likely to perish. If they lose land – if it is taken for timber, rubber or clearance for crops – they lose everything.'

But cultures live on beneath the surface, sometimes suppressed, as they were by invaders, missionaries and colonial authorities.

'People who survived the ravages of the rubber boom in the Amazon in the late 19th and early 20th century retreated into the deep forest. They are now thought of as 'isolated', even though they were violently exposed to the modern world. They have since settled on headwater land, which is less fertile, and have, as a result, become nomadic. They have changed; but they are still presented to the world as though they were remnants of the "Stone Age."'

Pressure on fragile cultures has increased dramatically with the spread of the global economy, faster communication, tourism and travel. On the other hand, institutionalized and official government violence against the occupants of forest and other fragile environments has been reduced. But this has not prevented the more 'benign' assimilation, generally in the guise of bringing economic advantages, the benefits of the modern world, to people. As the Dalai Lama has put it: 'No doubt that our religion and culture is our biggest strength, but at the same time we must not lag behind China in acquiring modern knowledge and skills as we must keep pace with the fast-changing world.'[4]

Those who resist are often painted, not as primitives, savages or brutes, as they were in the early colonial era, but as standing in the way of progress, as wilfully obstructing development. Their struggles are presented as the work of minorities impeding the wellbeing of the majority of the population. When they are abused, killed or poisoned, as in Papua, these are seen as human-rights abuses or environmental struggles. They are rarely presented as local skirmishes in the great global project of eliminating all economic dissidents, whose cultures have arisen around the answering of need outside the universal market.

The consequences for cultures

The biggest problem is that, of course, most societies want development. They want the economic gains of globalism, but they do not want the social consequences.

Tariq Ali[5] expresses the dilemma in his native Pakistan: 'Apologists of the American Empire often talk of hard choices in the world of market-states. For the Islamic world this means either a democracy decked in the chains of free trade and intellectual property rights and privatizing anything that matters, or a reversion to bearded barbarism.' (It should be remembered that Tariq Ali writes as an atheist). 'But the "bearded barbarians" rarely raise objections to the economic model of the West. What threatens them is the social side of the equation. They know that to concede on issues related to gender and sexuality would destroy their influence in the Islamic world. For this reason, they violently reject the freedoms permitted women, and more recently, homosexuals.'

> **The biggest problem is that, of course, most societies want development**

One of the reasons many of the supporters of Osama bin Laden were Saudis is because they saw in Saudi Arabia the most arrogant and obvious hypocrisy. While leading lives of sybaritic self-indulgence, the ruling elite were also the custodians of the holiest places in Islam. Their wealth, conspicuous consumption and submission to Western interests were paid for by their commitment to brutal laws, which decreed the execution, amputation and other barbaric treatments to those who did not conform to a version of Islam which the country's leaders themselves did not practice.

In the West itself, the social and cultural consequences of economic devel-

High roads to change

Do mountain peoples benefit from their territory being opened up?

'When I was a child I have traveled on foot to Kaskes. There was no road then. People carried food for themselves and for their animals and traveled for a week or a month through the forest and the desert. Some even died...' said Ayichesh, from Ethiopia.

Mountain peoples have always traveled, but their routes were often long and arduous, as they carried goods from some of the remotest places in the world across some of its most difficult terrain. But in recent decades, the scale and extent of road building has brought huge changes to the mountains. Roads have eaten up the distances between mountains and the lowlands. They have brought with them the many advantages of being connected to others more swiftly and simply, but also imported all the challenges and pressures that this implies. In this sense, the road serves as a metaphor for the changes facing many mountain societies today.

Many of these have been positive, as Ayichesh points out: 'Now, because there is a road, they brought barley from Addis Ababa and *dagussa* (finger millet) from Gojam by vehicles here and saved our lives when the land refused to produce food.'

For people living in previously 'isolated' mountain areas, roads can provide a range of benefits:

- increased employment and income opportunities
- access to health and education facilities and consumer goods
- exposure to the wider world and learning opportunities
- provision of external support during/after a disaster or famine
- greater opportunities for regional cooperation and economic exchange.

Improved access to mountain areas has made labor migration to surrounding areas easier and has also facilitated the development of markets, industry, and tourism, thus providing much-needed local employment and increased economic diversification. But the coming of roads has also made some mountain societies vulnerable to exploitation by outsiders.

Xuefeng, from Yunnan in China, notes: 'Before, when there wasn't the road, when people from the plains came to steal, they would steal only one or two trees. Now one truck can carry 10 people, [so] many trees were easily taken... Now it's barren. People are rich, but the resources are used up.'

The people complain there are no roads, no schools and no hospitals. People believe that if there are roads in the village, development has taken place. 'But what is the direct benefit of having a road in our village?' asks one Himalayan farmer. 'The people here are connected not with roads but with their forests. The grass will go, the trees will go, the stone will go from our village.'

He warns that only when the villagers can utilize their resources and have goods to sell – vegetables, woven baskets, carved stone handicrafts – would the road also bring them, rather than outsiders, economic benefits.

But ultimately, for mountain people who have had to carry sick people, women in labor, and all goods into and out of their communities, the benefits of a road are too great to turn down even if people are aware of the negative impacts.

'The hospital is far away... if a seriously sick person needs to go to the hospital, it takes at least 15 or 16 people to carry him or her... In this place, because there is no road, living conditions are worse. Everything needs to be carried by people. There are potatoes [to be sold] but they are too heavy to carry. If there is no horse, you cannot carry them by yourself,' says Guangzhen, from China.

Source: *High stakes; the future for mountain societies*, Katrina Payne, Olivia Bennett and Siobhan Warrington, Panos 2002, www.panos.org.uk and www.mountainvoices.org.

opment have also entailed some high (and non-economic) costs. The rise in crime, in psychiatric illness, in addictions of all kinds, social instability and the breakdown of relationships, not to mention the much-discussed dislocations brought about by the diseases of excess – commerciogenic malnutrition, obesity, the pollutants and gases that contribute to global warming – are generally thought to be a price worth paying by the beneficiaries of global integration.

While incomes continue to rise and people have more to spend on the goods and services of their free choice, the social and cultural fallout of these arrangements scarcely perturbs majority acceptance of whatever forfeits must be yielded as the price of 'progress'. What is clear is that no place on earth is immune to the negative social and cultural effects of global economic 'success' – hence the desperate efforts of governments and elites worldwide to keep all measurements of human wellbeing firmly within the indices that demonstrate permanent economic improvement, and not to stray into the areas of daily life where so much value-added misery accumulates, just as the waste and rubbish of industrial society pollutes the waterways, the air and forests of the earth.

1 Amartya Sen *Development as Freedom* OUP, 1999. **2** Survival International. **3** *State of the Environment of Tibet*, 1996. **4** www.tibet.ca/wtnarchive/2001/ 11/21_2.html. **5** Tariq Ali *The Clash of Fundamentalisms* Verso 2002.

JIM HOLMES / PANOS PICTURES

LOCAL AND GLOBAL

Plate 1 Under threat: markets like this one in Bangladesh are dying out as global goods and products replace local ones.
Plate 2 Barisal, in Bangladesh is a meeting place between city and country. Here a young boy works in a brick factory.

ALVARO DE LEIVA / PANOS PICTURES

THE INDUSTRIAL PAST

Plate 3 William Cobbett, who
charted the decline of the local
in Britain in the 1820s.
Plate 4 Bleak view: Industrial
landscape in Britain 1869.

3

4

THE AUTHOR
AND FAMILY

Plate 5 Jeremy Seabrook today. Inset: as a young boy.
Plate 6 His grandparents in Northampton.
Plate 7 His mother

5	6
7	

A HISTORY OF
CONQUEST

Plate 8 Columbus lands
at Guanhani in 1492.
Plate 9 Atahualpa, the
last Inca Emperor,
murdered by Pizarro
in 1502.

8

9

WORLDS OF
CONTRAST

Plate 10 McDonalds in
Kiev, in the Ukraine,
where the end of
communism has meant
increasing poverty.
Plate 11 Coke comes to
the Red Fort in Delhi.

ANDREW KOKOTKA

MARK HENLEY / PANOS PICTURES

DISAPPEARING CULTURES

Plate 12 A surveyor and a geologist at Grasberg mine in Papua New Guinea, where the local people have been displaced.
Plate 13 Children in Papua New Guinea take part in a local festival.

12

13

THE SAN

Plates 14, 15
The San of the Kalahari, whose culture is under threat. The woman is picking wild berries and the group below are performing a trance dance.

PAUL WEINBERG / PANOS PICTURES

14

15

PAUL WEINBERG / PANOS PICTURES

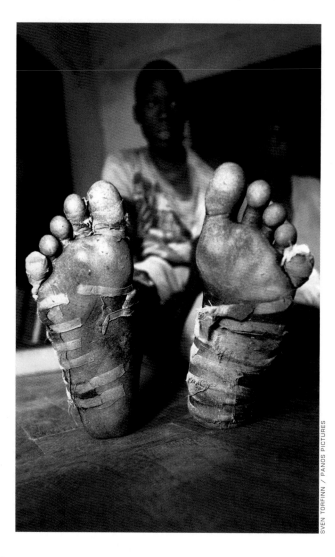

MILLENNIAL MOVEMENTS

Plate 16 Feet first – this boy walked through the bush for days to escape the Lord's Resistance Army in Uganda.

8 Our cup is broken:
the life and death of cultures

'All our gods are weeping. Idemili is weeping. Ogwugwu is weeping, Agbala is weeping... Our dead fathers are weeping because of the shameful sacrilege they are suffering and the abomination we have all seen with our eyes. This is a great gathering. No clan can boast of greater numbers and greater valor. But are we all here? I ask you: Are all the sons of Umuofia with us here?'

A deep murmur swept through the crowd.

'They are not... They have broken the clan and gone their several ways. We who are here this morning have remained true to our fathers, but our brothers have deserted us and joined a stranger to soil their fatherland.'

Chinua Achebe[1]

Today, all cultures could be considered hybrids, mixed by conquest, migration and intermarriage. 'Partly because of empire, all cultures are involved in one another, none is single and pure, all are hybrid and heterogeneous, extraordinarily differentiated and unmonolithic,' noted Edward Said. 'This, I believe, is as true of the contemporary United States as it is of the modern Arab world, where in each instance respectively, so much has been made of the dangers of "un-Americanism" and the threats to "Arabism".'[2]

As cultures form and reform under influences both from outside and within, no one can predict which elements are going to combine with others, or what the resulting mix will be. There is also a significant difference between what constitutes a culture (its origins, influences and the particular cross-fertilizations that have produced it), and what people actually believe it to be. Cultures are neither rational, nor are they necessarily amenable to co-existing with others in harmonious pluralism. Those who express the hope that the best of the global will merge with the best of what is traditional are unduly optimistic. There are no laws of cultural hybridization, and no recipes for the most desirable mix. Sometimes, the most outlandish beliefs and practices are, apparently arbitrarily, absorbed into another culture, while all that is noble and humane may be just as readily rejected.

Sometimes the most outlandish practices are absorbed into another culture

A sense of exile

One thing common to all cultures is the indivisibility of individuals from their social context. Migrants to other countries often stay together in order to reconstitute a sense of the community from which they separated. In certain cities of South Asia, whole slum areas are populated by people from the same villages, where they try to continue a version of the familiar life in the alien environment: parts of Delhi are a microcosm of Karnataka or of the area around Kanpur in Uttar Pradesh, or are mainly Tamil speakers. In the refugee camps of Lebanon, Palestinians who left their villages when Israel was created in 1948 still live in areas that correspond to those villages.

A common criticism of migrants to the West is: 'they speak their own language so you can't understand what they're saying'. Much resentment is engendered when groups try to perpetuate the values of home: I well remember the outrage of neighbors in Blackburn in Lancashire, when at Eid-ul-Azah, people, in conformity with custom, had sacrificed goats and chickens in the backyard. Indeed, so great is the desire to recreate home, that even tourists from Britain who go to the far-from-exotic cultures of Spain and Greece gravitate towards English-style pubs and fish-and-chip shops.

A majority of people are unable to transcend the values which they contract from the norms and values of the environment where they grow up as heedlessly and unreflecting as wild flowers take up nourishment from the earth in which they are rooted. Indeed, cultural diversity is a product of the same evolutionary chance that has created all other living organisms. That these should be treasured no less than other forms of biodiversity strikes against the human need to prevail, the totalizing tendency in all cultures to see themselves as the only truly authentic version of human beings on earth. It is this which has given globalization a truly awesome power; since it bestows upon its bearers the capacity to prevail over virtually all others. Resistance, as we have seen, tends to be violent and spectacular. When this is perceived as 'terrorism', it discounts the sheer terror and panic induced in people who see their own cultural (and that means social, religious and economic) values relativized and diminished by the more powerful. What is called terrorism does not necessarily arise, as the leaders of the US have said, 'because they envy us and hate us for our freedoms.' It is often simply reactive to what is felt as aggression, because they see Western concepts of freedom being imposed upon them, as when President George W Bush said of Iraq: 'We will impose our values but not our culture.' It is not easy for the victims of these processes to perceive the difference, while those who impose them have no need to wonder whether a distinction even exists.

Just how close is the relationship between an individual and his or her culture can be seen in what happens when the culture which formed them is broken, destroyed or degraded. The cost of individual survival – particularly the refugee, the exile, the victim of disaster that obliterates the sheltering environment – has yet to be calculated in the busy accounting-systems of globalization.

In the contemporary world, not only are millions of people entering the alien culture of globalism, but they are discovering that the places they have abandoned are also being transformed, precisely by the same forces they have encountered elsewhere. The culture of home, enfolded in memory, embalmed in spirit, nevertheless continues to develop in ways over which the 200 million people in the world who migrate each year have no control.

In the siteless yet universal locus of globalism, everyone ought, in theory, to feel at home; except that the culture of globalization is the negation of all earlier cultures, and is defined by an absence of place, the abolition of home.

This is perhaps why the theme of exile has become commonplace, and the image of the migrant such a powerful representative of the restless spirit of the age. It is the norm; and the new global anti-culture offers illusions, not of return, but of consolations for a generalized sense of eviction from belonging.

Lost worlds

Global culture now reaches into the most distant places of earth. It does not merely re-arrange relationships, hopes and dreams in the remote areas into which it passes with ease; it also seduces the able and talented, draws them out of the old ways, and promises them treasures unavailable to them at home – fame, wealth, recognition. Artists, writers, musicians may be taken up by a hungry, omnivorous globalism, and their story, their song, their dance will be consumed in the rich metropolitan areas to which they travel. They pay their cultural tribute to the more powerful, depositing their

Global culture now reaches into the most distant places of earth

lives and their art in the safekeeping of others. When they return to the place which nourished or stimulated what they have produced, the sites of inspiration have also themselves been transformed; at best, they have been modified, at worst, been irrecoverably lost.

Prafulla Mohanti is a painter and writer, who grew up in a village in Orissa, in Eastern India. The opportunity to study in Mumbai, later to work in England as a town planner, showed him the piercing beauty and strength of the culture which inspired him; but if it lives now, it does so primarily in his evocation of his village through words and color:

'Does 'culture' mean a way of life or high art? I understand it as a total way of life, and art and literature are an integral part of that life. They have not been separated from it, taken out of context as something to be consumed by people outside.

'I was saturated with our culture. It was life itself, from morning till night, through the seasons, the months and years. It was always exciting. It was rooted in the land, and we grew with it.

'The pattern of the year brought its own pleasures. If I start in the summer months when the fruits are ripe, mangoes and melons. There would be a religious ceremony, and the fruits were made into a drink with sugar and yoghurt. Teenagers upwards would use *bhang* and cannabis. Storms would sometimes come up in the afternoon, and the mangoes would drop from the tree.

'The entertainers came from outside: snake-charmers, actors, puppeteers. We had story-tellers who told their tales through poetry, singing and music. They educated the villagers by telling stories, the epics of the Mahabharata and Ramayana. Some poetry was Sanskrit, some Bengali, some Oriya, poets from different languages which flowed through them in a common culture, of which our Oriya was a tributary.

'When the storyteller speaks, he will describe the person in detail – the face of the heroine, her eyes, the shape of her face, her eyebrows, her hair, the arms and breasts, waist, legs, how she walks, how she moves. The character comes to life as he evokes her; he becomes that person. Sometimes the stories went through the night. There would be two or three groups. One group would leave the story unended, and ask some of the others to continue. People sat for hours, spellbound, lost in the wonder of it.

'With these performances, the village street, usually quiet and dusty, came to life with the actors. The whole place changed – excitement, color, movement. People got involved in the action; they believed in it. When it ended, it all looked empty again, dust and silence again, and sadness.

'At the beginning of the rains, there were three days of doing nothing – just eating and drinking. The rain meant crops would grow: it was called *rajo*, which was the menstruation of Mother Earth. We celebrated that the seeds would grow and feed us for another year. We felt the connection with fertility. Whenever a girl began to menstruate, she was kept in for seven days. A pudding made with rice was served to all the villagers, to signify she had reached puberty. The whole village knew: private events but a public celebration.

'During the monsoon there were many festivals. The cows' birthday, for example. The cows are garlanded and decorated. The day was designated as the birthday of all cows, in every village. And the cow would be worshipped. No one scolded cows that day; we drew pictures of them on the walls.

'Harvest was Lakshmipuja, the goddess of wealth. The walls are decorated with rice paste, and white footprints on the floor, indicating where Lakshmi should step. Lakshmi was represented in some places as the goddess herself, a yellow figure in a sari, but in our village we had a bowl of paddy with a red sari, and mainly yellow flowers around it. Lakshmi for us vanishes, and then re-appears in abstract form. I was fascinated by the way we gave life to the image. When the ceremonies were concluded, we withdrew life from the image and it became something ordinary and was thrown away. The imagination of the village invested it while we worshiped it, and then we took the power away from the objects and dispersed it again.

'But now many of those practices have been altered; degraded perhaps. The noise of loudspeakers has invaded our rituals. Modern techniques have taken away much of the spiritual content. The outward form remains, but it is for show. The inner celebration has gone.'

The persistence of cultures

A clear illustration of how cultures evolve, particularly under stress, can be seen in the emergence in the 20th century of what came to be called 'cargo cults' in Melanesia. Although examples had been observed in the 1920s, it was only after the Second World War that the 'cargo cult' was defined.

The term 'cargo cult' is itself derogatory, and others have preferred more neutral descriptions – millenarian or nativistic movements, crisis cults. These expressions are often appropriate to describe reactions to any violent disruption to cultures, reactions which appear incomprehensible to outsiders and to the agents of sudden change.

The principal element in cargo cults is material goods, sometimes particular objects from outside which had not been seen before. Adherents ritually prepared for the arrival of planes and ships full of manufactured goods – weapons, radio sets, canned fruits and other items which they associated with deliverance. Followers of the cults believed in the imminence of a new age of plenty and fulfillment, which would be heralded by the arrival of cargo sent to them by ancestors or supernatural powers. In a mixture of Christian millenarianism and animism, the cultists were persuaded that ancestral spirits would bring down from heaven goods which they had first seen

The noise of loudspeakers has invaded our rituals

through the military forces which had arrived on the islands in the mid-20th century. The cargo which accompanied the soldiers inspired in the people the idea that the end of time had come: they would be freed from work. Money would become irrelevant. Cultivation of the fields could be abandoned. Animals were slaughtered for feasts.

When the goods they desired failed to appear, it was assumed that the necessary rituals had been inadequately performed, or that others had schemed against them. Sometimes believers adopted what they thought was Western behavior and clothing. They built air-strips and wharves in readiness for the expected cargo. Crucially, the anticipated cargo was associated with the restoration of dignity, honor and pride in their identity. Ancestors combined with products of industrial society proved a potent mix.

The cargo cults are a slight carica-ture of the culture of globalization

Such cults have been treated with amused tolerance by Westerners. This is, perhaps, an error, given the cults that have arisen in the heartlands of globalism around items of consumption – the bush-fires of desire that sweep through whole populations for some urgent must-have item, the mysterious imperatives of a new fashion, the latest style, the most recent craze. After all, the English word 'fan', applied to followers of football or the enthusiasts of this or that pop- or film-star, comes from the word 'fanatic'. The Italian word, *tifoso*, means fevered, affected by the heat of typhoid.

The great enclosures of merchandise that now bestride most urban areas of the world stand at the center of our lives, because it is in them that the cultists of consumerism find significance and meaning. The cargo cults, far from being an absurd and peripheral obsession with goods, are only a slight caricature of the culture of globalization. As Emile Durkheim said, given the universality of the need to invest something with a sense of the numinous, nothing is exempt from being sacralized under suitable conditions.

Colonial legacy: laws on homosexuality

It is a familiar cultural oddity that colonized peoples often internalize and perpetuate values which pass away in the countries which originally imposed them; just as mid-Victorian leg-of-mutton sleeves still cover the bare shoulders of many African women, and as red tape is still used to bind up documents in Indian government offices while mildew and white ants eat away at them.

For example, colonial laws on homosexuality still stand in many countries.

In 2002, the NAZ Foundation, a non-governmental organization in India working on sexual health issues and AIDS prevention, sought to abolish colonial legislation by challenging the constitutionality of Article 377 of the Indian Penal Code, which forbids 'sexual acts against the order of nature'. This is aimed principally, but not exclusively, against homosexuality. The response of the central government to the Delhi High Court was to declare that homosexuality cannot be legalized in India, as society disapproved of such behavior. 'The purpose of Section 377 is to provide a healthy environment in the society by criminalizing unnatural sexual activities against the order of nature.'

That was stated shortly after the publication of a survey which showed that a higher proportion of Indian men who have sex outside of marriage do so with other men than with female sex workers. The role of social disapproval in promoting the spread of HIV/AIDS among men who have sex with each other seems to leave the government untroubled.

In Malaysia, as in India, the law is called Section 377. In India it is almost never used, whereas in Malaysia, it was employed recently, and to great effect, against the fallen former deputy premier, Anwar Ibrahim.

In Africa, the number of the article in the penal code outlawing homosexuality varies, but the wording of the offence is virtually identical. In Zambia, 'carnal knowledge of any person against the order of nature' is punishable; in Uganda, 'any person who has carnal knowledge of any person against the order of nature is guilty of an offence and is liable to life imprisonment.' Article 214 of the Nigerian Penal Code states that 'any person who has carnal knowledge of any person against the order of nature... is guilty of a felony and liable to imprisonment for 14 years.'

So in Botswana, in Zimbabwe, in Tanzania; but not in South Africa, which has one of the most impressive records in the world in recognizing same-sex relationships – perhaps as a consequence of the long experience of single-sex migrant labor camps under apartheid, where 'marriages' became institutionalized between the skesana, the feminized younger man and the *injonga*, or active partner.

'Carnal knowledge' of course stirs Biblical echoes. It evokes missionaries, fortified by Biblical revelation and shocked at the bare breasts and unselfconscious grace of African bodies, as they strove to bring decency, as well as tractability, to the wayward children of empire. The colonial legislation is also redolent of the conflicts within the British themselves – their fear and disgust, not only of the ungovernable Other, but possibly, too, of their own ungovernable desires. By projecting these fears onto their captive peoples, they first named something which, although familiar in all societies at all times, had not been cast in the particular terms framed by the colonialists in the faint light of their own experience. 'Carnal knowledge' is portentous and minatory compared to the enjoyment of sexual relations.

So now when the West revisits Africa or India, declaring that gays – not homosexuals – raise questions of human rights, who is to wonder if what they hear in reply are the fundamentalist preachings from the mouths of black bishops, fulminating in the frozen, blood-curdling rhetoric of the early missionaries? The penitent imperialists (many of whom have also repented their previous repressive sexual attitudes) are confronted by voices from the grave, the far-from-still tongues of their long-deceased predecessors. And they do not know how to respond to them.

Here is a strange paradox: societies which have internalized the norms of former imperial invaders now send forth their clarion calls of indigenous morality, claiming that 'homosexuality' is alien to the tradition and culture of India or Malaysia or Uganda. It is, they affirm, a Western 'contagion', a form of decadence.

Cultures do decline and die, although they often leave behind a precipitate

The legacy of colonialism produces more complex and enduring distortions than might have been anticipated in the early zeal of liberation movements. It is made more problematic by the fact that societies and cultures which have mutated under its influence cannot be restored, but must be remade, once more, in our image.

The decline and death of cultures

Cultures do decline and die, although they often leave behind a precipitate, a legacy that may be dispersed almost beyond recognition.

In *The City in History*, Lewis Mumford wrote: 'Human cultures do not die at a given moment, like biological organisms. Though they often seem to form a unified whole, their parts may have had an independent existence before they entered the whole, and by the same token may still be capable of continuing in existence after the whole in which they once flourished no longer functions.

'Even today, the Church of Rome, which dominated Western Europe for a thousand years, with its peculiar combination of authoritarian centralization, Roman absolutism, local autonomy, political resilience, and theoretic moral rigor, remains in operation on the dogmatic basis of the theology of St Thomas Aquinas, within the political framework of Gregory the Great: still holding

The decline of languages

There are 6,800 languages in the world

- 1,700 (27%) are under threat
- There are 357 languages with fewer than 50 speakers each
- 83% of the world's languages are restricted to single countries
- 10 languages are the mother-tongues of half the world's population.

TOP 10 LANGUAGES

(percent of world speakers
in parentheses)

1. Mandarin/Chinese (16%)
2. English (8%)
3. Spanish (5%)
4. Arabic (4%)
5. (tie) Hindi, Portuguese, Bengali, Russian (3% each)
9. (tie) Japanese, French (2% each)

Sources: http://www.cnn.com/2003/TECH/science/05/22/extinct.language/
and *Nature*, 15 May 2003

itself the sole repository of a truth and a faith essential to human salvation.'

Mumford analyses the way in which medieval institutions reconstituted themselves in the 16th century by adaptation. For example, monasticism took on a new life by organization along military lines, with absolute obedience to the head of the order (appropriately named 'Director General in the Society of Jesus'). He also traces the new cultural traits taking shape in Europe, how the culture evolved from within; the evolution of mercantile capitalism. The medieval order broke up through sheer inner corruption; 'and henceforth religion, trade and politics went their separate ways.'

During the period of European empires, ancient cultures were heedlessly disturbed, their means of survival destroyed, their economic arrangements re-made in order to be of more use to the invaders. Economies of subsistence were transformed into cash economies, old gods were overthrown, social relationships were altered and new forms of worship introduced.

But the imposition of these things did not dislodge what previously existed. Traditional cultures may go underground, or insidiously absorb outer elements of the colonizing culture, while re-affirming their own identity. Cultures have both an inner core of belief and an outer shell of ritual and practice. It is important not to confuse them. Cultures change and mutate, and even when apparently eclipsed by the more powerful, they sometimes strike back with astonishing force.

The death of cultures: the case of Yukio Mishima

Cultures do not die suddenly, although they may be traumatized by a sudden opening up to values and beliefs they had never before encountered. When Japan was compelled to confront the West in the 1860s, the repercussions on traditional culture were far-reaching. Those committed to older codes of what it meant to be Japanese never accepted the modern world.

The novels of Yukio Mishima embody his belief in imperialism, and represent an attempt to reassert Japanese warrior-culture against the power of the newly-encountered West. The values of honor, loyalty and patriotism which governed the existence of the ancient samurai warriors he also saw in the soldiers of the Imperial Army during the Second World War, even though he felt the militarists of the 1930s were corrupt and had betrayed the spirit of Japan.

Deeply disturbed by the Japanese defeat, and even more by its pursuit of what he saw as Western materialism and commercial values, in November 1970, Mishima committed *seppuku* – ritual suicide – imitating the protagonist of his story, *Patriotism*, in keeping with what he saw as traditional self-sacrifice. He was at that time at the height of his fame, and had just delivered the manuscript of his last volume in the series *The Sea of Fertility*. His work is suffused with ideas of the beauty of sacrifice, the nobility of submission, and a homoerotic preoccupation with a male-dominated culture of heroism. He saw the pathway to a return to the samurai ideal through militarism and Fascism.

Seppuku is a death-rite which involves inserting a sword blade into one's stomach. The act is completed when an assistant cuts off the head of the dying person. Mishima protested with his death against the whole process of modernization in Japan, the demystification of the Emperor and the imperial system. Although *seppuku* had been officially abolished at the time of the Meiji restoration in 1868, it was not extinguished, and significant numbers of the military chose to die in this way, in particular in 1895, as a protest against the return of conquered territory to China. General Nogi and his wife committed *seppuku* on the death of the Meiji Emperor in 1912.

Fallen civilizations bequeath elements of their beliefs to posterity

Such practices fill outsiders with horror and revulsion. Only in the context of Japanese cultural tradition do they make sense; even so, the majority of Japanese were scarcely shocked into returning to the ways of the samurai by the death of Mishima: Japan was already well on its way to becoming the second economic power in the world.

'The samurai's life was like that of the cherry blossom, beautiful and brief. For him, as for a flower, death followed naturally, gloriously.'[3]

The influence of culture through time

Fallen civilizations do not vanish completely, but bequeath elements of their knowledge-systems and beliefs to posterity. Sometimes these are rediscovered by later generations; and often the traces of apparently vanished cultures continue to enrich and nourish those which have supplanted them.

Sumerian civilization, which occupied the flood plain between the Tigris and Euphrates – contemporary Iraq – around 4,000 years BC, created city-states which were organized around a temple and ruled by a hierarchy of priests. The cultivators and craftspeople produced food and artifacts for the temple, particularly for the warrior-caste who guarded the community. As the settlements came under attack, the soldier-castes became dominant and the rule of priests was replaced by that of kings.

The Sumerians developed a sophisticated society. Their origins are unknown, but the prominence of animals among their gods hints at a pastoral background, and agriculture was practised within the cities. The language appears unrelated to any other in the region. The Sumerians disappeared about 2,000 BC, overwhelmed by invading Semitic peoples. Many cultural innovations are ascribed to the Sumerians, including writing in cuneiform script, the use of the plough, clearly recognizable social and economic organization, and the division of the day into time that we recognize – one day is 24 hours and each hour is 60 minutes.

Some aspects of its culture lived on through its influence in Babylon and Egypt. Its existence became known through excavations of the ruins of Babylon. Known only through the prism of less ancient civilizations, its emergence, flowering and decay are now beyond reach, but its influence was transmitted immense distances through time.

Our cup is broken

In *Patterns of Culture*, Ruth Benedict wrote of an encounter with Ramon, chief of the 'Digger' Indians, as the people of California called them. Although apparently integrated into the modern life of the US in the 1930s, he also represented an older culture.

'He was a Christian and a leader among his people in the planting of peaches and apricots on irrigated land, but when he talked of the shamans who had transformed themselves into bears before his eyes in the bear dance, his hands trembled and his voice broke with excitement. It was an incomparable thing, the power his people had had in the old days. He liked best to talk of the desert foods they had eaten. He brought each uprooted plant lovingly and with an unfailing sense of its importance. In those days his people had eaten "the health of the desert", he said, and knew nothing of the insides of cans and the things for sale at butchers' shops…

'One day, without transition, Ramon broke in upon his descriptions of grinding *mesquite* and preparing acorn soup. "In the beginning", he said, "God gave to every people a cup, a cup of clay, and from this cup they drank their life… They all dipped it in the water", he continued, "but their cups were different. Our cup is broken now. It has passed away."

'God gave to every people a cup of clay… Our cup is broken now. It has passed away.'

'Our cup is broken. These things that had given significance to the life of his people, the domestic rituals of eating, the obligations of the economic system, the succession of ceremonials in the villages, possession in the bear dance, their standards of right and wrong – these were gone, and with them the shape and meaning of their life.

'The old man was still vigorous and a leader in relationships with the whites. He did not mean that there was any question of the extinction of his people. But he had in mind the loss of something that had value equal to that of life itself, the whole fabric of his people's standards and beliefs. There were other cups of living left, and they held perhaps the same water, but the loss was irreparable.'

1 Chinua Achebe *Things Fall Apart*, Heinemann 1958. **2** Edward Said *Culture and Imperialism*, Vintage 1991. **3** http://personal.centenary.edu/~khowell/index4patriotism.html

9 Visions and despair: millennial cults

'Go, democratic demons, go!
In France your horrid banquet keep!
Feast on degraded Prelates' woe,
And drink the tears that Monarchs weep.
Our Church is built on Truth's firm ROCK,
And mocks each sacrilegious hand;
In spite of each electric shock,
The heav'n defended steeples stand.'

Joanna Southcott

Cultures are at their most vulnerable when the most marginal groups within them lose faith in their power to provide them with meaning. From among these groups arise saviors and messiahs, who threaten to overturn the existing order. This often coincides with times of crisis: change and upheaval, invasion or economic disaster. At such times, gods are questioned, the sustaining rituals no longer satisfy, meaning is lost.

In this context, sub-cultures, or microcultures, are generated when significant numbers of people feel they no longer have a place in the society that has borne them up. The evicted and the dispossessed form a separate culture, which may promise radical change, an overthrow of the existing order, the re-insertion of the marginalized into the center of culture. At the same time, more often than not, it incorporates aspects of the dominant culture which it has been called into existence to overcome.

In the Western world such millennial visions are part of a long Christian tradition of visionary and apocalyptic belief, grounded most clearly in the Book of Revelation. Prophetic visions continued to haunt the margins of the Christian imagination. After the Reformation, it was placed once more in a definable social setting, and a material and social objective could be defined, with the Catholic Church identified as the whore of Babylon.

Later apocalyptic movements would include the prophecies of Marx, for all their repudiation of any religious base, and possibly, in our own time, the denunciations and warnings of the Ecological Movement: both of these, one with its dictatorship of the proletariat, the other with its yearning to return to pre-industrial ways of life, also promise salvation, material or spiritual, or both.

Millennial cults

During the early industrial era in Britain, as people lost their attachment to the land and migrated into the raw new towns and cities, many millennial sects emerged. There was, in the presence of the sulphurous landscapes of the first industrial period, a sense of apocalypse. Indeed, people were entering into a new kind of society, one never before experienced on earth. As industrial culture emerged, partly from within (the development of manufacturing), partly from without (the wealth extracted from empire), a wasting and archaic peasantry looked beyond the squalor and exploitation of the new life into which they had been driven.

In order to make sense of the convulsions in their material as well as psychic landscapes, many turned to the revelations and promises of distinctly unorthodox prophets and visionaries, who saw in the new society evidence of the last days.

Joanna Southcott was one such visionary. Born in the mid 18th century, the daughter of a Devon farmer, at the age of 42 she heard a voice which spoke to her of the social chaos and unrest in England and the disorder feared from the revolution in France. She discovered in herself the power of prophecy, and sought acceptance in the established church and among the Dissenters. She gathered disciples, a group of preachers she called the 'seven stars'. Her teachings, although millennial, were also firmly anchored in revulsion against figures such as the egalitarian Thomas Paine, and she wrote songs and hymns against the French Revolution.

Rejected by dissenting sects, she gathered large numbers of believers. Her Spirit revealed to her that she was 'destined to vanquish Satan and deliver mankind from the thrall of evil.' How this was to occur was made clear in 1814, when the Spirit told her: 'This year, in the sixty-fifth year of thy age, thou shalt have a Son, by the power of the Most High.' The son was to be named Shiloh, and the birth was to occur in the autumn of 1814. Of 27 doctors who examined her, 17 affirmed she was pregnant.

She died at the end of 1814. Her followers were not shaken in their belief – the son had been assumed into heaven at birth and would return. Small bands of her followers still exist, and her box of sealed writings are in Bedford, to be opened with 24 bishops in attendance, according to her instructions.[1]

The ghost dance

Where cultures are threatened with extinction, more extreme reactions are only to be expected. In the late 1880s, under pressure from new waves of migrants to the US, the Sioux were left with 35,000 square miles of Dakota, land regarded as virtually worthless by the US authorities. Settlers bound for the North-west clamored for roads to be opened. Promoters eager to sell land wanted to break up the Great Sioux reservation.

'Our land is the dearest thing on earth to us', White Thunder told US officials. 'Men take up land and get rich on it, and it is very important for us Indians to keep it.'

It was not until 1888 that the land-grab attempt was made, when a commission from Washington proposed to carve up the reservation into six smaller reservations, leaving nine million acres for settlement. By threatening to take the land by force, the government hoped the Indians would sell at $1.50 an acre, thereby avoiding the need to break the treaty. The agreement was signed, without the consent of Sitting Bull, and the territory was split up, leaving it encircled by land open to white settlers.

A year after the breaking up of the great reservation, Sitting Bull received news of the Paiute Messiah, Wovoka. The Paiute told how the Christ had returned to earth, not as a white man, but as an Indian. He appeared before a gathering of Indians and told them that he wanted to talk to them about their relatives who were dead and gone. He would teach them a dance which would bring back all those who had died. The earth

Not even bullets could penetrate a ghost shirt

would cover up all traces of the white man, and out of it would grow sweet grass, clear water and trees. Herds of buffalo and wild horses would return. The Indians who danced the ghost dance would be suspended in thin air; and when the new earth had come they would be set down with the ancestors, where only Indians would remain.

The ghost dance spread like fire. The Indians believed that if they wore the sacred garment of the messiah shirts (painted with magic symbols) they would be invulnerable. Not even bullets could penetrate a ghost shirt.

The Indians were dancing everywhere, and all other activities came to a halt. The US authorities were alarmed, and sent a detachment to arrest Sitting Bull. In a skirmish, Sitting Bull was shot and killed.

The Sioux danced; so certain were they that with the next greening of the grass the white man would disappear and all their ancestors would return, they made no retaliation for the death of Sitting Bull.

The reservation was surrounded, the Indians disarmed of their guns. The people were to be removed to another reservation. Fighting broke out, but as the Indians had no arms, they fled. The soldiers turned their guns on them. At the end of a few minutes 153 Indians lay dead. Many crawled away to die later. It is estimated that about 350 men, women and children died. Many were buried under the snow; their bodies were later found frozen as they fell. This marked the final military defeat of the Sioux and became known as the Battle of Wounded Knee.

The ghost dance was inspired by the Indians' interpretation of the Christian faith. It is not unusual for colonizers to project their own destructive intentions upon those they seek to vanquish: the history of peaceable peoples gunned down by the superior fire-power of those who do not understand, or even feel a need to understand, the psyche of indigenous peoples who, they take it as axiomatic, are inferior to themselves.

The war of Canudos

The famines of 1877 and 1889 in the Brazilian North-east visited appalling suffering on the peoples of the *sertao*, the high rolling plains. This mobilized visionaries and saints who expected the cataclysm to be followed by the establishment of Christ's thousand-year kingdom.

One of the most successful of these was a former schoolteacher Antonio Conselheiro, who, instead of fleeing the *sertao* during the drought of 1888 and 1891 like most bureaucrats and missionaries, created at Canudos a remote place more than 550 kilometers inland from Salvador, on a ruined estate watered by streams and rivers, in which he established a self-reliant 'socialist' community of about 35,000 people. Its ideology was mystical and Catholic, but its practice was essentially both egalitarian and libertarian. It was, as writer Mike Davis describes it, 'a peaceful withdrawal into millenarian autonomy.'[2] However, like earlier attempts to create slave republics (following emancipation in 1888), Canudos was regarded by the government as a threat to social order.

At the end of 1896, following the landowners' demands for repossession, a battalion of troops from Bahia opened fire on a peaceful procession. Although 150 were killed, the soldiers were driven off by the enraged survivors. The following year, 500 federal troops were fought off. A third assault by crack troops was repulsed, since the site of Canudos made it into an easily defensible fortress. This was regarded by the inhabitants as a miracle, and evidence of God's protection.

The people of Canudos... fought to the last defender

A fourth expedition became Brazil's greatest military campaign since the war against Paraguay. Conscripts were told they were going to fight the 'forces of the devil'. The people of Canudos, aware it was a war of extermination, did not yield, but fought to the last defender.

Mike Davis observes: 'Conselheiro's premature experiment in a "Christianity of the base" was denounced by Salvador's savants as "communism", by the ultramontane bishops as a "political religious sect" and by the federal government as "seditious monarchism".'

The Lord's Resistance Army

Such curious cultural interactions are not confined to the past. The invasion of other people's territory, conversions from ancient animist and tribal religions, continue to work their strange consequences on the societies they have disrupted, and these sometimes erupt in spectacular and apparently incomprehensible forms.

Uganda, for example, has thrown up numerous charismatic spiritual leaders, who have swept up large numbers of their tribespeople in social and political revolts fed by millenarian and apocalyptic visions of deliverance.

The Acholi people of northern Uganda were persecuted by Idi Amin and have violently resisted the present government of Yoweri Museveni.

In 1986, a young Acholi woman in the north of the country declared herself under the orders of a Christian spirit called Lakwena. She raised an army called the 'Holy Spirit Mobile Forces', and waged war against evil; not only the National Resistance Army of Museveni's government, but also a series of enemies within – impure soldiers, witches, sorcerers. She promised her followers immunity from the bullets of government troops, which would 'turn to water' before they reached the bodies of her supporters. She almost achieved her aim of toppling the government; but defeated, fled to Kenya.

Out of this movement the Lord's Resistance Army (LRA) emerged. Led by Joseph Kony, a former altar boy, the LRA claims to wish to establish a society based upon the Ten Commandments. Kony was formerly a member of the Lakwena movement. Kony claims to be guided by spirits who permit him to see into the mind of his enemies. Among these are reported to be a Sudanese female Chief of Operations, a Chinese Deputy Chief, an American named King Bruce (after the martial arts film hero Bruce Lee) and the spirit of a former minister under Idi Amin.

The LRA has infamously become known for its abduction of child soldiers and sex slaves, and for the mutilation of suspected informers. Political aims, millenarian fantasies and the violence of despair make up this movement which is fed by the disturbance of ancient ways of life, alien faiths and fragments of global junk culture.

The government of Museveni has insisted it will seek a military 'solution' to the grisly uprising of the Lord's Resistance Army.

At the same time, Museveni's Uganda is presented to the world as one of the great success stories of globalization. It has duly privatized its resources, and diversified its crops to include flowers for the European market. It has created a rich entrepreneurial class. It has also managed to limit the spread of AIDS. Just how this will interact with the legacy of the first colonial era and the wreckage left by the aftermath of that unhappy time, it is perhaps too early to say.

The Jonestown massacre

The unforeseeable growth and development of such cultures gives a small insight into how unbiddable these are; how external influences disrupt and distort them; and they then play back to the dominant culture what looks like a caricature of its values and beliefs. It is a question of the profoundest meaning with which human beings invest their lives. Colon

The heart of America itself also generates some destructive cults

ialism was not an event. It was a contaminant that devastated the resource-base of lands, and the cultures that had grown out of them. The souls of the evicted remain homeless long after the conquerors have gone and 'given' freedom to the people. The new imperialists offer what they see as an extension of these freedoms. They wipe out the last vestiges of self-reliance and replace it with market-dependency. This they then call freedom.

These developments are by no means confined to the 'periphery' of the global community. The heart of America itself also generates some destructive cults, some of which have led to large-scale death and carnage. A powerful example occurred in 1978 with the People's Temple of the cult leader Jim Jones in Guyana, when almost a thousand people died by taking Kool Aid – a soft drink – laced with cyanide. This was perhaps the first mass suicide of the present age.

When the horror of what came to be called 'Jonestown' became known, it was represented to be a characteristic irrational cult under a charismatic but crazy leadership. It had used 'brainwashing'; it was scapegoated as a form of deviant organization, even though it both mimicked and absorbed practices from the wider culture.

Such movements do not occur in a vacuum. They may exhibit apparently incomprehensible and destructive features; but they do not come from nowhere. Almost all are a consequence of despair, and their adherents are those who feel they have no place in society; in other words, no cultural validation, no sense of belonging.

Where ancient cultures have been disturbed by colonialism, the economics of subsistence transformed into a cash economy; where old gods have been overthrown, social arrangements altered and new forms of worship introduced, these do not simply efface previously existing cultural formations. In the early colonial period, missionaries soon followed (sometimes accompanied) the merchants and adventurers across the globe, with the view of bringing light to the heathen. In some areas, mass conversions did occur. But where tribal and animist societies were Christianized, Christianity did not simply replace what had been there before. Its capacity to interact creatively – or destructively – with other beliefs sometimes came together to form new patterns of belief. Cultures mutate, particularly when apparently eclipsed by the more powerful.

1 www.rochester.edu/College/ENG/eng529/aeza/southcott.htm. **2** Mike Davis, *Late Victorian Holocausts, El Niño Famines and the Making of the Third World* Verso Press, 2002.

10 Bearing witness: Kashmiri and Yiddish

*'Exile is not only a displacement from one's culture of birth; it can
also be a displacement in time.'*

Barry Davis

Globalization is not the only force in the contemporary world that extin-
guishes cultures. Other forms of conflict, warfare and struggle also efface civilizations that get caught up in the places where these are fought. Regional
powers seek to extend their influence over adjacent territories; partly in imitation of the most powerful culture on earth, partly as a consequence of earlier
acts of colonial dominance. The ruined culture of Kashmir, ground between a
newly assertive Islam and the growth of Hindu fundamentalism, is a victim of
the distant consequences of colonialism and the hasty and incomplete dismantling of British rule in India.

Murtaza Shibli is a Kashmiri writer and poet, whose father is also a writer,
both in Persian and Kashmiri. The culture of Kashmir which survived –
indeed, evolved – through centuries of rule by foreign invaders, served as an
inspiration to many of those who resisted the accession of Kashmir to India at
the time of Partition in 1948 and who equally wanted no part in the entity
that Pakistan swiftly became.

'Of course, the distant past of Kashmir has become myth, a shadowy place
of heroic peoples in irrecoverable golden ages, from the early inhabitants of
the Indus Valley, Aryans, Brahmin learning and Buddhist wisdom. What we do

know is that it was subject to waves of invaders over centuries. Paradoxically, out of their efforts to impose themselves, a tolerant, eclectic culture evolved, uniquely Kashmiri.'

Murtaza looks at the successive waves of invaders of Kashmir, most of whom sought, with varying degrees of coercion, to impose their own culture on the people. 'Kashmiri is an ancient language. It was written in the *sardu* script, but this was sanskritized by the Brahmins, so that ordinary people could not read it.

'When the Persians came in the 14th century, they saw no reason to change what their imperial predecessors had done – they merely changed the ruling language to Persian. Most Kashmiri literature then was written in Persian. Some Sufis, who distinguished themselves from Islamic preachers, wrote mystical and religious texts in Kashmiri. These included Lal Ded, who, because she was influenced by Sanskrit, is claimed by the Hindus as a Hindu.

'Kashmir has been brutalized for 500 years'

There were close relations between Hindu Brahmins and Muslims; there were great Hindu writers who also expressed themselves in Persian. But this was privileged culture. They were out of time, it doesn't reflect the life of the people, offers no commentary on the times, except their detachment from those who spoke Kashmiri.

'Kashmir has been brutalized for 500 years. Mughal rule began in 1587 and ended with the Afghan invasion in 1752. Afghans were raiders. They invaded villages and took women. They introduced prostitution; and created a dance where prostitutes danced to tunes of Sufi poetry.

'Kashmiris were then taken as forced labor to Punjab by the Sikhs who dominated from 1819 to 1846. The Sikhs were a martial people. They were farmers. They had no respect for our culture, but burned mosques and destroyed libraries. They also taxed the handicrafts which had come with the Persians – shawl-making, rug-making, woodwork, papier-mâché. The livelihoods of the people who produced these things ceased to be viable, but they were not permitted by law to leave their craft, and indeed, sons had to follow their fathers. Craftsmanship became slavery. Many people died during famine and droughts.

'Then the British installed the Dogras as a ruling Hindu caste, which lasted till Indian independence in 1947. Independent India had no interest in the Kashmiri language, for fear it might encourage nationalism. It was seen as 'backward.' Many people tried to suppress the language, but couldn't, because it is the language of the people, in which they told their stories and expressed their frustration, grief and sorrow.

'Many Kashmiri Hindu *pandits* (learned Brahmin caste) didn't like Persian. Some wanted to Brahminize Kashmir culture again, with the result that even today there is a difference between the Kashmiri of Hindus and of Muslims. There are words and expressions which make each one recognizable. In Muslim Kashmiri we say '*tresh*' for water, but Hindus say '*poin*', like the Hindi word, *pani*.

'The tragedy for our culture is that all the books written by the Indian Government Central Board of Education are written by Kashmiri Hindus, so they are all written from the perspective of the minority.

'My father writes in Persian and also in Muslim Kashmiri. He will publish 500 copies of his books, and he'll give 50 to friends, while the other 450 lie in the dust in our house. He gets no money for his work, because he is anti-India, and for that reason, he gets no books in libraries. Hindus say he should write in Hindi. My father is culturally marooned.

'I feel very sad. I recognize the efforts he has made to enhance and give value to Muslim Kashmiri, and it is from him I get my love of the Kashmiri language. I absorbed the language from him. It is not fashionable. I took additional graduation in Kashmiri. Everybody laughed at me. If I hadn't known English, people would not have taken me seriously. It is only because I am secure in an alien culture that I can try to revive my own culture. That is the only thing that gives it credibility. Apart from me, only two others in my year studied Kashmiri, and they were linguistic scientists.

'There has been a long oral tradition in Kashmir. The folklore also has a political content. There are folk-poems, reflecting the cruelty of the Afghan rulers, the Sikhs or the *Dogras*. *Ladishah* is a form of folklore, a satirical poem about contemporary events. There is also *chumja*, which would comment on crime, rising prices, the inaction of government. These existed for centuries, but like the folk-theatre, have now gone.

'Kashmiri culture was influenced by Sufism, which is about human values, love and tolerance. I am a disciple of a Sufi, who teaches never to speak against anyone who preaches the rights of others. The Sufis were the only people who adopted the Kashmiri tongue and promoted the Islamic values of brotherhood and tolerance. Sufis still write and sing in Kashmiri; it appeals only to the few dedicated.

'At festivals in Kashmir, two or three hundred people will come and listen to and play music the whole night long.

'Since Indian independence, Kashmiri language and popular culture have been degraded by English, and more recently, by Hindi. In the past 10 years, people have TV satellite dishes. The Kashmiri exiles are not interested in the language. Persian is now dead. Even Urdu is dying, replaced by English and Hindi.

'The Islamists in Kashmir don't want the Kashmiri identity either. They want an Islamic identity. The secularists are pro-Indian, and they don't want Kashmiris to have a cultural identity either, because that is charged with political meaning. As for the Kashmiri nationalists, they don't know who they are. They say they want an independent Kashmir, that is, Kashmir to be governed by Kashmiris. What does that mean? It would be a US outpost. With Kashmiri culture and language on the margins, as they always have been. There is no idea of a Kashmiri identity: Islamists want Islam, Hindus want to saffronize Kashmiri culture.

'Although we have been invaded and raided for centuries, Indian aggression is different from that of the past, because it is on a greater scale, and it is an industrialized aggression, its influence more far-reaching.

'Jawarhal Nehru was a Kashmiri *pandit* – this is why the promised plebiscite after Kashmir was assigned to India never took place. Of course, the Kashmiri *pandits* have also lost their culture, just as we have. Although I am a Muslim, I don't demean our Hindu past or culture, or our glorious Buddhist past.

'At Independence, India needed Kashmir, because this was the only Muslim-majority state: it was vital to their secular credentials. It was vital to demonstrate their pluralism. Now they are using Kashmir to re-shape the Hindu identity, and to show that Muslims cannot really be Indians. It now has the very opposite function it had at Independence.

'Both India and Pakistan have spread so much hate. Trust has been destroyed. The youth of 18 or 20 have seen only murder. This is now their culture. Murder was a major sin, now it is a daily occurrence. Brutalization. The conflict has become pointless. What we saw – even as recently as 1989, when the new uprising against Indian rule began – as the defense of our culture has degenerated. It is now what India and Pakistan say it is – a dispute over territory. I would give my life for my culture, but not for the territory either of India or Pakistan. Children grow up to absorb hatred, resentment and frustration. The last poem I wrote was in January 2000.

> *Why for so many years*
> *has our backyard been*
> *the meeting-place of misfortunes,*
> *a laboratory to change souls,*
> *a carnival of suffering?*

'The culture I love has been annihilated. By holding Kashmir, India thinks it is defeating Pakistan. It does not see it is killing us – that is incidental to its rage against Pakistan. It has eroded our personality and collective sense of identity, so that all that is left is humiliation and despair.

'There cannot now be an independent Kashmir. It wouldn't be economically viable. It is our misfortune to occupy a piece of land that has been fought over for centuries, but which had forged a tolerant culture out of our defeats and sorrows. Even that is being extinguished. There is now no space between Islam and Hinduism for a fusion of cultures. This was the great beauty of Kashmir – an example of cultural eclecticism, syncretism and harmony is being ground to extinction.'

'I can't fight for something that has been destroyed'

'Murtaza shows a video of himself 10 years earlier. It is a TV interview, following a massacre by the Indian army, and he is describing what he saw. At that time, he was vigorous, youthful, passionate. In the intervening years, he has been imprisoned, tortured and is now in voluntary exile. He shows me the scars on his back where he was burned by the naked flame of blow-torches. The mark of a blow from a rifle-butt remains in his skull. He has lost much of his hair. He witnessed many murders and killings at close range. He says there is no reason why he should have survived: he has also been threatened and beaten by Islamic groups who see him as a 'traitor.' Poet, writer, journalist, defender of Kashmiri culture, he says there is no space for him in the struggle.

'The words used by India to de-legitimize Kashmiri Muslims become more and more extreme – we were anti-nationals, then militants, then Pakistani agents, then extremists, then terrorists; now we are even called Al-Qaida.

'I can't fight for something that has been destroyed. I have tried to make a living in Britain selling Kashmiri handicrafts. I have worked on market stalls, selling calendars, soft toys. I don't want to write any more, since the only language I can write in is the language of humanity; and that is now a foreign tongue.'

Yiddish – a way of bearing witness

Yiddish, the culture of the Jews in Europe, was violently suppressed by the Nazis. Associated now with powerlessness, defeat and resignation, it was repudiated by the new state of Israel, which now embodies a far more assertive and uncompromising culture. The destruction of Yiddish culture is a dramatization of the slower erosion of subordinate, minority and fading cultures in the world; but at the same time, its renewal and recuperation in recent years show the remarkable survival of the spirit of culture.

Barry Davis represents the desire and the will to remember and to recuperate a Yiddish culture, the destruction of which he has experienced all his life as a pervasive absence. Growing up in a Yiddish-speaking home in East London, it is not that he himself would have absorbed that culture, since he was a clever child and went to a very English-oriented grammar school. But the fact remained that that culture was no longer available to him. When his parents died – he was in his early twenties – not only was he prematurely cut off from the transmission of the culture, but the wider culture itself scarcely existed except in the memory of an ageing generation.

'Yiddish is the quintessence of being powerless. The diaspora Jew is depowered by the loss of his or her language. Hebrew was a symbol of the Jewish tradition, although it wasn't really spoken even at the end of the time when the Jews were in the Holy Land – it was Aramaic. But the myth that the language was Hebrew was very strong, so you were always in exile. You are in exile, you don't speak your language so you are punished.

'There is another kind of exile, which is not geographic, but a cultural or social exile, that is, of the Jews who are cut off from the surrounding population, because of say, the religion of the Middle Ages, and even in Europe up to the time of the French Revolution – their use of the vernacular comes to be associated with powerlessness, lack of control, absence of esteem. Living this mythology of exile, they believed that the true, the noble language was Hebrew, and they looked upon the language they spoke as second class.

'As I understand the word, a 'culture' is the expression of the way of life of a people. They express that culture through language, folk-ways, you could include food, religion – a whole way of life, Jewish, Sikh, Christian, Muslim. When people talk of Jewish culture, they usually subsume everything in it, but they usually mean the culture of the

'If culture gets too assimilated, it ceases to exist'

Ashkenazim of Eastern Europe. They forget that Jewish culture is tremendously varied – like Christian or Muslim. But Yiddish culture belonged to Eastern European Ashkenazim – their social relationships, how they lived. All that is described in the literature. If you read Sholem Aleichem or other writers, they are describing the culture as they saw it, and also criticizing it at the same time. Many intellectuals wanted the Jews to become modern, to assimilate, to become part of the modern world. They saw Jewish society as dominated by obscurantist religious beliefs, and Jews as cut off from the world around them, living in the ghetto – to use a modern world – the mindset ghetto as well as the physical ghetto. They didn't live in a physical ghetto, but in a society, as it were, that had walls around it.

'Of course the perpetuation of culture depends to some degree on its enclosed quality. If it gets too assimilated, it ceases to exist. This is the paradox of the Jews, the more accommodation they make, the more they cease to be themselves, the more easy it is for them to become like other people, and then to disappear. We all know the history of the Jews who were persecuted and who resisted the outside world, but it would be much more difficult to write the history of those many many Jews who were assimilated. Who writes the history of assimilated people?

'At the extreme moment, in Hitler's Germany, you see a reversal of the historical process of assimilation: you see people flee to tradition where they find meaning, if not safety. The dynamic of assimilation is carried on in the US. American Jews do believe they can become very American and they can be properly Jewish. They can achieve the genuine biculturalism which American society gives rise to – Italian/American, Greek/American and so on. The truth is, American Jews are assimilating rapidly. While some retain this biculturalism, many are losing their Jewish culture, because it is easy to get lost in the wider sea of US culture. You get a bland approximation of an older culture. In America, you get a kind of sentimentalism, a Fiddler-on-the-Roof imagined *stetl* (community, homeplace).

'Yiddish now only has a real meaning for the Hasidim, the ultra-religious, for whom it has an organic function. Stamford Hill in London and Antwerp have the largest concentration of Yiddish speakers in Europe.

'After Independence in Israel in 1948, Yiddish culture was harassed – there were laws forbidding Yiddish newspapers and theater performances. The transformation of the Jew which Zionism was supposed to have achieved had to be a new culture, a new set of attitudes, and Yiddish exactly represented all those attitudes that Zionism sought to put behind it.

'In America, the Yiddish sensibility lives on its humor. It's a cliché that American Jewish humor is often Yiddish – Woody Allen and co – that's the second generation after Jack Benny and the others. The entertainment industry is full of Jews; musical comedy too. The debunking humor of the powerless, this cleverly subversive humor is a very visible influence. It's there in language too. You hear expressions like 'I need it like a hole in the head.' *En loch in Kopf.* Yiddish has a direct effect on the way people speak English – words like *chutzpah* and *schmooze* which are used in Britain now, have come back via America.

'I always had an affinity for Yiddish. None of my aunts could speak English without a very thick accent. I had such a sense of this being normal, it was the English accent that sounded abnormal. But being brought up in London, you pick up what people feel about the Jews and the prejudice that goes with all that. This reinforced my father's view of the world, which was that everyone was against us. As a child I was caught between the desire to be safe in a secure Jewish world and to be safe in a desired world outside.

'The sensibility of Yiddish appealed, it was theatrical and warm. As a child, too, I identified with the powerless. I hated nationalism – look what German nationalism did to the Jews, and English nationalism was responsible for racism. Although my parents spoke Yiddish all the time, nobody thought of studying it. People who couldn't read Yiddish would bring letters to my mother to translate. I had a positive image of the culture from my mother. She was more active in Yiddish than my father, even though he was the real native speaker from Poland.

'I can't say my religious education gave me much idea of the spiritual values of Judaism. All I could see in the community was materialism, so I turned away from Jewish things after my bar mitzvah. I wanted to become more English, and followed a conventional academic path.

'My father died when I was starting university and my mother when I was in my mid-twenties. Then something within me asked: "What connection do you have with the past?" I thought, Yiddish. It was something you had to deal with on an emotional level. I went to a Yiddish course, and it all came welling up in me, it all came back. I took to it very easily, and discovered I could not only speak Yiddish but also sing in it. This gave me a voice – it was natural to sing in Yiddish. It was a sort of return unto the self.

'For me now, teaching and acting and singing in Yiddish is a way of bearing witness. The holocaust almost wiped out the culture of Yiddish, but not entirely. This is what I call the *davke* principle – in spite of. A lot of people say: "Don't give Hitler a retrospective victory". I'm a *davke* sort of person, people who are contrary as a matter of principle. Being contrary is an affirmation of the human spirit of resistance.

'I think the holocaust was part of my initial attraction to Yiddish, the more so since it occurred soon after my parents died. I was drawn to the murdered past. This is why I reacted against the Zionist idea, since it suggested a rejection of the past. Part of the contrariness of my being didn't want to forget the past, but to keep faith with it. If an obsession with death and loss was part of it, that was only appropriate in the face of the enormity that had happened in Europe. But it evolved into something much more positive, and it changed me. I found part of myself through it. Yiddish became an affirmation of the past. People talk about the destroyed culture. Yes, it's true, a living culture was destroyed, but the literature is still there, you can take the riches, the treasury of Yiddish culture. An antidote to sentimentalizing the past is to read the literature, to see how fresh it is. Whether a culture is destroyed or not, whatever was real is preserved in the literature, the modestness, the ordinariness of it…

'One of the sad things is the negativity towards Yiddish, because it was seen as the culture of those who went to their deaths. There are many cultures on the edge of extinction, but there isn't this negativity towards them. In Israel, the blame for what happened in Europe is attributed to the culture, this subaltern, subordinate culture. In Israel, it comes down to the belief that these people were weak, their language represented debility.

'Yiddish also had associations with the language of women, the language of the ignorant, and was often referred to as *Weibesloschen* (women's talk) or jargon. Yiddish occupied the status of being folkish. Many people comparing Yiddish with Hebrew say Hebrew is the stern father, Yiddish the loving mother. Therefore it is called *Mamaloschen*, which means mother-tongue.'

PART 3

Consuming
Cultures

**For and
against**

Globaliza
and Local
Lives

11 Arguments in favor of global culture

'It is true that modernization makes many forms of traditional life disappear. But at the same time, it opens opportunities and constitutes an important step forward for a society as a whole. That is why, when given the option to choose freely, peoples, sometimes counter to what their leaders or intellectual traditionalists would like, opt for modernization without the slightest ambiguity.'

Maria Vargas Llosa[1]

Human cultures evolve to deal with, to celebrate and to make more acceptable some of the unalterable conditions of our existence. The varying rituals around birth, rites of passage, marriage customs, taboos on sexual relationships between kinship groups, the status of the elderly, the inevitability of death and the way it is dealt with – the diversity of the cultures of the world are the legacy of responses by different human groups to the most profound and unavoidable certainties of life. It is perhaps strange that the basic sameness of our human existence should have been marked in so many diverse ways. The essential mystery of our being, our origins and destination – these remain constant in all societies and at all times; yet out of these, societies have conjured some strange interpretations, rituals and ceremonies, which they have so totally made their own that to all outsiders cultural forms appear bizarre, strange, usually incomprehensible.

Other people's cultures have served as justification for every kind of conflict, invasion, wars of annihilation, every imaginable act of destruction and revenge; since these cultures are always interpreted as symbols of the otherness of strangers and aliens.

It is significant that most of the severest quarrels and indeed wars, have arisen, not so much over the unyielding sameness of human lives (few people disagree on that), as over the fate of human beings after this life is finished. Such conflicts have not been confined to those who found differences between the notion of paradise or hell, of reincarnation or the transmigration of souls. Violence has been equally bitter among those who have denied that life has any meaning beyond itself, and have even preached a religion of humanity. A belief as vehemently atheistic as Communism killed, purged or annihilated millions of people in the godless gulags of monolithic certitude. Belief itself is an inextricable part of human societies.

It isn't matters of fact that create discord (a majority of people in the world recognize their own kinship with the child dying of hunger, or in the elderly infirm abandoned by their young), but matters of faith. This is certainly the greatest obstacle to the development of a universal culture.

What binds together cultures and societies is a shared system of belief. This is usually, but not invariably, a religious faith, which commands the respect of a majority of the people in order to survive. Emile Durkheim eloquently described the relationship between belief and society. Faith is the

Conflict-related deaths
There have been more conflict-related deaths, and more deaths of civilians, in the 20th century, than in all previous centuries put together

16th century	1.6 million
17th century	6.1 million
18th century	7.0 million
19th century	19.4 million
20th century	109.7 million

Source: *World report on violence and health*, WHO 2002

informing element, the cement which holds cultures together.

There are no secular societies. There are countries, or nations, which seek not to cede pre-eminence to one religion over another, just as there are societies in which the State separates itself from the religious beliefs of the people. But there is always an informing ideology, which gives coherence and meaning to the members of a society. This may be religious faith – Islam or Christianity, it may be a 'secular' ideology, like Communism or Fascism, but these invariably take on the totalizing aspects of more spiritual creeds; or it may be a cult or totem. It may be a flag, a virulent nationalism, a belief in racial supremacy, almost always a conviction that the particular group has been singled out by the gods, God, by destiny or Providence, distinguished from (usually above) all others.

Even the most assertive materialistic philosophies strain for transcendence; thus Communism rested in an act of faith of historical necessity. 'Secularism', in the sense of the co-existence of faiths within pluralist societies is, at best, only a temporary truce between majorities and minorities, as the periodic outbreaks of violence between Hindus and Muslims in India suggests.

A price worth paying?

If the culture of globalization promised deliverance from such bloodthirsty dispute, it might not matter if such a culture were reductive, bland or trivial. It would, perhaps, be of small importance if the diversity of the world was threatened by a truly global and inclusive culture. Even a leveling homogeneity might be regarded as a price worth paying, if it were to overcome the murderous hatreds that have set people against others in defense of (or worse, in the promotion of) a language, an ethnicity, a homeland, a belief.

However, discussions about cultural convergence are rarely conducted at this rather elevated level, in terms of conciliation and global harmony. They focus mainly on whether the universal model of development associated with globalization is leading all peoples towards an (admittedly distant) single culture. This prospect is usually regarded with alarm, since the loss of the richness and diversity, the colorful particularities of human cultures, appears as a catastrophe.

The remaining representatives of dying cultures leave their habitat, often involuntarily, and go to seek a precarious living in city slums. Ancient ways of life are brutally disrupted by warfare. Economic activity – excavating the earth for minerals, fishing, ranching, plantations, agriculture that has become a form of biological mining – turns people away from long-established practice. Migrations and wanderings of people across the globe are the defining element of a common uprooted-

Just suppose it was possible to unite everyone in a common culture and purpose

ness. The iconography of global affluence beckons; and it seems new genera-tions can hardly wait to wipe the native soil from their boots, and start over in the rich pastures fertilized by money, in which they will become the most lucrative cash-crop in the world.

But few really imagine this presages even the beginnings of a truly global culture. People, it is claimed, are never going to give up their language. Religions are not going to melt away. Hierarchies of skin-color will not be reversed. Nation states are not going to abandon their uniqueness. Efforts to create a single language – Esperanto, for instance – have not been encourag-ing. The British writer George Eliot (Mary Ann Evans), who, in the 19th century, preached a religion of humanity, was compelled to acknowledge that human beings appear to value the distinctiveness of their cultural heritage over their common fate.

A force for modernization

But just suppose it was possible to unite everyone in a common culture and purpose! Wouldn't this be preferable to the competitive strife between groups separated only by this dialect, that aspect of belief, some strange custom sanctioned only by time? Would the loss of these things really matter? After all, cultures have always been in a state of flux and movement, open to influences from elsewhere; sometimes whole civilizations have been swept away by conquest, or have been driven underground; faiths have been supplanted by the revelations of later religions – animists were banished from Britain by Christianity, the polytheism of Arabia ousted by Allah, the gods of ancient empires were dethroned; languages mingled with those of invaders, customs were modified and rituals changed beyond recognition. Why would anyone want to assert the primacy of this set of beliefs and practices over another? Would it not be better that they should perish, be melted down in a shared worldwide culture?

No-one has argued more persuasively in favor of global convergence than the Peruvian novelist Mario Vargas Llosa. He sees the resistance to globalization as the reaction of stifling and oppressive nationalisms. According to him, globalization is a vehicle for modernization, and the free market a force for economic, social and cultural liberation.[2]

He says that the most powerful attack on globalization has not been in the economic sphere, but in the area of society, ethics and culture. He concedes that the idea of an assault on customs, values and traditions may be damaging to local identities. The critics, he says, see the culture of North America imposing itself, crushing diversity and transforming vibrant cultures – not all of them small-scale – into empty replicas of the dominant power, which imposes, not only its capital, military strength and knowledge-system, but even its own language, its way of thinking, believing, enjoying and dreaming.

Llosa says resistance to globalization comes from both Left and Right, not only from threatened small-scale cultures but also from the developed world. France is the most conspicuous embodiment of this. It has always promoted itself as the supreme protector of civilization (which happens to be French), including in its own imperial territories, where '*la francophonie*' was perceived as a badge of belonging to the most superior intellectual and artistic culture in Europe. Many French activists feel they are under siege from 'Anglo-Saxon' culture, which they characterize as fast food, junk culture and the global media transnationals, with the resulting debasement of the French language and a loss of its cultural self-expression.

Llosa accepts that much which is 'picturesque', folkloric and distinctive in the world will vanish; but this will be replaced by beliefs and practices more suited to contemporary reality. The disappearance of quaint cultural survivals is a consequence of modernization, and globalization is only one manifestation of this. If any isolated society − a remote tribe in Africa or the Amazon − wants to preserve cultural identity by remaining cut off from other nations, it would 'take that society back to prehistoric standards of living'.

The views of Llosa are worth dwelling on, for they represent a powerful strand of thought in the world, perhaps a dominant one. Culture, he declares, is not static, but a living entity, evolving and changing through contact with others. Those that remain unchanged 'live in caves, worship thunder and beasts, and, due to their primitivism, are increasingly vulnerable to exploitation and extermination.' He claims all modern cultures have been so spectacularly altered over the past two or three generations that France, Spain and England would scarcely be recognizable to Marcel Proust, Federico Garcia Lorca or Virginia Woolf who, nevertheless, did so much for the renewal of these cultures.

For Llosa, the idea of 'cultural identity' is dangerous, because it is reductive. It leads to the predominance of the collective over the individual. True identity lies in the ability of people to resist these determinants and to 'counter them with free acts of their own invention.' Cultural identities are an ideological fiction, rooted in nationalism. Globalization, argues Llosa, gives individuals the opportunity to construct their own chosen cultural identity. People do not have to live within the constraints of language, nation, religion and custom of the place where they were born. Globalization 'notably extends the horizons of individual liberty'.

> **Cultural identities are an ideological fiction, rooted in nationalism**

In Latin America, cultural arguments have been polarized between the *hispanists* and the *indigenists*. The former see earlier cultures as a fusion with the Spanish and Portuguese languages and Christianity; while the latter seek to retrieve from native languages, the beliefs, rites, arts and popular mores that resisted Western cultural oppression. Llosa sees both as reductionist, an inadequate account of the diversity of Latin America, since both seek to contain it within their particular ideological straitjacket. The mixture of indigenous, European and African cultures is a rich and varied treasure; and all contribute to the multiple identities of Latin America. To narrow down one aspect is to imprison people. A great liberating potential lies at the heart of globalization, the emancipation of the human person from the confinement of one arbitrary and restricted identity.

Llosa says fear of the Americanization of the planet suggests 'ideological paranoia'. He acknowledges that English is indeed the dominant planetary language, as Latin was in the Middle Ages. (This is, of course, highly ethnocentric and ignores the linguistic diversity of the wider world). This does not, he argues, destroy other languages, but opens up young people to the absorption of other languages and cultures. 'The best defense of our own cultures and languages is to promote them vigorously throughout the new world, not to persist in the naïve pretence of vaccinating them against the menace of

English.' Cultures must live freely, 'constantly jousting with other cultures in order to remain alive and exuberant.' Llosa believes in a kind of cultural Darwinism – what deserves to survive in local cultures will find ample space to flourish.

He sees in globalization the potential for the dissolution of nation-states, a process which will give back identities annihilated by the promotion of 'national' cultural identities in the 19th century. This permits silenced, oppressed and marginalized regional cultures to flourish as never before.

Homogenization as freedom

Arguments for cultural convergence promise an enlargement of freedoms, because this emancipates humanity from parochialism and the limitation of lives bound by a specific value-system. It will open wider horizons, and offer choice in place of an unquestioning acceptance of custom and tradition.

When asked 'Who are you?' even English speakers say 'We are Inu'

In this view of the world, the threat of 'McDonaldization and Disneyfication' is as crude as it is false. These have, in any case, only a superficial impact on people's lives. They do not disrupt the foods of other cultures, nor do they interfere with the transmission of older values.

Jonathan Mazower, of Survival International, says: 'The Inu in Northern Canada have been in contact with whites for hundreds of years, maybe even since the time of the Vikings. Although they have been integrated into Canadian society, the language remains, values and customs are still observed. When asked 'Who are you?' even English speakers say 'We are Inu'. In North America people cannot easily make a living on reservations, particularly a traditional living, but where they still occupy ancestral land, it still serves to make a livelihood. The Inu may eat Canadian breakfast cereal, but this doesn't mean that their culture is under threat any more than the existence of McDonald's in Prague or Porto Alegre means that the culture of the Czech Republic or Brazil is about to collapse.'

Cultures are more resilient than is often assumed. The use of English does not necessarily cancel local languages, and the 'mother-tongue' remains the language for the most intimate and homely responses of people to one another. Such languages are reinforced, not undermined, by English.

In any case, it is possible to see in the use of English as the language of business, commerce, the internet, diplomacy and to a considerable extent, of the global entertainment and music business, the growth of 'biculturalism'; a condition which already affects many people whose local culture has existed for centuries side by side with wider national cultures. If a single global culture were to be established, all the hostilities based upon the impenetrability of other cultural forms might be dissolved. If this has been the dream of imperialists, it has also been the aspiration of internationalists.

The multicultural individual

These are not abstract or theoretical arguments, for they touch upon an increasingly widespread feature of the present world, namely societies in which sizeable minorities from different cultures live together in varying degrees of acceptance and tolerance. Many individuals in such groups often become bicultural, adept both in their native tongue and in the language of the host community, learning to dart and dive nimbly between them with a supple cultural athleticism.

They often develop critical insights into both; and in Britain, this has produced an enormous number of writers and artists, many of whom have used English creatively, absurdly, inventively in a way which native speakers cannot. A generation of writers – Wole Soyinka, James Ngugi, Chinua Achebe – emerged from the direct colonial experience, whereas the voices of Salman

Rushdie, Rohinton Mistry, Monica Ali are some of the voices of globalization.

There are many millions of such people in Western Europe and North America. Their testimonies should be heard, for these tell us a great deal about the relationship between individuals and cultures. For instance, some migrants or refugees adapt very swiftly, quickly become fluent, and learn to operate very effectively in the new culture; others cannot overcome their sense of exile, and may remain embittered and estranged for the rest of their lives.

That different cultural beings can co-exist within the same person does not necessarily imply some form of schizophrenia. Those who have come from minorities in their homeland had already adjusted to the need to be both the local self and the national self. Salim, a Berber from Algeria, learned to be not only Berber, but also to express himself in Arabic, and

Different cultural beings can co-exist within the same person

equally, to be educated in French. Each identity lives within him, called forth by the context – of home, of the street, of the educational institution. When he came to London as a refugee in 1997, he knew no English at all. He acquired the language within a year, then continued his education, doing a master's degree in chemical engineering (in English), and then trained in IT. He worked, in restaurants, bookshops and later in an IT company. He has no difficulty in switching from one language to another, although there are certain elements in his life which remain constant. He is not going to change his religion, and the language of home is still the Berber dialect which, he says, is nevertheless fading. This is a terrible loss, since language is the key to the inner world of a people, and once it has gone it cannot be artificially restored.

I spoke with Choman Hardi, an Iraqi Kurd, a poet and writer who came to Britain when she was 19 after the gassing of Kurds in Halabja in 1989. She came with her parents to join a sister who had married and come to Britain at the age of 19 in 1976. Her parents never learned English, and with the passing of time, her father, a poet, became more sad in England, more distressed by exile. They returned to Iraq in 2003, and this has given them a new lease of life despite the difficulties of living under occupation.

Choman's sister, too, although a teacher, retained her Kurdish identity inviolate, spending her time with other Kurdish refugees. 'They would move from one house to another at weekends, holding parties, playing the *tabla* and the *daf*. She did not allow herself to be caught up in the culture of exile; and when she went back to the Kurdish area of Northern Iraq in 1998, she threw herself into welfare work with women and children, and now runs a major non-government organization.'

Choman describes her own experience. 'I couldn't speak English. I pretended I was 17, so I could go to school. I was in a class of 16-year-olds. When you arrive in a country whose language you cannot speak, you are perceived as stupid. I started to behave in the way I was seen by others. Also, I soon became aware of the different standards of beauty here. I saw all these self-assured young women with blond hair and long legs. At home I had always been thought OK, but here I also felt ugly. Ugly and stupid. For a time, I also became convinced that I smelt, so I stayed in a corner.'

Within a year, she had become fluent in English, within three years had gained a university place at Oxford. She married in Britain, and has become truly bicultural. 'I resent the sexism in my culture and the racism of this one. Working, as I do, as a translator for refugees, you can feel the perpetual hostility of some officials towards asylum seekers.'

Choman says that cultures do not exclude each other. They are not rigid. 'Being bicultural is great. It means you have two homes to go to. I do become a different person in each one, or rather, different aspects of myself emerge. In my culture, if you don't cry, you have no heart. As a Kurd, I am noisy, demonstrative, but with my British friends and relatives I am more polite and reflective. I am still the same person. Some people find it impossible to find room for another culture. It is partly a question of temperament and adaptability.'

One of Choman's poems expresses the futility of borders. As a child, her family had been in exile in Iran. Recalling this, she wrote *At the Border*:[3]

> My mother told me: *We are going home*.
> She said that the roads are much cleaner,
> The landscape is more beautiful, and people are much kinder.
>
> Dozens of families waited in the rain.
> 'I can inhale home' somebody said.
> Now our mothers were crying. I was five years old,
> Standing by the check-in point,
> Comparing both sides of the border.
>
> The autumn soil continued on the other side,
> The same color, the same texture.
> It rained on both sides of the chain.
>
> We waited while our papers were checked,
> Our faces thoroughly inspected.
> Then the chain was removed to let us through.
> A man went down and kissed his muddy homeland.
> The same chain of mountains encompassed all of us.

The co-existence of cultures, whether in societies or individuals, is not the culture of globalization. But the ease with which they can live together suggests that perhaps even a dominant culture does not have to crowd out others. There is, according to the enthusiasts of globalization, no reason why a global culture should not pervade the world, while people at the same time retain the distinctive features of their own tradition.

Towards a more stable world

In an article in *Foreign Policy*,[4] David Rothkop, Managing Director of Kissinger Associates, sets out clearly the credo of the less reticent proponents of global cultural convergence. He uses many of the arguments of Maria Vargas Llosa. What he lacks in literary refinement of a Llosa, he makes up for in exuberance.

He deplores the 'chants and anthems of nationalism' which are raised by demagogues, decrying new risks to ancient cultures and traditional values. Rothkop identifies the resistance to cultural globalization as the work of 'new nationalists and cultural romanticists'; claiming that globalism works towards integration rather than division. It removes not only cultural barriers, but also many of the negative dimensions of culture. 'Globalization is a vital step toward both a more stable world and better lives for the people in it.'

Cultures, he insists, are not static, but grow and develop. Attempts to confine or preserve them are doomed. Conflicts may erupt along cultural fault-lines, as Huntington says: 'Cultural differences are often sanctified by their links to the mystical roots of culture, be they spiritual or historical. Consequently, a threat to one's culture becomes a threat to one's God or one's ancestors, and therefore, to one's core identity. This inflammatory formula has been used to justify many of humanity's worst acts.'

Rothkop believes the erasure of cultural distinctions may indicate the progress of 'civilization', and offer evidence of greater understanding. He attacks the exclusionary aspects of religion/language, political/ideological beliefs. He speaks of eliminating those characteristics that promote conflict or prevent harmony, citing the European Union, India, South Africa and the US as examples of tolerant, multicultural diversity. (The inclusion of India was perhaps premature, in the light of the 2002 carnage in Gujarat and its after-math).

This benign project, Rothkop admits, may take centuries. The US is 'the indispensable nation' in the management of global affairs, and the spearhead of this integrative model. It is obvious that those who develop and deploy the most effective means of communication, the technologies of information, the means of rapid travel, will use these to propagate their values. 'Satellites carrying television signals now enable people on opposite sides of the globe to be exposed regularly to a wide range of cultural stimuli. Russian viewers are hooked on Latin American soap operas, and Middle Eastern leaders have cited CNN as a prime source, even for local news... The United States dominates this global traffic in information and ideas. American music, American movies, American TV and American software are so dominant, so sought after, and so visible that they are now literally available everywhere on earth.'

The efforts by France and Canada to preserve indigenous cultural content of films, TV and popular music are, according to this view, like King Canute who commanded the sea to recede. The convergence of lifestyles from Sao Paulo to Tokyo, from Frankfurt to Bangkok, from Johannesburg to Detroit, suggests that 'in order to compete in the marketplace they must conform to the culture of the marketplace.' Although business is the primary engine of globalization, its effects are not confined to commerce. National sovereignties must be partially ceded to international organizations co-ordinating policy on trade, the environment, health, development and crisis management.

It is in the interests of the US to ensure that if the world is moving towards a common language, that language should be English. If common telecommunications, safety and quality standards are to be adopted, they should be American. If the world is linked by television, radio and music, the programming will be American. If common values are being developed, they should be values with which Americans are comfortable.

The US must do everything in its power to shape the development of the global information infrastructure, the rules governing it and the information traversing it. Rothkop refers to the 'infosphere' as the crucial area for US dominance. Those who claim this culture will overwhelm the cultures of others are mistaken: since US culture is an amalgam of global influences, it allows individual freedoms and cultures to thrive. 'The United States should not hesitate to promote its values. In an effort to be polite or politic, Americans should not deny the fact that of all the nations in the history of the world, theirs is the most just, the most tolerant, the most willing to constantly re-assess and improve itself, and the best model for the future… Americans should promote their vision of the world, because failing to do so or taking a 'live and let live' stance is ceding the process to the not-always-beneficial actions of others.'

'The United States should not hesitate to promote its values'

Historical precedents

Contemporary proponents of a single culture have some unexpected historical allies. The hymns to globalism are strongly reminiscent of the lyrical paeans of praise of Marx and Engels to the radical power of global capital. In the *Communist Manifesto* in 1848, they wrote:

'The bourgeoisie has through its exploitation of the world market given a cosmopolitan character to production and consumption in every country… All old-established national industries have been destroyed or are daily being destroyed. They are dislodged by new industries, whose introduction becomes a life and death question for all civilized nations… industries whose products are consumed, not only at home, but in every quarter of the globe. In place of the old wants, satisfied by the production of the country, we find new wants, requiring for their satisfaction the products of distant lands and climes. In place of the old local and national seclusion and self-sufficiency, we have intercourse in every direction, universal interdependence of nations.

'And as in material, so also in intellectual production. The intellectual creations of individual nations become common property. National one-sidedness and narrow-mindedness become more and more impossible...'

The immediacy and familiarity of this argument makes one wonder why capitalism expended so much money and blood in its desire to destroy a socialism which, whatever heresies it propounded, never seriously questioned the industrial paradigm.

Radicals and reactionaries

Irving Kristol, repentant radical, sometimes described as the 'godfather' of the neo-conservative movement in the US, edits *The Public Interest*, a publication dedicated to the study of culture and 'values'. Writing in the *Wall Street Journal*, he expresses a kind of ingenuous astonishment that the United States 'has come to dominate the world militarily and culturally without clearly intend-ing it or fully realizing it.'[5] The amazement of Kristol is probably not shared by those in the US administration of President George W Bush, who have worked so long precisely for this; and it certainly comes as no surprise to those who have been on the receiving end of its imperial pretensions. Kristol believes that: 'no European nation can have – or really wants to have – its own foreign policy... Europe is resigned to be a quasi-autonomous protectorate of the United States. For the moment, Washington is not demanding Europe's quasi-automatic support of US foreign policy. But pressure towards this end will become irresistible.'

These words, written long before the events of 11 September 2001 and the war on terror, were shown to be prophetic at the time of the invasion of Iraq. While the British Prime Minister was eager to demonstrate the protected status of his own country, France and Germany, supported by Russia, sought to express their independence. The US made support of its policies the price to be exacted for the preservation of the 'credibility' of the United Nations. When France refused to comply, a wave of anti-French sentiment in America led to the renaming of 'French fries' as 'freedom fries', sales of French wine and cheese plummeted, and many Americans canceled their vacations in France.

The war in Iraq also clearly showed that, although the 'Pax Americana' had governed the early period of globalization, the cultural carrot having been offered in place of the military stick, the US had by no means renounced its willingness to return to more classic imperial forms of dominance.

Irving Kristol sees the decline of European independence as 'signs of Europe's cultural decadence. Its version of the welfare state and its radically secular society are no longer any kind of model for the rest of the world, where economic growth is favored more than 'social security' and where religion is an ever more vital force.' More prescient words, although not, perhaps, quite in the way they appeared then.

Anti-French sentiment led to the renaming of 'French fries' as 'freedom fries'

Kristol finds evidence all over the world of the voluntary submission of the peoples of the world to the 'US imperium'. The expansion of the North American Free Trade Agreement is not simply a matter of commerce. 'Free trade is followed by large American investments, which Latin America badly needs, and these investments lead inevitably to a gradual Americanization of Latin America's popular culture and way of life.' Kristol claims the nations of South East Asia are far less fearful of a 'light-handed American imperium' than of the prospect of Chinese domination. 'They're involving us, and we are permitting ourselves to be involved.' Kristol claims 'a great power can slide into commitments without explicitly making them.' He concludes: 'The world has never seen an imperium of this kind, and it is hard to know what to make of it. In its favor, it lacks the brute coercion that characterized European imperialism. But it also lacks the authentic missionary spirit of that older imperialism, which aimed to establish the rule of law while spreading Christianity. (Our missionaries live in Hollywood.) What it does offer the world is a growth economy, a 'consumerist' society, popular elections and a dominant secular-hedonistic ethos. It is a combination that is hard to resist – and equally hard to respect in its populist vulgarity. It is an imperium with a minimum of moral substance. While the people of the world may want and need it now, one wonders how soon they will weary of it.'

11 September 2001 changed this complacent sense of the US as a benign and unstoppable force welcome everywhere. The sympathy generated by the attack on the twin towers was swiftly dissipated by the war in Afghanistan, and even more by the invasion of Iraq. Meanwhile, the economic model also took some battering with the Argentinean crisis, the sudden impoverishment of half the people in a country that had not only been a prize pupil of the West, but was also near the top of the list of 'developing' countries. The coming to power of Chavez in Venezuela, popular protest in Bolivia and the election of Lula da Silva in Brazil suggest that the easy passage of the American way of life even into its own cultural backyard may be less easy than they had imagined.

To the rest of the world the violence against Afghanistan might have been understandable ('Doing nothing is not an option'), but the assault on Iraq, under cover of the phantom threat of weapons of mass destruction, which had been brandished by the Bush administration at the world to beat them into compliance, suggested that the time for cultural dominance might be giving way once more to the time of military conquest and control. Just how radical a change this represents in the perception by the world of the US, it is difficult to overstate; especially since Vietnam, it had eschewed the pathway of open militarism and offered its irresistible economic, social and cultural package of freedom, democracy and consumerism.

It is clear from the writings of the great majority of US conservatives before 11 September that the concept of culture is central. This had always situated itself alongside military and economic methods for achieving dominance, primacy, hegemony, or whatever nuance US preponderance cares to assume. The idea of 'cultural' penetration is altogether softer and more acceptable – since it is there for people to accept or reject – than military occupation.

Thus, the cultural power of America is by no means an afterthought, an add-on to its strategies for supremacy. The US had contemplated a diminished military role, its former coercive might giving way to the milder dispensation of the superiority of its culture. That this has been disrupted since 11 September and its consequences is a severe blow to the more lenient face it has sought to show the world. For the war against the 'axis of evil' is at odds with the global cultural seduction on which it had embarked. Whether fear can be an adequate substitute for persuasion remains to be seen: what the US gains in control may be offset by what it loses in legitimacy and popularity.

1 From a speech delivered by Mario Vargas Llosa for the Cátedra Siglo XXI lecture series at the Inter-American Development Bank in Washington DC on September 20, 2000. **2** http://www.iadb.org/idbamerica/English/JANO1E/jan01e1.html. **3** These poems are being published in September 2004 by Bloodaxe Books **4** *Foreign Policy* 22 June 1997. **5** *The Wall Street Journal* 18 August 1997.

12 Arguments against: the creation of a global monoculture

'Economic globalization has become a war against nature and the poor. But the rules of globalization are not god-given. They can be changed. They must be changed. We must bring this war to an end.'

Vandana Shiva[1]

Opponents of globalization claim that economic globalization has repercussions on every aspect of life, including the cultural. This, they say, will produce a global monoculture. This process is clearly visible as cultural activity and exchange are transformed into industrial products, which can be bought and sold, and are subject to 'regulation' like any other commercial commodity.

The World Trade Organization (WTO) imposes the rules of its agreements on trade in culture as rigorously as on any other traded item. Efforts by individual governments to protect their own cultures have been defeated. It seems none of the countries signed up to the WTO is to be permitted to protect its publishing, broadcasting or film industries. Negotiations over the General Agreement on Trade in Services (GATS) and Trade-Related Intellectual Property Rights (TRIPS) have ensured that the whole realm of communications, including the internet, TV, radio, trademarks and copyright law are subject to rules similar to those governing garments, coffee or guns. This remains one of the many highly contested areas of the 'rules-based system' which the WTO represents.

The relationship between economic homogenization and cultural leveling is complex and contested. Diversity scarcely exists in the economic arena, as defined by the masters of globalism. Economic arguments may rage around the mix of the public and private sectors, tax regimes, the extent of liberalization. But there is no longer any official dispute that the economy of every country, region and territory is in the process of 'integration' into a single economic entity.

But if economic diversity is now virtually meaningless, how can cultural diversity persist? As we have seen, the development and growth of cultures has usually been intimately allied to the unique resource-base out of which they grew. The elimination of all ways of answering need, providing goods and services for oneself and others outside the global market are deviancies which must be remedied. In that sense, the argument of the cultural homogenizers has already been conceded, even though on the ground, in the places where people actually live, the situation may be quite different.

We have seen that globalization will not limit itself, cannot be limited, to the economic arena alone. The crucial line has already been crossed; and it is ingenuous to believe that a protective cordon can be constructed around 'culture', when land rights, as it were, have already been ceded to the single global economy. When commerce itself has become the dominant culture, defensive efforts to preserve other cultures may already be too late.

This has been widely recognized. Former US Trade Representative Charlene Barshefsky stated in 2000 that the US would use the WTO to promote US corporate-entertainment interests around the world.[2] These are not really mere cultural products – they are the reinforcements, as it were, of conquests already made. They represent the new temples built on the site of ancient structures where other gods were worshipped – the mosque on the site of the demolished temple, the Christian cathedral that sought to extinguish the mosque at Cordoba, the Palace of Culture where the orthodox seminary used to be, the Adventist church in the sacred grove, the shopping-mall on the site of yesterday's paddy-fields.

Maude Barlow, chair of the Council of Canadians, has proposed that culture should be exempt from trade agreements, especially those emanating from the WTO. Cultural diversity should be regarded in the same way as biodiversity (to which it is intimately related). The fact that biodiversity comes under the WTO has been heavily contested by farmers and growers worldwide, who believe that neither biodiversity nor cultural diversity should by subject to the superintendence of any international bureaucracy.

The International Network for Cultural Diversity represents growing resistance to the specifically cultural aspects of globalization. Formed in 2000, it is 'a worldwide network of artists and cultural groups dedicated to countering the homogenizing effects of globalization on culture'.

It believes in 'a different kind of globalization: one which encourages cultural production within nations, and authentic exchange among them; one which encourages the dynamic coexistence of a diversity of cultures. As pressure grows to include more cultural sectors in bilateral, regional, and global trade agreements, cultural groups around the world are uniting to make a counter-proposal: the creation of a new international instrument for cultural diversity.'

The Network constitutes a considerable part of the more general anti-globalization movement, which is itself dedicated both to safeguarding local cultures, while at the same time helping to create a culture of tolerance and internationalism in contrast to a mechanistic industrial monoculture.

It believes that every act of encroachment upon people's capacity to do and create for themselves and others is an act of enclosure and a measure of unfreedom. As more and more activities are passed over to the market, a growing sense of subjective impoverishment accompanies the rising levels of consumption; and human wellbeing is effectively by-passed. Monoculture is a process. It is fluid, constantly expanding, sweeping up more and more human occupations into its control. This culture of impoverishing enrichment is now poised to engulf all humanity.

Missionaries of globalism

The missionaries of today's global culture are far from the earnest Victorian bearers of truth, with their mosquito-bitten red faces, distributing bibles to children in jungle clearings and urging women to cover their breasts. Indeed, the proselytes of this age are barely even creatures of flesh and blood – they are the shadowy emanations of the great media conglomerates, the larger-than-life figures whose supreme purpose is to beckon a new generation away from the muddy earth of home, to be resurrected in the instant eternity of the industrial Elysium.

> **The proselytes of this age are barely even creatures of flesh and blood**

The 'conversion' of the peoples of the world, set in train during the colonial era, has been intensified in the age of globalization. And the culture of globalism takes on a far more seductive guise than anything that has preceded it, for it promises earthly, not celestial rewards. It is also more systematic and self-conscious. 'Modernization' does not mean that people become wise in their own way, it means they acknowledge the superior way of the great powers of the world.

The fervors of wealth-creation require less florid exhibitions of worship than the Jesus-died-on-the-cross-that-we might-live exaltations of an earlier age of zeal. Today's converts have only to adhere to the solemn admonitions of the global financial institutions. This is apparently an altogether more prosaic form of conversion, although it actually involves converting the accumulated riches of the ages – the currency of human wisdom one might call it – into money, at an exchange-rate which does not figure in any published tables of convertibility.

The language of business

Edward Said says that the 19th century pattern of dominions or possessions laid the groundwork for what is now a fully global world. Within this world, the language of the imperium has numerous dialects. One of the most potent of these is the idiom of business and finance. When this reaches the aspirants to a better life, it flows through the ideologically-charged pedagogy of Business Studies.

The cities of the South are full of unemployed graduates. Many of these have dutifully followed the prescriptions and exhortations of voices that have urged them to join the modern world. They find themselves educated, qualified, but unfit for employment. Some of these have been sufficiently disillusioned to let themselves be recruited into the armies of drug-lords, criminal gangs, political hoodlums or religious fundamentalists.

A new generation has learned a new lesson. They have heard the seductive language of global business, and believe that this will be their passport to individual advancement, wealth and freedom. The imagination of a whole world of young (mainly) men all over the world has been seized by a new hope, which has come upon them with the force of a revelation.

It could be Lagos or Nairobi, Managua or Mexico City. There tens of millions of hopeful young men clinging to the hope that their MA in Business, Personnel or Management will ease their passage into the better life, for the sake of which their parents have sold land, wedding jewellery, property and have wagered their own future. For many, this means 'going out' to the West, the enticing imagery of which has beckoned them with a promise of personal deliverance.

Farooq, in Dhaka's Ramna Park, almost 30, is still giving 'tuitions' to younger students. He has never worked. Now pursuing his masters in Business Administration, he says: 'I hope to obtain a management post in a company. I shall be highly qualified for this. I know English, which is the international language. The world is becoming smaller. We must compete or die.'

COLLIDING CULTURES

Plate 17 Punk girls in Tokyo, Japan.
Plate 18 Side by side: Elvis and Mao in Shenzhen, China's richest city.
Plate 19 Cecilia, a young asylum seeker in Britain, in Maasai costume.

MARK HENLEY / PANOS PICTURES

MARK HENLEY / PANOS PICTURES

RORY CARNEGIE

DERMOT TATLOW / PANOS PICTURES

**COLLIDING
CULTURES**

Plate 20 A man paints a
satellite dish in Ethiopia.
Plate 21 An unusual ear
ornament on a Maasai
man in Tanzania.

ALASTAIR McNAUGHTON / PANOS PICTURES

WHAT PRICE DEVELOPMENT?

Plate 22 As a boy in Mauritania races his donkey, which is used to transport fish, local fishermen struggle to compete with huge foreign fleets.

Plate 23 Development grants have funded houses, schools, water and electricity. But the pump for this well in Nigeria is broken and villagers have to use a rope and bucket.

22

23

THE QUECHUA

Plate 24 Out of the window: Quechua woman in Peru watches a bullfight.

KASHMIR

Plate 25 The beauty of the
Kashmiri city of Srinagar.
Plate 26 An Indian solider, one
of 500,000 sent to Kashmir.

25

26

PROTEST!

Plate 27 Drop the debt: anti-globalization protesters in Prague.
Plate 28 Banner people: marchers at the World Social Forum in Mumbai.

27

28

Plate 29 Against the IMF: indigenous people's banner.
Plate 30 Our world is not for sale banner at the World Social Forum.

BRIGHT LIGHTS

Plate 31 In Bangladesh, the lure of the city brings many to find work. **Plate 32** Hoping for a better future; one that means more than mere survival, India.

31

32

Not only is he speaking a foreign language, but he is also speaking a new dialect, the clichés of global business culture. He sounds like the reports from the World Bank, which have formed a significant part of his curriculum.

How many times, in India and Bangladesh, have I been approached by these hungry young men, with their scuffed shoes and frayed trousers, the plastic wallets with the copies of their biodata folded so many times they have almost fallen apart! The easy intimacy, the avowals of friendship, the eagerness to express themselves in an English discolored by the utilitarian banalities of their studies. The professions of lasting friendship are soon followed by the stories of their family circumstances – the mother in urgent need of an operation, an illness that has led to unpayable medical bills, a younger brother to be kept while he studies, the money to be found for a sister's dowry, the ancestral land lost, false court cases laid by people who want to evict them…'Employ me', they implore, 'I'll be your cook, your driver, your servant; sponsor me, get me a visa, find me a place.' I have even been asked: 'Adopt my child, so he will have a better start in life.'

I have even been asked 'Adopt my child, so he will have a better start in life.'

I sat one day on a bus next to a young man on his way to sit his final examination. Fastidiously placing a handkerchief on the seat, he explained that he was wearing his best clothes, 'because today is the most important day of my life. What happens today will make the difference between success and failure.' I asked what failure would mean. He said 'To follow my parents.' His father is a teacher in a government primary school; an underpaid functionary, neither respected nor rewarded.

The new devotees of the business cult are conspicuously carrying text-books, mostly published in the US, in an impenetrable style which suggests the study of hermeneutics rather than the prosaic realities of business. And indeed, it is a form of alchemy: their faith is absolute that the certificate will open doors for them and provide them with opportunity, wealth and work for life.

It is the more poignant since many are from poor families, from distant villages and small towns, who have come to eke out a living while they study: to study in the big city enhances prestige. Distance from home adds value, no matter how academically thin the object of study. It is unlikely that a majority of these young people will find a place in the global culture to which they aspire: the promises of Business are merely the latest version of a foreign ideology, calculated to pacify yet another generation.

Thirty years ago, their equivalents were studying politics and sociology; and their grandparents would have been avidly reading Karl Marx and Franz Fanon, secure in the conviction that the liberation movement of their country would propel them into a future of socialism, justice and plenty. It is significant that all the ideologies are from elsewhere, indeed, the same elsewhere. All were formulated in the heartlands of an imperialism from which – at least this is new – they no longer feel the need to be free. The

The novelty of business culture is that it promises global inclusion

novelty of business culture is that it promises global inclusion; and in this lies its fresh appeal to a new generation in its credulous and vulnerable innocence.

They dream of success, lifestyles fed by the imagery of ancient TV re-runs of *Dynasty* and *The Bold and the Beautiful*, and of the imagined lives of ruthless tycoons and their glittering women, who fly in private jets from ranch to city boardroom rooftops, where fortunes are made by dynamic people who live in a happy-ever-after of lottery-winner materialism and cartoon infantile omnipotence.

Their study of business is as remote from their experience as the study of Tudor history was during the colonial era. Their English is a mixture of Victorian archaisms and marketing jargon, an alien tongue which teaches them also to despise the culture and values of their heritage.

It is unfortunate that I, who am far from an embodiment of the exalta-tions of business culture, should nevertheless be seen as an emissary of the culture which the young men attribute to all Westerners. They are caught up in other people's dramas, which are not even dispelled by the presence of flesh and blood which repudiates them. At first, it seems simply absurd, but it soon becomes increasingly uncomfortable. I with my white skin and English language, a graying figure, find I have become an emanation of their fantasies, the unwilling ambassador of a global market, business deals, a commuter between the capitals of the world; and by a repelling inverted racism, the vehicle of their imaginings and object of their myth-making – as potential patron and benefactor. I am appointed to rescue them from the culture into which they were born, sad changelings, stranded on the margins of the global market to which they desperately seek admittance and belonging.

Many who actually do 'go out' and reach the invented lands of promise, learn some brutal lessons. I met one man at Kuwait Airport, a Bangladeshi doctor, who had emigrated to America in the 1970s. His children were born and grew up there. When his son was 17, he demanded that his parents provide him with a new car, as the parents of his friends and peers had apparently all done. His father told him he could use the family car when it was not required, but had no intention of buying a new one. Enraged, the boy went to the local newspaper and complained that his parents had abused him. There were police investigations. His parents were briefly arrested and then released. The father took the boy to Bangladesh to meet his relatives. He tore up his son's passport, told him to learn about life by surviving on the streets of Dhaka, and left him there.

The channels of cultural leveling

It is necessary to look at what are usually seen as the 'culprits' of global mono-culture – the internet, global communications and entertainment conglomerates, the power of the symbols and brands of transnational companies. These are not, however, the primary agents of the wider penetration of the world: they are the vehicles of dominance.

The channels and instruments of the globalizing culture – cyberspace, the products of the transnational media conglomerates, the branding of space, the universal ideographs of publicity and advertising – bear the values of cultural transmission, but the consequences are in fact psychological transformations of the people. One cannot read into technology changes of the heart and spirit. The great majority of humankind remain embedded within their own cultural tradition and practice. They still speak the mother-tongue. Most people still move only tens of kilometers from their birthplace during their lifetime. People are not easily dislodged from ancient traditions; and it is tempting to take superficial changes for something more profound and far-reaching. But those traditions may also be less firm and stable than they appear; cultures, mobile and dynamic, are always changing; and the nature of that change, especially under the powerful promise of relief from poverty, cannot always be foretold.

To claim that modes of communication are the cause of cultural change is to attribute to them a disproportionate weight and power. Naomi Klein's 'incorporeal corporation' comes close to defining the kind of relationship that takes place between powerful producers and people: the ideology is absorbed, since it fills the air, as elusive as sound and pervasive as sunshine. The question is, not so much what do the messages say, but rather how do they alter the practice and behavior of those who are on the receiving end?

It is naive to assume that the sensibility and psyche of people may be deduced from the products they consume. These do not create a culture; but neither do people remain unaffected by them. It is common to hear people in the South, for example, speak of how TV has disrupted traditional customs and celebrations; while in the West, TV is regularly blamed for increases in crime and violence, an alleged deterioration of civility and innumerable other social evils. It is tempting to assign too great an influence to symptoms of change; while the underlying causes, too opaque or complicated, go unexamined.

People are not *tabula rasa* on which the media inscribes its messages at will

In their polemic, *The Case Against the Global Economy: And for a turn toward the Local*, Jerry Mander and Edward Goldsmith write: 'Although hundreds of millions of children and teenagers around the world are listening to the same music and watching the same films and videos, globally distributed entertainment products are not creating a positive new global consciousness – other than a widely shared passion for more global goods and vicarious experience... So far, commodity consciousness is the only awareness that has been stimulated.'[3]

People are not *tabula rasa* on which the global media inscribes its messages at will. But neither is it an adequate explanation to claim that people interpret the messages after their own fashion and integrate them into their own worldview. It is more complicated. People do assimilate images and information according to their own experience, but, particularly in cultures where until recently people have remained closed to the assault of efficient technologies of cultural dissemination, this is scarcely an encounter of equals.

If this is true of adults in cultures sheltered by the remoteness or inaccessibility of where they live, it is even more true of children who, all over the world, and from early infancy, are exposed to the brandings of consciousness by the global market. These then become major determinants upon their growth and development. When I was a social worker in East London, mothers of very young children frequently said: 'They're very clever. They know what they want.' Few people paused to reflect that in what William Leiss called 'a culture of wanting', learning to want represented little more than obedience to the values of their society.

Nor are the mechanisms of dominance a one-way process. The very conduits that reinforce existing economic, social and cultural structures can themselves be subverted to create alternatives. The power of technology should be neither denied nor exaggerated; the important thing is the context in which it is deployed, and how it may be diverted so that it ceases to be an instrument for manipulating the people.

The internet

The internet now has hundreds of millions of users; it is estimated that about 200,000 more people gain access each day. It permits the spread of information, ideas and knowledge across all boundaries. Efforts by governments to control access to it are both clumsy and ineffective, as attempts to censor it have shown. Singapore tried to monitor and remove all illegal websites coming into its territory. It has strict legislation against pornography, libel and attacks on race or religion. Although committed to the use of the internet for economic purposes, the government of the small city state (with its population of a mere four million) wants to conserve a culture which it defines as one of 'family-oriented values', while remaining at the cutting edge of business competitiveness. This balance is maintained with some difficulty.

The internet is a powerful force for popular instruction, by-passing official ideologies; but at the same time it has become a major channel for pornography and the dissemination of ideologies of hatred. Many Western countries have closed down chat-rooms used by pedophiles to 'groom' children for sex; while the use of the net for coded communication between criminals, ideologues and terrorists has subverted it in ways that could scarcely have been foreseen. It has also proved to be as vulnerable to hearsay, rumor and superstition, as the old-fashioned and archaic means of communication, word of mouth.

Internet access reinforces existing inequalities

Eighty per cent of websites use English, although less than one-tenth of the world's people speak it. This does not, of course, mean that mother-tongues are abandoned, but the pervasiveness of English – both on the net and in the language of advertising, popular culture and so on, imparts another sensibility to other languages.

A friend of mine is a writer in Kannada, the language of Karnataka, the Indian state of which Bangalore is the capital. He says that people writing in Kannada now do so, not only with an eye to being translated into English, but in a style also influenced by the inflexions of that future translation. They are writing original works in a sort of provisional tongue, knowing that only its appearance in English will guarantee them a 'market' beyond the local and parochial.

Internet access reinforces existing inequalities; it divides privilege from poverty, young from old, urban from rural. The expression the 'digital divide' is sometimes used to recast the whole idea of social injustice, so that this means the distinction between those who do or do not have access to a certain kind of technology.

The internet is a powerful generator of convergence, but at the same time, it serves as a potent instrument for dissent. The anti-globalization movement has used the instant communication it provides to organize its demonstrations at meetings of the G-7, the European Union, the World Trade Organization, the World Bank and International Monetary Fund. It offers a capacity for popular interaction. There is no centralized power-location, and anyone can communicate by means of e-mail, chat-rooms and websites. The information is selected by the recipient and is not imposed by the programming or decision-making of others.

If the internet helps to magnify one element of the oral tradition – it globalizes gossip and rumor – it nevertheless deals yet another blow to the most ancient form of cultural transmission, the word of mouth, the song and the story told and retold through time by succeeding generations. It interrupts inter-generational communication of beliefs, values, behavior and customs; some of these were, doubtless, harmful, but the discontinuity does not distinguish between the damaging and the life-enhancing. And oral tradition, the most ancient and rooted of all vehicles of cultural continuity, has also been displaced by the authority of visual communication channels: the image predominates over the word, the picture over the idea.

Of course, the context in which the facility comes into play is not neutral. The global market has, to some extent, already done its work before the inquiring operator sits in front of her computer. It is no accident that shopping, sex and celebrity gossip are the most sought-after subjects on-line.

This raises, perhaps, the most significant criticism of the very paradigm which creates that context, what Illich calls the 'radical monopoly', which he refers to: 'When one industrial

The internet
In 1995, 6 million people used the internet. By 2002, it was 605.60 million. And by 2005 it is expected to top a billion

World Total	605.6 million
Africa	6.31 million
Asia/Pacific	187.24 million
Europe	190.91 million
Middle East	5.12 million
Canada & US	182.67 million
Latin America	33.35 million

Source: www.nua.ie/surveys/how_many_online

production process exercises an exclusive control over the satisfaction of a pressing need, and excludes non-industrial activities from the competition... Radical monopoly exists where a major tool rules out natural competence. Radical monopoly imposes compulsory consumption and thereby restricts personal autonomy... radical monopoly reflects the industrial institutionalization of values.' The enthusiasts of information technology claim that individuals are empowered to overcome precisely this by means of the internet. This discussion is far from concluded.

China, for example, has sought to limit access by its people to subversive or dangerous ideas on the internet. In January 2004, an Amnesty International report called for the release of 54 people imprisoned in China for expressing opinions on the internet. Amnesty estimates this to be 'a fraction' of the real number. The report notes: 'There has been a dramatic rise in the number of people detained or sentenced for internet-related offences. China is said to have the most extensive censorship of any country in the world.'

The report states that prisoners include those who signed online petitions for reform, published non-official news about the Sars virus, communicated with dissident groups overseas, or called for a review of the 1989 crackdown in Tiananmen Square. Among those detained there are also members of the Falun Gong movement.

As internet use grows in China, the government increases its efforts to control it. Officials try to block access to all sites that discuss sensitive issues. Amnesty said that the 54 detained – all 'prisoners of conscience' – had received sentences of between two and twelve years.[5]

The entertainment transnationals

Critics of global monoculture see the great concentrations of the entertainment and information conglomerates as vehicles shaping the sensibility of peoples – the power of Time-Warner, Disney, News International, and the increasing speed with which they dominate what people see and hear, and crucially, what children learn, all over the world. The word 'Disneyfication' has entered the language to describe a certain re-presentation of the world in the image of a sanitized theme-park. This, it is often alleged, replaces a messy, often chaotic reality with a cozy, predictable place of perpetual escape and distraction.

Even the apparent growth of Western culture is fragile

But reality can be less predictable than it seems. Even the apparent growth of Western culture is fragile. Disney, for example, has suffered the fall-out of the events of 11 September 2001 and in 2004 was faced with a takeover by Comcast. Who would have thought this in 1998, when Disneyworld in Orlando, Florida, was the biggest tourist attraction in the world, with more than 30 million visitors each year? At that time it employed 50,000 people.

The company has all the rights and powers of an independent municipal government. It can build its own roads, operate its own sewage and water-treatment plants, run its own police and fire stations, administer its own zoning and planning and employ its own inspectors. It is an autonomous entity within the state.

The recreation of exotic landscapes – African villages, a giant concrete baobab tree with a cinema inside the trunk, a rainforest café and Asian Adventures Area – offer artificial environments from all over the world. These have transformed the original orange groves, wetlands and palmetto scrub of Florida.

Disneyworld is serviced by employees who are assigned to jobs according to their age and experience. The company calls this 'casting'. It means that the most attractive young people get the frontline jobs. One employee said: 'Old ladies sell the merchandise, old men work in security, Haitian women work in housekeeping, Puerto Rican young people work in food services and preparation. And all the "less-than-presentable" people get stuck in the third shift, from 11 at night to seven in the morning.'

The Disney model increasingly animates the design and conception of parks, shopping malls and gallerias globally; it permeates chains of fast-food outlets and entertainment complexes. In Jakarta, Manila and Lagos, these are enclaves of privilege, set in cities of poverty, where they stand out like the brilliantly illuminated craft that have landed from other planets; in fact, they have merely arrived from another culture.

But how perishable, how flimsy and evanescent, are those cultural forms which seem as though they are sweeping the world.

Colonizing the imagination

I observed two little girls, seven and eight, in a middle-class Indian family. They were playing with Barbie dolls; not the models that had been specially fashioned for the Indian market, but pink, impossibly slender, with a floss of blond hair and a distinct swelling to mark the breasts. They had a doll's house, furniture, all the surroundings created by an inventive grandmother. These home-made items appeared shabby and ill-contrived compared to the high-gloss appearance of the shining little icon, which they picked up, handled, dressed and undressed with a tenderness they didn't show towards the hand-made house, the little pieces of furniture shaped out of patches of fabric, matchboxes and colored paper. This was clearly a learning experience; but one of the things they were learning was to look down upon the familiar and everyday. They were receiving instruction that the most beautiful, desirable things come from afar, a mythical and fabulous elsewhere, the elusiveness of which, in due course, will also provide them with experiences and hopes which they can scarcely expect to realize in the shabby, over-exposed and imperfect place called home.

The fascination of these concentrated distillations of an industrialized global perfectionism lies, not so much in the meaning conjured out of these objects as in their capacity to swallow up the disappeared significance of the local. They are sponges, absorbing, mopping up even memory of self-determining amusement and play.

This is what a 'culture of consumption' suggests. It is a process whereby ancient practices and ways of answering need – and the need to play and invent is as profound as any – dwindle away, are consumed, literally, by the intensity of the ardent products that replace them; a kind of spontaneous cultural combustion, which strikes the placid sensibility of tradition with the force of a revelation. Only when the moment of dazzling illumination has passed is the true convulsion of the psychic landscape made clear: places of ashes, funeral pyres, where the ability to make, create and provide has been used up, and the human imagination, raw, unpredictable, limitless, has been laid waste by the wildfires of industrially generated desire.

This culture, consumerism, creates and sells goods and services increasingly by harnessing signs and symbols that have no meaning in any traditional culture, no social anchorage, no identifiable roots. These take on a life of their own, and become the 'intellectual property' of the company that markets them. These are transformed into sacred objects; and as such, must be protected from attempts to abuse, misuse or bring them into disrepute or ridicule.

The holy iconography

In 1997 the Mattel Corporation, which owns Barbie, filed two lawsuits within a week, claiming trademark and copyright infringement. The first was against MCA records, for distributing the popular song 'I'm a Barbie girl', by the Dutch group, Aqua. Mattel claimed the song infringed its copyright and its 'most valuable trademark'. The lyrics, it was claimed, were damaging to Barbie's pure image. The back of the album contained a disclaimer, saying that the song is a social comment and 'was not created or approved by the makers of the doll.' The second suit was against Nissan, for a commercial that used plastic figures resembling Mattel products, including Barbie.

In the same year, the Body Shop displayed a poster with an exaggerated image of a woman with a faint resemblance to Barbie, and a caption which read: 'There are three billion women who don't look like supermodels and only eight who do.' A banner at the bottom of the poster read 'Love Your Body'. Mattel successfully convinced the Body Shop to stop its campaign by threatening them with a lawsuit.

While no one contested Mattel's right to profit from its own product, a ban on public criticism of icons that belong to the culture extends the power of owners of trademarks in such a way as to infringe the right to comment and freedom of expression. Discussion of the meaning society attaches to Barbie is, surely, admissible. Mattel sees a source of profit, society sees an image of unattainable perfection promoted as a model to young girls. The meaning beyond the product cannot be the property of Mattel alone – this suggests corporations may extend their power into the realm of the metaphysical.

> **Mattel sees a source of profit, society sees an image of unattainable perfection**

It is clear that 'culture' is not simply an addition to globalization, a frivolous luxury item or optional add-on. It is at the heart of the project; the materialization of a global ideology.

Market-driven news

The power of supranational companies in the management of global news helps them prioritize the issues which serve the interests of proprietors of TV and radio stations, newspapers and magazines. This creates forms of censorship far more subtle and effective than anything exercised by tyrannical governments which have sought to limit the access of their people to news that directly concerns them.

It is paradoxical, though scarcely surprising, that as global economic integration proceeds, so news, and especially foreign news, becomes of decreasing interest to the people in the rich countries, from where most of the information conglomerates operate. News that has been dominated by politics and by stories of poverty, violence and inequality in the world commands a declining market. Consequently, the news media, which must survive in a competitive global marketplace, must also give the people what they want. And if people do not want to know something, and vote by canceling their newspaper or turning off their TV set, then the damaged company will change its policy to ensure they are served with what they do want.

This has led to the mainstream media giving greater prominence to lifestyle and leisure, show-biz and sports gossip, celebrity and personality-cults that make Imelda Marcos or Kim Jung II look like shrinking violets. It sometimes seems that the right not to know what is disagreeable or makes us uncomfortable has now superseded the right to know of an eager generation which was resistant to manufactured news. It is now axiomatic

Commercial breaks have become a new art form

that the news is the big TV turn-off in the West, and that this is the time when people leave the room to make a cup of tea or go to the lavatory, and not during the commercial breaks, which have become a new art form, and therefore the object of interest and scrutiny.

Nowhere is this more true than in 'coverage' (significant word) of the news from the South. First of all, these are still, for the most part, classified as disaster areas. The capsized ferry in the Congo rates scarcely three lines, even though the death-toll may be several hundred. The earthquake in Turkey or Iran or the hurricane in Nicaragua focuses upon the elderly survivor, the miracle of the child drawn out of the wreckage ten days after the catastrophe; the recurring hunger in Ethiopia or southern Africa is treated with perfunctory and the now obligatory imagery of the emaciated child, the wailing mother, the outstretched hand. This is a fixed iconography, and it tells the people of the West less about international solidarity (although that, too, still exists, and 'compassion-fatigue' is not yet the debilitating numbness it is sometimes claimed to be), but more about how lucky we are to live in the lands of good fortune, prosperity and comfort. The corollary of this is that we would be foolish indeed to jeopardize it; so while we may place our coins in the charity envelope or make our tax-deductible standing order, we are not going to question the wisdom of a global dispensation which favors us so conspicuously. This, we soon learn, is ascribable to our merit and virtue, and we do not repudiate these self-attributed qualities.

Secondly, since the countries of the South have become major players in the global game, they cannot be ignored completely. This is why news from Namibia, China or Peru is more likely to be either picturesque, an illustration of the bizarre and droll customs of others, or representations of convergence, how 'they' are doing their best to become like 'us'. Images of the global middle class now make the news; and this has the effect of eclipsing the poor, consciousness of whose existence has virtually disappeared from the imagery of globalism, except when they become objects of endeavor – say, the UN goal of reduction by half in the numbers of poor by 2015 – and then they are more likely to appear as statistics of poverty than as themselves.

This, of course, leaves us in a state of extreme suggestibility for when important events occur, such as the invasion of Iraq. Then, it seems, anything that leaders choose to tell us can take root in the fertile ground of our suggestibilty, which they have so sedulously fostered until that point. The invasion of Iraq, although it had little popular support in Europe, was transformed by the dominant media into a fight against weapons of mass destruction which threatened us and all that we stood for. Saddam became the new Hitler, the incarnation of evil, the mother of all tyrants who must be brought down; while such upholders of human rights as Pol Pot and Idi Amin were permitted to die peacefully in their beds.

The war in Iraq demonstrated not only the power of the US and its allies to do as they wished, but also the limits of the ability of the global media to colonize the hearts and minds of the people at home, let alone in the country it became necessary for them to occupy. Skepticism, dissent and other ways of seeing are not obliterated, even when it seems the long nimble fingers of the existing vehicles of information can reach into our brains and re-configure them in accordance with the necessities of global privilege.

Tourism: a cultural contaminant

One of the most significant contributors to the undermining of traditional cultures has been the promotion of tourism to those (hitherto) 'unspoilt' places, where 'primitive' or 'picturesque' environments have been tended by the people who have occupied and sustained them – and been sustained by them – for centuries.

Tourism has become the biggest industry in the world, with slightly less than 600 million arrivals in 2003, generating $450 billion.[6] Many countries have seen tourism as a major – and relatively painless – means of earning foreign exchange. They have, accordingly, marketed their 'scenery', their landscapes, beaches and wildernesses, and often, the customs and festivals of their people, to the rich world, in the hope of attracting the free-spending well-to-do. This, it is claimed, creates jobs, spreads wealth and brings prosperity to places that would otherwise have remained impoverished and backward.

In the 1950s, only 25 million people a year traveled to a foreign destination. In the 1960s, this grew to 70 million. While the figure dropped slightly after 11 September, figures for 2003 were 694 million. The World Tourism Organization predicts 1.56 billion by the year 2020.

Tourism is also a big employer. It is now estimated that 260 million are employed, either directly, or indirectly – one in nine jobs – in the global economy. Tourism is now pursued as a major strategy for development in the South. Under IMF and World Bank prescriptions, tourism is classified as an export strategy; and is seen by the international institutions as a beneficial means for indebted countries to repay their debt to them.

Liberalization has made it easier for transnational travel companies to invest in 'Third World' countries, hotels, holiday complexes and leisure facilities. The protection formerly provided to local tourism industries by the General Agreement on Trade in Services has been abolished, so the transnationals now enjoy the same benefits as local enterprises.

Tourism is the mirror image of economic migration: the privileged may pass through any borders they choose, while those who actually seek to put into practice the core ideology of globalism – that it is the right and duty of the individual to seek her or his economic salvation – are stigmatized as illegal migrants, refugees, or asylum-seekers; so that the persecuted, as well as the dispossessed, are denied the right to seek security or livelihood.

Tourism
The numbers of tourists worldwide continue to grow, despite a 1.2% downturn after 11 September 2001

1950	25.3
1960	69.3
1970	159.7
1980	284.8
1990	455.9
1995	550.4
2000	687.3
2001	684.1
2003	694.0

Source: World Tourism Organization

In any case, tourists are more often than not sequestered in fortresses of luxury, where many of the comforts they find indispensable to their well-being are brought from home – including food, beverages and entertainment – so that their contact with the culture is, to them, invisible.

But the host community certainly sees them; *their* extravagance, *their* expensive undress, *their* leisure, *their* capacity to summon local people into the livery of servitude to wait on them are very conspicuous. They bring an aura of glamor and wealth. If Goa, or Acapulco or Rio or Bali are the object of their dream, this has the opposite effect on the young people in the resorts – where the rich come from is their 'elsewhere'. The money-power of tourists permits them to pre-empt the best of everything; and villages are deprived of water so that the lawns of the hotels are kept green. The

People consume the blueness of the water, the innocence of the people

travelers are not going on holiday in the traditional sense, they are on a hedonistic spree in the Third World. Tourism is an industry more extractive even than the mining of industrial conglomerates: people consume the blueness of the water, the innocence of the people, the land that no longer produces rice or fish.

Sex tourism is only an extension of this. In Thailand, the story is of delighted Western men, usually older, who discover with astonishment the tenderness and solicitude of young women. The men feel rejuvenated, alive, above all, wanted. It is as different an experience from the sex industry in the West as can be imagined. Only later, when it appears the girl – or boy – has a mother who needs an operation, a brother to be put through school, a house destroyed in a cyclone to be rebuilt – that the demands for money become

more insistent. Where the visitor sees himself as involved in a personal relationship, his partner is already inextricably caught up in a web of relationships,
whereby a dozen or more people depend upon her for survival. It is then that
the client declares he has been cheated, conned. She made out she wanted me.
I didn't know I was taking on a whole family. The encounter with the culture,
so sweet, so beguiling, quickly reverts to racism, and the rich men see themselves as the victims of the duplicity and selfishness of the young men and
women they found so charming and attentive.

The monoculture of money

These are only a few of the channels through which a globalizing *tendency*
undermines local cultures. They are not the causes. The causes lie embedded
in the logic of economic reason, which is often at odds with common sense,
humanity and even reason itself. But if we are moving towards a unified global
culture, this is the truly compelling, irresistible force which is leading, slowly,
unevenly, and certainly not without resistance, towards it.

The erosion of cultural diversity is accelerated by the employment of technologies in the service of economic dominance: societies and cultures that
have survived for millennia are attacked at their roots.

This has been the great insight which Vandana Shiva has brought to the
discussion: how the modification of culture is inseparable from changes
imposed from outside, in the economic sphere. One of the most telling
examples she cites is the way in which traditional ways of answering the basic
human need for food have been subverted and replaced by industrialized
food-production.

Shiva argued, in her Reith Lectures in 2000, that the obsession with the
quantity of food production in the world is reducing the diversity of food
production, and in the process, vital alternative sources of nutrition. 'High
yields' of industrial agriculture tell us nothing about the variety of nutrients
required by the human body, which have traditionally been answered by the

work of women agriculturalists, who have planted pulses, fruit and vegetables on the margins of the principal crop. 'Planting only one crop in the entire field as a monoculture will of course increase its individual yield. The obsession with productivity creates blindness towards the higher diversity of productivity and leads to the 'monoculture of the mind'. It is this which makes people more receptive to the monoculture of globalization, which is the monoculture of money.'

She states: 'The Mayan peasants in the Chiapas (in Mexico) are characterized as unproductive because they produce only two tons of corn per acre. However, their overall food output is 20 tons per acre when the diversity of their beans and squashes, their vegetables and fruit trees are taken into account. In Java, small farmers cultivate 607 species in their home gardens. In sub-Saharan Africa, women cultivate 120 different plants. A single home garden in Thailand has 230 species, and African home gardens have more than 60 species of trees. A study in eastern Nigeria found that home gardens occupying only two per cent of a household's farmland accounted for half of the farm's total output. In Indonesia 20 per cent of household income and 40 per cent of domestic food supplies come from home gardens managed by women.'

Shiva says what is needed to feed the people of the world is the maintenance and enhancement of biodiversity, not more intensive chemicalization or the genetic engineering of crops. The truly productive are made invisible by the industrialization of agriculture. The self-reliant, those who feed themselves, are seen as non-productive, or economically inactive; science and technology makes the true 'feeding the world', mainly undertaken by women, disappear.

Monoculture defines as inferior everything that is local, homemade, familiar. 'Human hands' says Shiva, 'are being defined as the worst contaminants, and work for human hands is being outlawed, replaced by machines and chemicals bought from global corporations. These are not recipes for feeding the world, but for stealing livelihoods from the poor to create markets for the powerful.'

In other words, the destabilizing of local cultures touches them at their material base. Once this has been damaged or degraded, the propaganda of a seductive and intensifying industrialism merely does its work more effectively. The communication conglomerates, the iconography of advertising, the publicity machines and propaganda mills simply serve to support this process.

1 Reith lecture 2000. **2** www.uschina.org/public/wto/b4ct/barshefsky.html **3** *The Case Against the Global Economy: And for a Turn towards the Local*, by Jerry Mander and Edward Goldsmith, Sierra Club Books 1996. **4** *The Homogenization of Global Culture* edited by Jerry Mander and Edward Goldsmith. **5** *The Guardian* 28 January 2004. **6** The Economist Intelligence Unit.

13 The gods, the Quechua and the Maasai

'When the gods made the world, the sky was not distant as it is today. It was just above the heads of the people, and it was there for them to reach up to and take what they wanted. Sky could be used to create clothing, for food, for shelter. It was everywhere and within their grasp. But unfortunately, the people became too greedy and were tearing down pieces of sky beyond their need. So the gods decided they would teach them a lesson: they raised the sky to its present height, where people can no longer abuse it, and to remind them of the beauty and plenty they have lost.'

Story of creation

Many cultures have, as part of their founding myth, the story of some special distinction conferred upon them by their god or gods. Privileges were taken away often as a result of the failure to observe the sacred laws; which plunged the people into the present darkness, which accounts for sin, death and time; and the dream is of a return to the golden age, the time of universal peace and harmony, when everything will be restored to its original condition.

The myth of a golden past makes cultures vulnerable to efforts at purification and renewal; to movements that seek to recapture a distant, vanished era. Such movements seek to return to literal prescriptions embodied in holy texts, to alter behavior, to enforce conformity with traditions which, they believe, will redeem or reinstate the age of universal contentment. This leads to forms of revivalism which can be extremely violent, particularly when evil forces are believed to be at work which must be exorcized. At such times deviants, witches, unbelievers or those who infringe the obligations and duties of the culture will be treated very harshly indeed; as will all 'outsiders', the bearers of other faiths. These will be persecuted and may be put to death. Those to whom the 'cause' of want, poverty or violence is attributed lead to purges, evictions and expulsions. Someone must be made to pay, to expiate and to reconcile the people to the irreconcilable, that is, the inadmissibility of the finality of death.

Cultures seek to explain the basic riddles of existence: while we long for immortality, our tenure of life is brief. Our inability to transcend nature creates the need to explain these fundamentally unsatisfactory circumstances of our lives. The contradictions are reconciled in the great stories we have narrated to each other about eternity, living on, transmigration, the indestructibility of the soul, paradise, after-life, renewal and the return of the ancestors, the apoc-alypse and judgment, or the attainment of eternal peace.

The ambiguities in these tales both satisfy and disturb: they give meaning to the incomprehensible; but at the same time, do not assuage the anger and resentment at the restrictions imposed by mortality upon our poor brief lives. Since we cannot attack the gods (although we might blaspheme, and declare our unbelief, convert or abandon our faith), there is one thing we can do; and that is, recognizing our captivity within nature, nature that gave us life and will take it away again, seek to become like the mysterious forces that hold us in their power. We can, even if only for a moment, usurp that power: we can harm, we can fight, we can kill: when we have others at our mercy, we feel an access of pride and power, a sense of invincibility. If we can conquer others, we become briefly like the very forces that will vanquish us in due course. But not today. Today we can put to death the those-who-are-not-us, the inferior beings, the followers of alien beliefs and outrageous sects. We come to resemble Nature itself, that from which our frail existence is held on lease, and which will claim us in the end.

Diversity in sameness

Cultures exhibit great diversity in their sameness: the ways in which the fundamentally identical experiences of all humanity may be celebrated, elaborated and decorated by ritual, magic and symbolic actions. All have some form of myth of origin – how the group, the tribe, the race came into its privileged existence. But the way in which power is distributed, how rulers reflect the divine or cosmic order, how we mark the passage of time, birth, growth, maturity, sex and procreation, ageing and death, patterns of kinship, belonging and collective re-affirmation of order – these are common to all cultures, but the forms they take appear strange, barbaric and incomprehensible to outsiders.

Even recent, materialistic cultures do not fully free themselves from these antique forms.

Cultures exhibit great diversity in their sameness

How can they? They simply re-interpret ancient myths and serve them up in a form more acceptable to changing sensibility of the people. New meanings are sought, and perhaps even discovered; but these do nothing to alter the ancient unchanging puzzles, and even less to alter the facts of decay and death. For instance, industrial culture with its myth of progress, could not, apparently, be more different from cyclical notions of time that characterized older cultures, the eternal recurrences that reflect the seasons, night and day, the mysteries of the natural world. Progress is simply the memorializing in material form of the achievements of a transient humanity. It doesn't stop people dying, even though industrial technology promises life prolonged into a tenth or eleventh decade. It has learned to mine the present, the curious cultural phenomenon of seeking to cram eternity into a single lifetime – to do everything, go everywhere, so that the accumulation of experience in a finite life-span reflects the economic order, which states that growth is unending and human appetites without limit. It merely re-arranges ancient stories in a different shape; there are no new elements. In any case, we still die, despite the life-lengthening possibilities of technology, medicines and drugs, spare-part surgery, cryogenics and all the other forms of pseudo-resurrection-ism.

Even when cultures appear to be overwhelmed by more powerful and empowering revelations, they do not simply fade away. In February 2004 the grave of an Anglo-Saxon king was discovered in an area close to Southend-on-Sea which was being surveyed for road improvements. It was one of the most perfectly preserved tombs ever found in Britain. The burial was in a large chamber, and among the perfectly preserved artifacts were bronze cauldrons, gold foil crosses and blue glass vessels, copper buckles, a sword and shield. The crosses indicated that the king was a recent convert to Christianity, but he was also taking with him everything he needed for an afterlife which had nothing to do with his recent conversion. Older beliefs remain; and, particularly when new beliefs are in their early stages, many people propitiate both the old and the new religions.

Nowhere is this clearer than in places where ancient beliefs have been under assault for centuries.

The Quechua

> *¡Pachakuteq Taytallay! ¡Kamacheqniy Inkallay!*
> *Maypin kashan munaykiki? Maypitaqmi khuyayniki?*
> *Mark'aykita mast'arispan Tawantinsuyuta wiñachirganki,*
> *auqa sonqo runakunataq llaqtanchiqta ñak'arichinku.*

Qolla suyoq yawar weqen Inkakunaq unanchasqan,
qantapunin waqharimuyku Perú Suyu nak'ariqtin.
Maypin kashanki Pachakuteq? Maypin llanp'u sonqo kausayniki?
waqmantapas sayarimuy llaqtanchis Suyo qespirinanpaq.

Father of our nation! Creator of the Incas!
Where is your love? Where is your compassion?
You extended your arms, and made our nation grow into an
empire.
But now, cruel men make our people suffer.
Tears of blood now flow in the venerated land of the Incas.
We call upon you, because our people are suffering.
Where are you Pachakuteq? Where is your noble heart?
If you were alive today, our nation would prosper.[1]

The Quechua-speaking people of the Andes are the descendants of the Incan
Empire, whose language it was. In fact, the Quechua were simply one group
which formed the Inca empire, but their language long preceded the imperial
venture. There are still around 10 million speakers of Quechua today; and
about three million ethnic Quechua remain, in Ecuador, Bolivia and Peru.

The Incas had a highly organized society. At its apex was the emperor,
whose power was divine and absolute. The imperial government demanded
absolute obedience, and everything was owned by the state, except houses,
movable goods and small pieces of individual land. The people were
compelled to labor in mines, construction and military service, although
provision was made for the sick and aged from state storehouses. Mines
provided copper and bronze for everyday goods; gold, silver and tin were
reserved for the emperor and higher nobility and the decoration of temples.

The empire was of relatively brief duration – from the early 1400s until its
conquest by the Spanish conquistador Pizarro in 1532. The area expanded

beyond Cuzco under Pachacuti, the first emperor; and for the next century grew to cover about 3,500 kilometers of the western coast and mountains of the continent from what is Colombia in the north to Chile in the south.

The Quechua language existed perhaps 1,000 years before the empire. The creation myth of the Incas has a number of variations, and combined much of the lore and beliefs of the Aymara people. One version begins with the god Viracocha who emerged from Lake Titicaca. He created the the coast. But the people living around the lake had offended the god, so he destroyed them and they turned to stone; and from him later Inca rulers descended. Viracocha was served, primarily by the sun, but also by the moon, the gods of thunder, stars, earth and sea. Divination, healing, sacrifice (which could be human at times of great stress or insecurity), ceremonial and ritual were part of the religion.

Stone — the great monumental structures of the Andes — not surprisingly played a major role in Inca culture: the mountain contained a spirit which could transform itself into human beings, and human beings could be turned to stone. It was believed that sacred stones could be turned into an army that defeated invaders. Machu Picchu remains as the great testimony to their reverence for stone, with which they built temples and made sophisticated artifacts. Machu Picchu escaped the attention of the conquerors, and it was here that many refugees fled after the invasion.

The collapse of the central and south American civilizations was hastened, not only by the ferocity of the faith of the invaders, but equally, by the spread of diseases to which the people had no immunity. When the emperor Atahualpa was captured in 1532, the symbol of power and prestige was broken; and the outer trappings of a civilization were doomed. Although there were rebellions against the Spanish, it was not in the military sphere that resistance continued: the culture occupied the deep recesses of the heart and sensibility, just as the people lived on in the mountains, caverns and hillsides of the topography of the Andes. The Quechua language was banned as the Andean republics became independent republics, and the indigenous peoples increasingly pauperized and victims of discrimination.

They are not 'Indians'. They call themselves *runa*, the people; like all cultures, they saw themselves as the supreme people, the only authentic people created by the true gods, adhering to the true religion, following the only admissible culture.

Old skills die hard

The Quechua system of agriculture, terracing the steep slopes of the mountains, together with a highly developed irrigation system, permitted them to grow a wide variety of produce, through different climatic zones, which changed with altitude. They knew how to freeze-dry food in the cold upper slopes. Many vegetables familiar all over the world today originated in the Andes – notably the potato, tomato and corn. The Incas herded llamas and vicunas, producing meat, wool, grease, fuel and leather. They produced textiles of vivid dyes and in geometric patterns, and of course, ceremonially used the coca leaf; that symbol of prohibited mind-altering states in a quite different contemporary culture of North America and Europe. Many of these elements remain in the life of the Quechua today: the fabrics, the traditional dyes; the Quechua suggest an inner dignity enfolded within the psyche, the resistance of mountain cultures and a defiance of the attempts of outsiders to efface it.

The Quechua were a pre-literate people. With no written language, oral tradition and memory served to preserve culture; and indeed, this means of transmission has remained embedded in language. Their system of denoting significant events was through the celebrated *quipu*, tying of knots in rope, which served as accounts and record of events and transactions. Many words have been absorbed into Spanish from Quechua, and some have migrated into English, including coca, condor, guano, gaucho, llama, puma, lima (bean). In 1975, after years of suppression, Quechua became one of the official languages of Bolivia. In Peru, the population today consists of about 15 per cent *crollo* (white), 37 per cent *mestizo* (mixed race), 45 per cent indigenous and three per cent other.

In the 20th century, migrations to the cities of Quito and Lima have depleted the rural areas and led to the growth of city slums, as elsewhere in the world. The Quechua language remains, and many of the older beliefs linger beneath the official Catholicism which was imposed upon the people by the zealotry of the colonialists; and

'In my heart I'm still a little girl from the Andes'

these sometimes appear in syncretic festivals and rituals which blend Catholicism with an older religious sensibility. A report by Indigenous Peoples of the World describes the annual two-day festival of La Virgen de las Mercedes (known also as the Fiesta de la Mama Negra) in Latacunga, Ecuador.[2] Although this is ostensibly a Roman Catholic festival, on the second day after mass, a statue of the Virgin is carried through the town. People throw flowers in the hope of receiving a blessing or good fortune. Then, cross-gender dressing and masked street-dancing become the main activities. There is a procession of sacrificed animals, and liquor and cigarettes are also offered up: these gifts to the spirits are carried by men on their backs, mingling with the dancers and musicians.

'I lived in the Andes until I was 12 years old, then in the city of Lima another 12 years before coming to the US. But even though I've lived here many years, in my heart I'm still a little girl from the Andes… Whenever I heard a native Quechua language song, I used to listen attentively to learn the words, because I might not hear the same song again for a while (there was no electricity for radios or CDs to play the songs over and over again). While at home I liked to sit in the yard, and my animals would come to me and lay down around me, maybe to be friendly, and I would sing to them some

Quechua songs,' wrote Ada Gibbons.[3]

Yet paradoxically, although the meaning might have been drained from the heart of the culture, conquest, poverty and oppression often sustain traditions rather than eliminating them; especially where, as in the Andean region, there are places of refuge from other invading or encircling cultures. Of course, in the 20th century and after, once in the slums of Lima or Quito, many indigenous peoples become detached from their own culture, and learn to adapt to newer cultures of market-engendered poverty. Indeed, the long time-lapse since the culture of the Quechua-speaking peoples remained the principal animating force in their lives, the culture has itself slumbered on; and in recent years, the people have been on the receiving end of evangelical Protestant missionaries, who speak of 'untouched' peoples, and considerable conversions have been made of nominal Catholics; how far this will eliminate older animist indigenous values remains to be seen.

The Maasai

'It takes one day to destroy a house but to build a new one will take months, perhaps years. If we destroy our way of life to construct a new one, it will take thousands of years.'
Maasai belief[4]

The Maasai are pastoralists who have occupied the Rift Valley of East Africa for three millennia. Their migration into southern Kenya is more recent – perhaps half a millennium ago. They occupy arid lands, with little surface water, a terrain unsuitable for agriculture, but well adapted to cattle. The Maasai created a delicate balance between environment and culture: indeed, the culture served ecological integrity in the particular climatic zone in which they survived. Equilibrium had to be maintained between herds which did not overuse resources and yet did not fall below the level of necessary subsistence. It was in their interests to protect the commons on which they depended.

Both religious and cultural practice tended towards maintaining the sensitive interaction between place and culture. Social life consisted of a series of transitions between different age-groups, each one attended by great ceremony, from youth into adulthood, and thence to maturity and on to become one of the respected elders, which, in turn, brought them closer to God. The crucial aspect of each ceremony was the sharing of meat. Each step indicated the enhanced status of the age-group as it passed through time. The rituals regulated the cattle population, and kept it within the bounds of the grazing potential of the region.

The older age-groups formed alliances across different areas and communities. Women acquired a higher 'age-grade' after marriage, and were accorded increasing responsibility for herds, land and families.

Young children stayed in the enclosure – temporary structures suitable for the semi-nomadic life – which safeguarded both people and cattle from raids by rival groups. Children looked after the small animals, women milked the cattle, took them to graze and distributed the milk. Between the age of 15 and 18 both girls and boys were initiated into adulthood by circumcision; this gave them the right to marry and to own cattle.

Boys also became warriors. It was their function to steal livestock from others and to protect their own animals. Raiding cattle was sanctioned by religion, since the Maasai believed that the cattle had been given to all people as part of the heritage of common resources.

The society was polygamous: each wife had her house within the family homestead, and lived off the cattle she was given at the time of marriage. The wider family shared resources during times of scarcity. Birth rates were fairly low. Men had to acquire cattle as warriors before they could marry; and this then required permission of elders, who remained the owners of the family herds. This led to late marriage age for men. There was also no sexual activity for six months after the birth of a child, and while the woman was breast-feeding sexual abstinence was required. Drought also played its part – in times of scarcity people suffered lower nutritional status and this limited fertility. In the colonial period, the spread of sexually transmitted disease further reduced fertility.

Animal husbandry, raiding cattle, the tending of animals by women and children and foraging – these were the principal elements of the indigenous culture. In the colonial era the cash economy became significant; but it was only towards the end of British rule that new forms of land tenure were compulsorily introduced; and since Independence a more intensive penetration by the market economy has ruined self-reliance and impoverished many Maasai. Dependence on livestock was almost total – up to 80 per cent of the diet was milk, and most of the remainder, blood and meat.

Tourism has had a harmful effect upon the lifeways of the Maasai

Trading and barter in the 19th century opened up the society to a wider range of goods. Since the colonial era, the story of the Maasai has been one of continuous erosion of culture, alienation of land and degradation of their condition. Reserves were set aside under the 'Treaties' of 1904 and 1912; and individuals received titles to land. This undermined the idea of shared resources – water, land and beasts. Land has been subdivided, and many Maasai settled in more or less sedentary households, although seasonal grazing still takes place. Maize is now cultivated, but sub-division of land into small privately owned plots makes them too small to be economically viable. The number of cattle per person has been significantly reduced. Boreholes have lowered the water tables. Traditionally the Maasai moved to lowlands in the rainy season and highlands in the dry period – this dispersal permitted regeneration of the resource base.

In recent years, tourism has had a profound and harmful effect upon the lifeways of the Maasai. Elephants, rhinoceros, lions and other large mammals have attracted visitors, and on the Maasai Mara Reserve – formerly dry season grazing land – grazing is now banned. Many Maasai today sell handicrafts and beadwork at the entrances to the reserve parks, from where they too are banned. Park and 'conservation' management has imposed an alien culture on the Maasai. The preservation of habitat and wildlife, principally for the benefit of Kenyan entrepreneurs and foreign tourists, has been at the expense of the people. Trackers, conservators and wardens are brought in as outside professionals, whereas in fact, the Maasai were themselves the guarantors of stability and harmony between wildlife, the fragile ecology and humanity. In an epic act of injustice, the very people whose care and husbandry have preserved the land for centuries are being blamed for overgrazing, cattle overstocking and environmental damage.

This is because game reserves have been called 'protected areas' and the Maasai must remain in areas which are 'non-protected'. Wildlife recognizes no such boundaries, and grazes across borders, using up the pastureland to the detriment of the original cattle-herders. This introduces new concepts of land use, contrary to traditional customary law of the people. The market economy offers them no benefits; only the poverty of exclusion, both from their traditional way of life and equally, from the market.

The Maasai have inferior schools, small access to secondary schooling and virtually no opportunities for further education. Healthcare is unsatisfactory, health centres distant, and neglected sicknesses like TB and HIV receive little help. Although a major water project runs a pipeline through Maasai land, they must use contaminated boreholes which are shared with cattle.

Cultural *bomas* have been set up, which are artificial Maasai villages for tourists. The Maasai who sell beadwork and handicrafts outside the lodges where tourists stay serve principally as a photo-opportunity for the visitors. Very few are employed in the lodges, and when they are it is as security guards, or as groups of traditional dancers. The market economy introduces a foreign culture, in which they are left behind, since none of their skills of ancient sustainability of the savanna landscape has any place in the new society.

Surunkai Ole Kimurua is an elder of the Maasai, 90 years old. His family lived in the Oloirien region for generations but have now been forced to leave:

'... My father migrated to this region before I was born. He told me that our great, great grandfathers – they passed this land to us and I was hoping to do the same thing to my children – to have them occupy this land. As far as the current situation goes, I can forecast that my children will not be able to walk on our family's remains. Our ancestral remains are now being dug out by modern machinery (tractors).'[5]

The Maasai illuminate the unresolved argument between the benefits brought by 'modernization' – or is it cultural dominance? – healthcare, dietary improvements and the advantages of traditional society. The failings of the new are glaringly obvious – they create inequalities, individual ownership of shared resources, inequality and a terrible loss of meaning. The failings of the old are also clear – scarcity and periodic hunger from times of drought, practice of circumcision, especially of young women, the hierarchy of age. There are clearly powerful arguments in favor of 'integration' into the modern world; but to those who bear the values and traditions of time out of memory, this is experienced as a violation of everything in which they have believed. There is, it seems, no obvious way in which the best of the old and the best of the new can be synthesized. Even if the Maasai are given 'fair' access to the market economy, this can never be sufficient consolation for the loss of meaning of their world.

'A Maasai without culture is as a zebra without stripes. If we abandon our way of life, our next step could be extinction,' says Kakuta ole Maimai, who hosts a website about the Maasai.[6]

1 www.peoplesoftheworld.org/text?people=Quichua **2** www.peoplesoftheworld.org **3** www.andes.org/chickens.html **4** www.maasai-infoline.org **5** www.maasai-infoline. org. **6** www.maasai-infoline.org

PART 4

Consuming
Cultures

Reclaiming
hearts and minds

Globaliza

and Local

Lives

14 Cultures of resistance

'The most effective attacks against globalization are usually not those related to economics. Instead, they are social, ethical, and, above all, cultural.'

Maria Vargas Llosa

Resistance to globalization has come in a number of guises; the anti-globalization movement being perhaps the most well known today. But attempts at resistance have taken many other forms, from the Islamic Revolution that overthrew the Shah of Iran to the partial globalization espoused in Malaysia.

Many saw the Islamic Revolution in Iran in 1979 as the first significant reaction against neo-colonialism, as globalization was called at the time. The revolution not only ousted the Shah; it also rejected the market economy that he had embraced. The story of the circumstances that led to the revolution is of more than historic interest, since the developments that led up to it are repeated in many countries today.

The rise in oil prices of the early 1970s made Iran rich. But since the money came from the sale of a single basic commodity, and was not generated within the country, the ruling elite had no reason to concern itself with what happened to its own people. Banks gave loans to urban businesses, to the detriment of the countryside. This threw rural laborers out of work, and they migrated to the shanty-towns that developed around the major cities. Local small-scale producers were undercut by imports of Western goods.

At the same time, the Shah encouraged a class of transnational rich, who sent their children abroad for education and sought medical treatment in the West. An extensive middle class emerged that was highly educated, although there were few jobs for them within Iran, since there had been little indigenous development. The position of Iran made it the ideal

The new elites mimicked those which had been overthrown

location for a US-supported power that would protect its interests in the region. Unlimited arms supplied by the US created a state increasingly dependent upon the US.

The revolution followed a big rise in taxes when oil prices fell; and the chief participants were a coalition of industrial workers, the urban poor, the small producers and shopkeepers of the bazaars, the Shi'a clergy to whom the ostentation of Western consumerism was anathema. At least in the early stages the rebellion had been fuelled by a national alliance against the Westernized elite, the transnational companies, arms dealers and the culture of inequality which these promoted.

The Shah fled in 1979. Within two years Iran became a Shi'a theocracy. There was a redistribution of wealth, and welfare nets were provided for the poor. Ayatollah Khomeini sought to inaugurate a 'reign of virtue', by contrast with a rule contaminated by what he called '*gharbzadigi*' or 'Western toxicity'.

But a new kind of autocracy emerged: political parties were disbanded, the communists and secularists outlawed; so that, in the end, the new elites mimicked those which had been overthrown with the ousting of the Shah. The Islamic Revolution, institutionalized, presented itself as a successful overthrow of Western-inspired development. However, even after a quarter of a century, the outcome of the Iranian alternative is far from certain – the struggle between reformists and conservatives continues. Whether this will result in the victory of the supporters of theocracy or in a re-making of the Islamic state, or whether Iran will be re-absorbed into the global economy, it is too early to say.

Resistance by social tradition

Other governments – particularly those of South and East Asia – have boasted of the power of their social traditions to overcome some of the most malign consequences of globalization. Networks of kinship and family remain more or less intact, despite long exposure to liberalization. Some, including Malaysia, have taunted the West with the survival of their human safety-nets, scorning the dependency of the people of the 'developed' countries on the costly apparatus of State welfare.

Their confidence in the capacity of these cultural traits to endure shows how little they know of Western history. In Britain, in the early industrial period, the support of flesh and blood was the only recourse of the poor against utter destitution. These were undermined by the uprootings of industrialism, and began to decay only when a measure of security was provided by the State, a process accelerated by the setting up of more comprehensive welfare programs after 1945.

Few Asian leaders appreciate that their countries are the site of a vast, untried social and cultural experiment: there, too, the bonds of kinship are also being eroded by the migrations and disturbances set in train by urbanization and global integration.

Yet there is little chance these countries will be in a position to afford even the most rudimentary social security systems for the poor. In the villages, where seasonal migrations were limited and controlled, the sick and the elderly were readily tended by those who remained behind. But with the scatterings of human beings all over the globe, the migrations of both hope and despair, the trafficking of women and children, the global sex trade, the commerce in domestic servants, the buying-in of care by the rich West for their children, the labor-exporting reservoirs of Bangladesh, Indonesia, the Philippines, Thailand, Burma, China and India, Guatemala, Mexico, as well as the draining of talent which takes medical, nursing, academic and highly qualified personnel from all over the world for the benefit of the rich countries – all this disrupts settled patterns of living, leaves people high and dry, disturbs the upbringing of a new generation, creates incalculable costs to the vulnerable and abandoned.

Selective globalization

Malaysia has been at the centre of an effort to achieve this kind of selective globalization, which would take advantage of the economic advantages, but keep at bay some of the undesirable social consequences. The *Washington Post* reported on efforts by the Malaysian government to turn back the enthusiastic popular embrace of American culture.[1]

'The result is a mixed message. Lewd jokes are censored from the David Letterman show, and the sex scenes snipped from *The Man in the Iron Mask*. Malaysian pop-charts feature home-grown soundalikes of Mariah Carey and the Backstreet Boys... The government is like a stern parent, reviews every movie, television show, book and performance, deleting violence and sex, and guarding against perceived violations of Islamic values, like bare female shoulders or long hair on men... It also protects – or tries to – Malaysian producers, requiring, for example, that television commercials should be made locally. Yet most TV ads are modeled on American versions and usually feature actors of indeterminate ethnicity.'

The *Washington Post* journalist, Megan Rosenfeld, judges the culture to be 'a hybrid, a synthesis'. She believes definitions of national cultures are becoming more and more difficult. Her analysis may be shallow, based upon the evidence of objects of instant consumption. She shows little understanding of the fragile ethnic mix of Malaysia – 60 per cent Malays, 30 per cent

Chinese, 10 per cent Indians, the latter descendants of indentured laborers brought by the British. Malaysia has maintained communal harmony for almost 40 years by favoring the formerly economically disadvantaged Malays. Unparalleled prosperity in a country rich in resources, but with a population of only 20 million, has made this easier. The theory (which is also the Western model) that social peace can be maintained principally through a constantly rising disposable income has also supported the

Mainstream culture in Malaysia is a bland version of transnational pop culture

Malaysian experience. Heavily interventionist, it has re-directed resources to the majority Malays. Whether this can be replicated in countries with fewer resources and much bigger populations is another matter.

Mainstream culture in Malaysia is a bland version of transnational pop culture, without the sex and with only some of the violence. The authoritarianism of government has been at war with a rather tepid version of youth culture: this is reminiscent of the relatively modest 'excesses' of emerging teenagers in the 1950s in the US and Western Europe.

Malaysia has tried to mould 'development' so that it mimics the US, but is devoid of its vigor. The result is a curiously imitative and bloodless version of the West, underpinned by some Islamic pieties. Mohammad Mahathir, Prime Minister for two decades until 2003, declared his independence from the Western model of development. (At the time of the financial crisis in Asia in 1998, he refused to devalue the currency and controlled the exchange rate, in defiance of the IMF/World Bank recommendations.) But it is not the Western model itself that has been criticized by Malaysia. It is, rather, the arrogance of the West and the financial institutions it controls in its effort to impose identical policies on all countries. Certainly Malaysia has grown rich, but inequality is also conspicuous – the Indians, mainly Tamils, are still by far the most disadvantaged group. Nor do changes in the material fabric of the country show any remarkable difference from that of the West: the intersecting highways, the economy built around the needs of the motor-car, the suburbs, the shopping malls and fast-food centers have given the country the aspect of a vast new town, conservative, unadventurous, with a few gestures to national grandeur, most notably the towers of the Petronas

Today's anti-globalization movement has its roots in the 1960s

Building in Kuala Lumpur, now the tallest human-made structure in the world. The prohibition on sex, drugs and alcohol has driven them underground, so that they exist in the shadow of the contrived wholesomeness projected to the outside world.

Malaysia has re-created itself as a careful and slightly overwrought make-believe. Its 'independence' is as synthetic as its hybrid culture; and it shows above all the limits of imagination of those who claim there are other versions of 'modernization' than those embodied in the familiar images of globalization.

Cultures of resistance

Today's anti-globalization movement has its roots in the 1960s, and has been defining itself for at least the last quarter of the 20th century. In 1973, Ivan Illich used the word 'conviviality' to designate the opposite of industrial productivity: this means supplementing a modest dependency on material resources from within the incomparable treasure-house of human resourcefulness.

This slowly emerging culture also inherits features long familiar in the Western tradition, even though it formally repudiates many of them. It is visionary and apocalyptic; it foresees planetary extinction unless the changes it advocates are brought about. It is evolving in opposition to a materialist doctrine of secular salvation; although it, too, is concerned with secular, as well as spiritual, survival.

In the late 1980s, Mats Friberg sought to place the new cultural movement in its historical perspective. He saw the 'Green Wave' as the fourth in a series of revolutionary changes in Europe, beginning with the Protestant reformation, identified with the 95 Theses of Martin Luther in 1517. The core of Lutheranism was the idea of a direct relationship between the individual and the Godhead through scripture and personal faith (which became grounds for the growth of individualism and potential egalitarianism). It preached, not withdrawal from the world, but engagement with it. Its spiritual preoccupations had a powerful influence on social and economic relationships: Puritanism, for instance, played a major part in early modern European revolutions.

The liberal wave was the next revolutionary movement, originating in the Enlightenment of the 18th century. The rationalist radicalism of the *philosophes* applied natural sciences to social problems; and out of their teachings came the revolutionary ideas of liberty, equality and fraternity. Out of this emerged a vision of a society of free men (not yet women) equal in rights, the notion of popular sovereignty, and ideas of economic freedom. This was embodied in the reform movement in England, although in Europe the conflict between liberal and conservative forces was more violent.

Partly overlapping the liberal moment was the socialist wave. The early ideologists were utopians, children of the Enlightenment, who wanted to transfer the means of production from private control to the community. Experimental communes in the first half of the 19th century generally failed. Marx's socialist doctrine, which was later to become ossified into State

The survival of Cuba

Sixty per cent of the vegetables consumed in Cuba today are organically grown in city gardens. With the disintegration of the Soviet Union, Cuba was denied access to pesticides, fertilizer and tractor fuel, on which its agriculture had depended. This, together with the trade embargo by the US, ought to have ensured the collapse of the regime: the gross domestic product fell by one-third between 1989 and 1993.

That it didn't is a tribute to the ingenuity and creativity of people who have lived for half a century in a state of siege. In place of industrialized agriculture, Cuba has developed a low-input sustainable system. In the countryside, organic sugar, coffee and orange farms have been set up; but the real triumph has been Cuba's ability to mobilize popular support for turning unused city land into small vegetable plots. There are now more than 60,000 *huertos*, or gardens, growing food in Havana alone. People have drawn on their memories of the countryside to revive old skills, and the people of Cuba, despite their poverty, now enjoy one of the healthiest diets in the world.

When Cuba was compelled to de-link itself from a moribund socialism, it could not, as happened almost everywhere else, enter into the global capitalist fold – a 'punishment' which has been turned into a blessing. It had to find its own pathway to self-reliance. And this makes it an even bigger threat to the only industrial system remaining, for it shows that there is indeed an alternative, and it is to be found, neither in learned theories nor in advanced market societies, but in the resources of home.

Cuba shows that human resourcefulness is one of the earth's greatest treasures; when this is allied to sustainable agriculture, the wounds to the planet may yet be healed.

Cuba holds out hope to the world. Its journey towards self-reliance has been peaceable, without fanfare. It has taken place despite the silence of the media, and the switching off of the engines of global publicity. But there it is. It has happened. It has also drawn increasing numbers of visitors – nearly two million in 2003.

What a contrast with the US, which has invaded Iraq to seize the resources that will maintain its version of sustainability. This locks the US into a mechanistic conservatism, whereby the future represents only more, much more, of what we have already seen. This creates a determinism that thwarts true inventiveness and imagination. Cuba, supple and ingenious, tells a different story, and shows that the loss of dependency upon industrialism doesn't have to mean chaos and ruin. Cuba, not for the first time, and despite many mistakes and blemishes, shows the way towards a different culture; the blending of abundant human resources with limited material advantages, combined in a version of Illich's truly 'joyful austerity'.

ownership and control, commanded the faith of millions of people world-wide. The Paris Commune of 1871 initiated the first phase of European socialism. The Russian Revolution split the movement into two, although both currents depended, however distantly, on an authority borrowed from

Marx. The high point of the socialist wave came in the struggle with fascism; and after 1945, seemed to have been settled in favor of socialism. The countries newly emerging from colonial rule almost universally identified themselves with the Soviet Union and its version of state socialism.

The power of this ebbed rapidly; partly in response to the power of capitalism to produce the goods which socialism, for all its theory, could not. Socialism decayed as a mass faith. The increasing transnationalizing of capitalism, the productive power of which vanquished even the Soviet Union, set the stage for globalization, which has meant the further consolidation of global capital.

The Green Wave

The Green Wave aims at nothing less than the replacement of industrial growth with an ecologically sustainable and decentralizing society, based upon human development and the restoration of community. It is internationalist, non-patriarchal, spiritually open, with a concern for global social equality and non-violence. The components of the Green Wave have a common belief that technological-industrial society is flawed.

Although it is seen as an ecological movement, it actually brings together far more diverse strands of resistance to the dominance of globalism. The movement is converging – albeit slowly – towards a new vision, which has already produced many prophets and visionaries (among them, Lewis Mumford, E F Schumacher, Ivan Illich, Rudolf Bahro, Fritjof Capra, Andre Gorz, Murray Bookchin, Johan Galtung, Vandana Shiva).

The movement is converging – albeit slowly – towards a new vision

Many of these draw on the inspiration of traditional sustainable cultures, whose animating principles include sufficiency, the revitalizing of human resources as opposed to growing dependency upon the material resource-base, and a joyful modesty and respect for that which sustains all human cultures. Such principles serve as a guide for sustainable, non-violent societies. It isn't a question of going back, much less of nostalgia or the worship of the primitive; but of supplementing a more modest material resource-use with the uncounted treasures of the human resource-base.

It is not through the revival of older cultures that the culture of globalism will be defeated, although these may inspire the growth of what is coming to be seen as the ideology of anti-globalization, or more positively, of localization. Since this is opposed to the overarching existing centralizing culture, it is scattered and fragmentary. This is not necessarily a disadvantage. For what the rhetoric of globalism proclaims – that it is pluralist, diverse and respectful of the richness of human cultures – is false; and it is in the celebration of the local, the everyday, the familiar, the ecologically specific that the growing counter-culture is embodied.

Its apparent negativity – it is against globalization, and resisters are stigmatized as wreckers and anarchists – is in fact its most powerful characteristic. It is not in the realm of theory that the new culture is developing, but in practice, worldwide, in the lived experience of people who have been marginalized, excluded, abandoned or trampled beneath 'economic forces' which appear as irresistible as a phenomenon of nature.

It has not, so far, coalesced into a hardened ideology. This is both its strength and weakness: strength, because it remains fluid and open, weakness, because it is slow to make headway against the ideological certainties of the economic mythology of global wealth-creation. It is essentially a culture, formed in opposition to that of globalization. If people complain that it lacks coherence, it should be remembered that socialism was also almost a century in gestation before it became a mass movement.

Alternatives

The supreme resistance to early capitalism lay in the monumental power and poetry of Karl Marx. His great epic, *Das Kapital*, continues to influence efforts to reshape the global order – not by following the prophecies and predictions of Marx (that is left to sectarians, the Jehovah's Witnesses of socialism), but in the sense that people believe that in order to promote other ways of being in the world, these must have a watertight and all-embracing theoretical basis. In other words, the ghost of Marx haunts the efforts to formulate a myth of resistance to equal the great myth of Marx.

The opponents of the global adventure, and of its leveling culture, have been eager to define a new paradigm to justify their challenge. The search for 'an alternative' has at times been almost obsessive. It is, perhaps, surprising that theory should preoccupy the enemies of capitalism, that most promiscuous of ideologies that will couple with anything that yields profit. A model of alternativism that seeks to equal the monstrosity that confronts the world is not needed. After all, it is not the theory of globalization that threatens humanity. Quite the reverse. Its crudeness and inconsistency are visible everywhere in its instruments and institutions. It preaches free markets but seeks to contain people within random national borders, often scribbled by colonial pirates on virgin maps. The rich countries demand that the poor liberalize, while they protect their own agriculture and industry. The global institutions disingenuously impose policies on the poor that will maintain and exacerbate their subordination.

The cultural power of globalization lies, not in the rags and patches of its theories, but in the *practice* of its productive power. And an ideology promoted through its iconography of hope, through images of plenty and affluence, hold out their beguiling promise of liberation to the poor of the earth.

This has important implications for an effective culture of resistance. It tells us that anything so neat and comprehensive as a *paradigm* is unnecessary and should be abandoned. Alternative practices, pathways to disengagement, other ways of answering need – real pluralism and diversity – are the only answer to the reductive monoculture.

Let the practice flourish, then, and theory will take care of itself. We will be enriched by the search for other ways of being in the world, the cultural experimentation, not by the working out of new dogmas.

Let the practice flourish, and theory will take care of itself

The young people who journey to the places in which the G-8 holds its imperialistic cabals have succeeded in banishing those macabre conclaves to unvisitable mountains and island retreats, beyond the reach of the people whose lives are affected by their desiccated calculus of gain – they have done more to isolate the manipulators, the engineers of human souls on the global sale, until they appear as they are: beleaguered, alone with their blueprints and conspiracies of injustice and pain.

The work of the anti-globalizers is supported by a deeper resistance in villages and neighborhoods, in schemes where people exchange goods and services without monetary transactions; in protests against GM crops, in the rejection of the terminator gene in seeds, in slum-dwellers fighting evictions. Every local triumph of people over the moneylender and land-grabber; every small victory over the industries that have turned food against nourishment, health against well being, education against understanding, livelihood against life. Such movements are sometimes heroic – the Landless People's Movement in Brazil, the Zapatistas in Chiapas, those who struggle against the large dams that will destroy thousands of people's livelihoods, the marchers in South Africa who took to the streets to protest against the pharmaceutical companies' patents on essential AIDS medicines – and won. Then there are the millions who marched all over the world against the Iraq war; the thousands

'I came for a week and stayed 30 years'

Reynaldo is from Uruguay, but has lived in London for a good part of his life

'I grew up in Uruguay, but the origins of my parents were Basque and French Catalonian – marginal European cultures that spilled over the Pyrenees; I have always been a borderland person. My father's family was also radical – one brother was communist and two were socialists.

Uruguay itself was an unusual state. It gained independence in 1825. We abolished slavery in 1830. Uruguay was ultimately created by British diplomacy as a wedge between Argentina and Brazil. We are a small state. We had progressive labor laws, a 40-hour week in the 1920s, and women were enfranchised here before anywhere else. Artigas was our national hero, a socialist opposed to the Creole elites and patricians who ruled the continent. He died in exile in Paraguay before Independence; and we were occupied by Brazil until 1825, to which we lost half of our territory.

The indigenous people of Uruguay were exterminated by the end of the 19th century. They were smaller in numbers than in Brazil, and when the railways were built, the second President of independent Uruguay made an effort to kill them in the name of progress. Uruguay had no minerals, no oil, no gold.

We were prosperous in the 1940s and 1950s, because we supplied Europe with food; but since then we have been in decline, and are now an economic satellite of Brazil and Argentina. The Tupamaras guerrilla movement was a response to economic decline in the sixties. Some of them trained in Cuba. They were urban – the countryside was too empty, the land had been enclosed in vast *estancias* at the end of the 19th century. The idea came from the Algerian independence struggle. They never had a great deal of popular support.

I started out not very politically minded. That changed after a student was shot in a demonstration against rising transport prices. Then I became angry. I joined the March 26 Group, and we co-operated with the Tupamaros, hiding weapons for them, helping their wounded. I was arrested, beaten up and taken to the military barracks – that was before the coup in 1973. I got a political education in prison. I had been a spoiled middle-class kid, living with my mother, grandmother, cook and maid; but I learned the meaning of sharing.

I also liked smoking dope. This created tensions, because the Left were puritanical. Even on the Left, I remained borderline. I felt that dope enhanced my ability to learn, my relationships, even my political awareness. I was arrested again and tortured. The military became more skilled after they had been trained by the US. I was kept in the dark, blindfolded, given electric shocks, ducked in water. Later, after the coup, I was arrested again. Now they wanted names. My girlfriend was tortured in front of me.

I left for Argentina, then to Paris, where I had friends. I came to London, arrived on Victoria Station with £10 in my pocket. I had contacts with Amnesty International and got a job as a translator.

I felt an enormous relief in London. I felt comfortable. I came for a week and stayed 30 years. I liked the music, the cannabis, the squats I lived in. I was always keen on meditation, I made connections through the squatting and peace movement. I became a vegetarian – the opposite of carnivorous Uruguay. London was like the dream of the sixties. It wasn't an alien culture. It was for me a kind of utopian socialism. I found acceptance and a solidarity I hadn't known in Uruguay. I became part of the movement, the ecology, the green, the peace and personal liberation movements – I was part of it. It seemed natural to me; I had left socialism and discovered I was part of a wider internationalism. To become part of the anti-globalization movement was a natural step.

I feel nostalgic for Uruguay, not patriotic. I feel loyalty to Britain, because it gave me freedom. Uruguay is *el paesito*; a suburb of Sao Paulo. But above all, I feel part of a worldwide movement.'

who attend the World Social Forum; the hundreds who protest in many smaller ways against the violation of their rights or in solidarity with others.

Every act of local self-reliance and solidarity is a challenge to the vast concentrations of economic power.

Small acts of charity and courage

The question also arises, what culture do the people in the West, in the heartlands of the globalizing power, reclaim as our own from the wastelands of universal industrialism?

Cultures are organic. They rise and fall, borrow from and influence others. But they require at their root an underlying belief which gives meaning and coherence to their rituals and celebrations, the re-affirmation of their uniqueness. We are familiar with the myth of globalization: mastery of nature, technological progress, 'economic reason' in Andre Gorz's phrase. We see its rituals everywhere, its deregulation of desire, the cycles of getting, spending and having, the orgiastic worship of celebrity and money.

At the beginning of the 21st century we are responding to a dominant – indeed, overwhelming – culture. In reacting against it, we experience only modest and provisional triumphs, small successes that are in themselves only pinpricks, which can scarcely be expected to overturn the global order. But they do yield a growing sense of confidence and self-esteem in the places where they are practised. They strengthen faith in our own ability to do, make and create things for each other; our capacity to serve, tend and cherish one another; to provide stimulus, amusement, support: this represents a rudimentary and scattered, but growing, response to the stifling monoculture.

The new culture arising out of globalization's dance of death respects other ways of life rather than marketing them; promotes diversity in ways of answering human need rather than forcing them through the global economic machine; resacralizes the elements without which life is impossible.

In the culture of globalism, every act of humanity, every effort to answer need locally, every shared gesture, every pooling of resources, every act of giving out of the generosity of the unsubdued spirit is a form of resistance.

It is impossible to *prescribe* cultural alternatives. Cultures are organic, living processes. Nor can you will cultures: values in the abstract have no value, but express themselves through the sometimes harsh materialities of daily life.

But the loosest ideology binds together the dispersed and sometimes chaotic movements, the small acts of charity and courage. For together they constitute a powerful impulse towards retrieval. Just as it is now recognized that the polluted landscapes, poisoned soils and damaged airs must be restored and rehabilitated, how much more true is this of the occupied territories of the heart and spirit, the alienated internal landscapes, the reclamation of land rights to the disputed terrain within.

This is not weak or sentimental. Absence of ideology means only that there are no dogmas, revelations or doctrines in the name of which more human beings must be made to suffer.

The unwieldy structures that do not answer our needs, but hold them hostage, can be made to perish from neglect. It requires only 10 per cent of the business of any mighty transnational corporation to fail for its profits to be wiped out. We can easily find the equivalent – and a great deal more – within the rich storehouse of our own generosity to each other: the unbought gifts and uncalculating mercies, the commitment and succor we can offer one another. In a world which has used up so much of its material riches, it is out of the neglected inner resources that a new culture is being shaped; not the market-filtered illusion of diversity, the leashed cultures of universal commerce, but a culture in which true diversity will flourish.

1 The Washington Post 26 October 1998

15 The bankruptcy of the soul

There are many macro-economic accounts of globalization; but we rarely learn how this affects the psyche and sensibility of lives uprooted and radically re-shaped by the penetration of their world by the market economy. This chapter is an attempt to convey the common subjective experience of people all over the world as they enter the global market.

In many parts of the world, people are still entering the market economy for the first time; or at least, are coming into more direct contact with its compulsions. For some, this is no longer a consequence of migration from farms and villages to urban areas. The market economy thrusts itself into their lives, whether they want it or not. Sometimes, it happens violently, as when the natural resources of traditional cultures – forest-dwellers or slash-and-burn cultivators – are enclosed and taken for an omnivorous market. For others, it takes place by stealth, as has occurred with millions of subsistence farmers through the industrialization of agriculture. The Green Revolution, with its hybrid high-yielding seeds, and the chemical fertilizers and pesticides these required, created hybrid societies, neither truly rural nor urban, as an ancient peasant psyche collided with an invasive industrialism.

The erosion of rural life all over the planet, and the movement to cities, has been a matter of dispute since the time of early industrialism in Britain. There has been continuous – and unresolved – argument over how far industrialization raised the living standards of the people, particularly of the generations who were the first to experience it. E P Thompson pointed out in his *Making of the English Working Class* that the early 19th century saw the final abandonment of the values of an older moral economy – the notion of the 'just price' fell into decay, as did the idea of a wage determined by social or moral sanctions, as opposed to the operation of free-market forces. Thompson asserts that even if it can be statistically proved that the real income of industrial workers rose between 1790 and 1840, they may still have felt that the non-economic losses – the uprootings and migrations, the impersonality of industrial relationships, the hostile environment of raw city slums – were more significant; indeed, so traumatic that they could scarcely be compensated for by any rise in wages.

This argument is significant, for it recurs in the contemporary world, although in a slightly different form. The question of the one-way movement of people from country to city has been framed in the context of the attraction of the city, its job opportunities and 'bright lights', against the declining power of poor farmers and the degradation of rural life. The seductions of the town are invoked to 'prove' the revulsion of the young against traditional country life and custom: they cannot wait to leave home and take up residence in the nearest city slum.

That this is happening, and at an accelerating rate, is undeniable. But how decisions to depart are arrived at is more complicated than any sudden revelation to the young of the wonders of city life. In the slums of Mexico City, Johannesburg and Jakarta, most people say they prefer life in the city for the simple reason that in the city they do not go hungry. If they had been assured of sufficiency in the village, they would never have thought of leaving. As for the brightness of lights, country people are rarely so foolish as to believe that these are likely to provide them with sustenance. They leave a ruined subsistence only for the sake of survival.

The gaudy attractions of the city only mask less visible pressures on the life of the countryside – the cheating of farmers by middlemen, the pressures of declining productivity and falling income, the degradation of village life. Since farmers must bring their crop to market as soon as it is harvested, they have no option but to sell when the price is at its lowest; whereas those with warehouses and godowns can afford to wait until prices rise before they release goods onto the market.

The promise of the city

Once in the town, it is always possible to find work. In Barisal, an overblown country town of about 400,000 people in the south of Bangladesh, thousands of former farmers have found employment renting and driving cycle-rickshaws. They can be seen, waiting on every pot-holed street-corner, at the bus stand, close to the river terminal, standing in rain and sun along the main roads. The vehicles, with their colored plastic canopies and painted panels, are curiously dainty, even picturesque, objects. Yet each delicate carriage represents measureless pain; the experience of lost land and ruined livelihoods. No one would take up such arduous and uncertain labor if there were an alternative. The stringy bodies of the drivers, many of them young men prematurely used up with work, speak of demands on human energy with which no one can keep pace. Indeed, the dispossessed come to resemble the land they have forfeited: they cannot maintain their energy any more than they could keep up with the fertilizer and pesticides for the earth they tended.

Land was lost because a dowry had to be found for the marriage of a sister or daughter. Land was lost because the rich took advantage of the illiteracy of the owners to cheat them of it. Land was lost because it was mortgaged at a time of sickness. Land was lost because it had to be divided between too many heirs. Land was lost because it became waterlogged, saline or unproductive as a result of developmental projects nearby. Land was lost because money was required to pay an agent for a job in the Gulf. Land was lost for the sake of the children's education – that wager that sets continuous harvests against the regular income from secure employment in government or private service.

But there is always work in the town. Labor is required to push carts, to break bricks, in transport, on construction sites, as guards and security personnel in private houses or places of employment; to sell fruit and vegetables; to offer roses to transients in five-star hotels. Women and children can work as domestic labor or brick-breaking, or making festival decorations or paper bags at home. Women are needed as sex workers to service hungry male exiles, a peacock-blue cloth on a wooden bed in a dim windowless room. If that fails, work can be created — credit for a handful of overripe bananas, a tray of combs, some chewing gum or cigarettes, selling newspapers at the traffic lights, plastic goods, toys; mending cycles, umbrellas, shoes; in small workshops making metal goods, repairing engines and machines. Boys crouch over ornamental grilles in a fountain of blue and gold sparks on the sidewalk. Children collect and sell firewood, plastic, cloth; they can carry bags at bus-stands and railway stations. They recycle all kinds of garbage in cities in which nothing is wasted but their own skinny bodies: each day thousands of children turn out the thin pickings from their jute sacks — rusty cans, broken plastic, old springs, bones, splinters of glass gleaming in the sun. But the city holds the promise of a daily income.

Children recycle garbage... nothing is wasted but their own skinny bodies

And those too frail or too weak for work beg. Even the grudging streets are not empty of compassion. The men with features or hands worn away by leprosy, elderly women sent to beg in the park to augment the family income, the young woman whose body is a torso on a wheeled platform, and who propels herself by *chappals* (sandals) which she wears on her hands, the mothers with their crumpled babies in grubby bonnets on the river terminal, the disabled children abandoned at the bus station, are usually fed by stallholders or by passing strangers who throw coins onto the sack spread on the pavement. There is always something in the city to sustain those at the edge of destitution.

The costs of market freedom

The freedoms bestowed by the market economy are tangible. But they depend upon a continuously rising disposable income which enables people to keep pace with the necessary goods and services enclosed and commoditized within it. If the market frees people from the anxieties of traditional subsistence and ancient arts of eking out a living, the maintenance of that freedom requires uninterrupted economic growth. And as we have seen in our time, this necessity for growth may subvert some of the very freedoms for which the market is celebrated: the consequences of economic 'success' involve serious social and environmental costs which confront the 'advanced' economies at every turn.

In the early stages of entering the market economy, the gains are usually clear, and seem significantly to outweigh any losses. It is the objective of the managers of the global economy to play down the latter, indeed, by ingenious accounting-systems, to make them invisible. They prefer to dwell only upon the emancipatory power of the market. This is dangerous, as is dependency upon any other fragile ideological construct which risks, at any moment, coming into collision with direct – and disconfirming – experience. When the market economy falters and contracts, whenever it is inflected by technological change, people who lose income become angry and resentful, in ways which they do not in subsistence economies. Of what use is it to curse a spoiled harvest, a late frost that ruins the crop, rains that fail to arrive when the fields are ready for planting? The market, being a human-made artifact, is perceived to be within human control, whereas everyone knows that the vagaries of climate are not susceptible to our will.

The invisible frontier

And what rich possibilities the market economy offers to new migrants to the city, particularly to those who receive, occasionally for the first time in their lives, cash-money (as they call it in Bangladesh) for their labor! With what sense of liberation and wonder they discover that the money in hand can procure the food, clothing, housing and other necessities of life, when, until this moment, they had labored under a burning sun, ankle-deep in water in the paddyfields, constantly scanning the skies for signs of advancing storms, and inspecting leaves and stalks for pest or blight.

The first thing the city offers is shelter against nature

The first thing the city offers is shelter against nature and its unpredictability. Indeed, people feel they are out of reach of its sometimes cruel power. All you have to do is pass over the price of the goods you want to a shopkeeper, and you will receive whatever you ask for. The ease, the absence of effort − market transactions banish what was once our own labor to a distant and unseen elsewhere.

To move into the market economy is to pass an invisible frontier into another country, where everything, at first sight, represents clear improvement and progress. What can be easier than buying? Whoever needs instruction in shopping? As the rice cascades into the scales from the worn shiny scoop, the money you have earned gives you permission to forget the effort required for its cultivation. And then, to make clothes at home was always laborious and time-consuming for women, and the end product always appeared rough and improvised. When there are so many cheap and colorful garments in the local market, why waste time stitching and mending shabby homemade things? Indeed, the very words 'homemade', instead of meaning a guarantee of freshness and self-reliance, take on an aura of faint but unmistakable shame.

The fabric of the city itself, the sights and sounds, speak of variety and diversity which strike the psyche of peasants and country people with the shock of a revelation. So much is going on! A rich and simultaneous tumult of activity, of excitement, of energy. They did not realize how poor they were, until they see it made material; what stares at them out of the glittering imagery of the riches of the city and the kaleidoscopic confusion of its streets is a growing awareness of their own impoverishment.

It takes some time before the first disadvantages appear, and even then, they do so only at the margins, as minor irritants in the journey of discovery which this epic transhumance of humanity has been. First of all, the money earned, the daily wage, is always insufficient for necessities, or more mystifyingly, for what have become necessities since farm and village were left behind. The actual power of the money you hold always lags behind what it promises. Money in hand always appears substantial; only when set against prices does it seem to melt away. It dawns upon newcomers that survival within the market imposes different burdens from those demanded by subsistence survival.

Of course many of the skills that came with them from the countryside can be used in the city. The men, who came first, found lodgings in shared rented rooms; three or four from the same village living together in the feral loneliness of a tin-and-bamboo slum house or a crumbling tenement in the old city. When it is time for the family to join them, they want to build their own house. In the village, wood, bamboo and woven bamboo panels, palm leaves, clay and cow dung were always available, and houses could be constructed for next to nothing. In the city, each bamboo stave, each rectangle of corrugated metal, every plank of wood, every sheet of polythene and plastic is rigorously costed. What is more, the only places in which people are permitted to build (or rather, are not prevented from building) are those required for no other purpose. This usually means dangerous terrain – an unhealthy area of marshland susceptible to flooding, beside railway tracks and polluted ponds, on arid rocky land exposed to sun and desiccating summer winds. Drinking water may have to be bought or carried long distances. And even this land belongs either to some government department or to private individuals; or ownership may be disputed, the subject of long court battles. The unsafe site will not, however, prevent slumlords from demanding protection money, or stop unelected gangs from regulating the lives of the people. The police, too, must often be paid simply to allow residents to remain in peace.

Despite all this, new settlements are appearing all the time; if no longer in the central areas of the town, then on the outer edges, where amenities are non-existent, from where transport to places of work is costly and slow. But still they persevere; and one day, they go to the bus stand to meet their family, with the battered cases and trunks, the few articles they have brought from home, after tearful farewells to mothers and aunts and grandparents, whose eyes follow them until the bus has disappeared over

Newcomers fall silent at the recognition that this is now to be home

the bumpy road behind the last cluster of trees shading the devastated landscape. And the newcomers look with the same wonder at the soaring buildings, the treeless concrete, the tangled skein of wires above the city streets that carry light and voices through the air; and they fall silent at the recognition that this is now to be home.

New forms of insecurity

It soon occurs to recent migrants that life in the city is attended with new forms of insecurity, some of which arouse familiar echoes of those they remember from the village. There are, it seems, even here, the equivalents of big landowners, local elites, upper castes and classes, in whose fields they had to work, even if this meant the neglect of their own patch of land, who paid them only in rice, whose sons sometimes molested their daughters. All are busy also in the city, even though they may take on a new guise, as bosses, employers, supervisors, bureaucrats, politicians. Their rule, it soon becomes clear, is scarcely more merciful than that of their rural counterparts.

And then, everything costs money. All that was freely given, exchanged between villagers, offered up out of the uncalculating generosity of subsistence, no longer exists in the city. Neighbors here come from all over the country; you rarely hear the familiar village accent in the voices around. Everyone is too busy. The bus fare to work is inescapable, and it soon eats into the precious wages that chase prices that leap and jump, agile as goats, from week to week. Surely, last time the notice on the piece of cardboard read 40 cents a kilo for sugar, and this week it clearly says 42; while vegetables that were virtually free at home, especially the gourds and cucumbers that came up almost overnight in the rains, have here become almost a luxury.

In the city, new forms of ill-health appear, to add to those already known. Who would have thought city air would be so difficult to breathe, the bluish haze trapped between buildings in the main streets, which gives you a permanent cough and leads to persistent infections in eyes and throat? Expensive medicines are required for the children's respiratory problems, antibiotics, remedies for asthma, tonics after the strange fevers that come and go with the rains. And then, there are so many voices telling you what your children should have if they are to remain healthy – how can you not give them the vitamin supplement, the syrup that will make them strong, the preparation that will strengthen their bones, the formula that promises they will be free from any dietary deficiency? Advertisements are everywhere in bewildering profusion. They make you wonder how children ever survived at all before their parents had learned these important messages and urgent instructions. Something unsettling, which gnaws away at the faith you had in your ability to care for the children. It was bad enough to abandon the growing of food for them; now it seems, even home-prepared meals cannot compete with the value-added bounty of food manufacturers.

Other, unforeseen expenses are incurred. Bolts and padlocks are required to secure even the smallest and most insignificant possessions against thieves. Who would have thought a colored plastic bowl or a metal bucket would be worth stealing? In the village, theft was almost unknown, and when it did occur, everyone soon knew who had done it, and that person was dealt with by family, by the elders, without the involvement of the police at all. And for the most part, doors had no locks. Neighbors came and went; and even if they were not always welcome, you certainly didn't bar your house against them.

Who would have thought a colored plastic bowl would be worth stealing?

New, troubling questions arise. Should we allow our daughter to walk on the streets after dark? Who are the shadowy young men standing like ghosts on street-corners, and what are they offering in their whispers to adolescents who pass by? Why is there always a group of youngsters on the local station, ragged and dirty, with matted hair, and why are they sniffing fumes that rise up from a square of silver paper, beneath which trembling hands hold a lighted match?

With the passing of time, even the food purchased so easily in the street-markets and small shops seems less varied and not so appetizing as it was in the beginning; and it is certainly less fresh than the food eaten in the village. More than this: the flour tastes chalky; the rice is full of small stones, each one of which must be picked out by hand, so your teeth do not break on them as you eat; the chili powder looks like brick dust. The newspapers are full of a scandal that a banned and poisonous vetch has been added to the pulses. And as for the withered yellowish leaves that are sold as vegetables, you would be ashamed to give them to animals at home, let alone pay money for them to feed your family.

One daughter has already been taken out of school to work as a maid in one of the big flats. She lives there, sleeping on a verandah. Up at dawn, she is always the last to rest in the household. She stands in the afternoon looking through bars onto the street, and the sun throws the pattern of her ornamental imprisonment upon her small face. She is not paid money, but at least there is one less mouth to feed, and when she comes home once a month she may bring a few old clothes and some leftover delicacies given to her by the mistress of the house. But now the oldest boy, too, must be taken out of school and sent to work in a metal workshop. He will be an apprentice for two or three years, but he will receive a little money, and will be fed on the premises. Maybe in time he will become a skilled metal worker. The ambitions you had for him that he might become an engineer or a doctor, have been reduced.

Many women also become domestic servants in the adjacent well-to-do suburbs, which are protected against strangers by yellow-and-black barriers on the road, frontier posts of the land of the rich. Watchmen in sentry boxes guard each house, so that the quarters of bureaucrats and business people look like an occupied country. Sometimes, when the poor women sit together in a rare moment of rest late in the warm night, they wonder how the money–power of the rich can call them away from their own families at the very moment when their children need their care and attention most. It is one of the most mysterious aspects of the city, that rich women who spend their time in beauty parlors, at kitty parties or in afternoon card games, should prefer these occupations to looking after their own children. Working as a maidservant also means taking one of the other daughters out of school so that she may mind the little ones. Of course, you can always ask a neighbor to keep an eye on the small children, but she has her own cares; and then you are always preoccupied, praying there will be no spillage of kerosene, as happened in a neighboring slum, when fire raged through the densely packed houses and an old woman and a child were burned to death.

Spirits in the twilight

Then, sometimes, late in the night, they remember. Those with land might have chosen to sow some new crop this year – millet or sorghum perhaps, some different vegetables, tomatoes and cauliflower instead of aubergines and potatoes. And then, the mango tree planted five years ago must be yielding by now. Mango-time, in any case, was always an informal local festival, as the children climbed the trees and shook the branches and the fruit fell, mellow half-moons, into the cloth their sisters held beneath. The green guavas, the rich smell of jackfruit, soft flesh of tender coconut, the senses were overpow-

> **They yearn to hear the flutter of a bird's wing beating the air**

ered by them. Newcomers to the city – was it really only two years ago? – are seized by fierce nostalgias, a desire to see again the pattern of dew on the winter grass, the distant hills stained with the fleeting gold paint of sunset, the darkness thickening visibly around the banyan or the raintree, as though spirits were gathering in the twilight. They yearn to hear again the sounds of the countryside, the dry leaves crushed by the bare feet of the homegoing laborers, the flutter of a bird's wing beating the air, the scrapings of insects in the thatch, the melancholy cry of a night bird; so different from the unquiet nights of the city, the clatter of trains, the traffic that subsides only for an hour or two before dawn, the sound of other people's TV sets, the family quarrels of neighbors, the relentless barking of the half-wild dogs that scavenge the streets.

And as the deeper lessons of this transplantation of humanity are slowly absorbed, its irreversibility also sinks in. Money, it seems, is not, after all, a means of making life easier; it is a costly input required to nourish urban life, like the bags of fertilizer which it was necessary in recent years to spread on land that had become less productive. And money has different seasons and other harvests from those familiar to country dwellers; and although vital to survival, it is as unpredictable as the weather. You do not know if the livelihood that sustains you will continue to do so: the cycle-rickshaws are now banned from the main city streets. The people in the big houses no longer require hawkers selling vegetables from door to door, now they can buy what they choose in the new supermarket. Is it time to join a gang of laborers who move from construction site to construction site, living in makeshift metal and straw barracks in the shadow of a big board, where an artist's impression of the new condominium gleams, white as snow on the winter hills?

Money must also be tended, just as the staple crop once had to be

Money must also be tended, just as the staple crop once had to be; but it is a different kind of nurture. Livelihood has become detached from life. In the fields, you never had to ask what was the purpose of the ripening grain that hung in fine beads from the graceful stem. Here, you wonder what the anxious crowds are doing as they make their way through the city streets, swallowed up in factories and foundries, where children can be seen blowing great golden bubbles of glass beside red furnaces, and whole families sit breaking bricks into fragments, their faces, arms and clothing covered with rust-colored dust. It wasn't like this at home. Home! This is now home, this poor shelter between the canal and the cemetery wall, where the rain drips through the rusting corrugated metal, and the food hangs in bags from nails driven into the wall where the rats cannot reach it.

People feel, not so much that they are still poor, but that they are poor in a different way. Poverty, like oppression, comes in new forms. Sufficiency remains elusive, satisfactions fugitive and provisional. As time passes, the children grow up and contribute to the family income. The loan is eventually paid on the handcart, a cycle-rickshaw, a three-wheeler taxi. Women have worked in garment factories, or at home making incense sticks or rolling cigarettes, sewing pearl buttons and silk bows onto dresses. A brother and his wife have come from the village after marriage, and their earnings can be pooled to build a better house, cement and bricks taking the place of palm-leaves and tin. In some cities it is possible to move to a dilapidated tenement, apartments with crumbling ornamented facades that once belonged to merchants or bureaucrats who have long moved on.

The realms of the impossible

But for the improved accommodation rent must be paid, or another loan taken to buy the small plot of land, the ownership of which is, in any case, unclear. It seems that however hard you work, the earnings are all used up in advance. Whenever you look at the goods in the shop windows – especially in the air-conditioned mall, where you sometimes take a few minutes' refuge from the heat or the rain – it strikes you afresh how poor you remain in spite of the striving. In the village, you knew what you needed for survival; and although you might have wished for some small luxuries, you never allowed your imagination to wander in the realms of the impossible. In the city, you are taunted with the absences in your life every time you pass through the central shopping area, with its glass and marble enclosures, and windows full of thin papier-mâché models wearing fashionable clothes for a foreign autumn, the array of dazzling white refrigerators and washing machines, the rows of flickering TV screens all showing different channels – ospreys in flight, speedway racing from Minneapolis, Alpine peaks in Switzerland. At night, the street-lamps and advertisements shimmer in the wet road, so that even beneath your feet a chasm of magical color reflects your own diffuse feelings of inadequacy and dissatisfaction.

Time, too, is different in the city. The hours of labor are measured and rhythmic. Sometimes, before it is light, you still wake up with a start, and sit up in bed, wondering whether it is time to milk the buffaloes, before you remember they were sold long ago, and even the names you had affectionately given them are forgotten. Morning tasks here are not the same. The front door does not open onto the glassy field where the heron stands motionless in the still water, and the tiny green bird sits on a blade of rice that does not even bend under its weightless presence. Here, the channel of indigo waste water makes its crooked way through the stones, the overhanging eaves of rusty tin threaten to cut your face, and only the blue-black crows wheel over the slum looking for discarded fragments of food. The women at the single tap that serves 40 households rattle their buckets and wait for the thin trickle that reaches the slums at last. Someone has beaten to death a sleek rat, and its entrails lie, an open red fruit, ants dark seeds in its ripeness.

Time here has no spaces, no intervals. There is no chance to sit with others, reflecting on the past, and listening again to familiar stories of the spirits of the locality, the ghosts and hauntings, and wondering at the pervasive presence of the dead among us. It seems the dead have, like the past, been banished from the city. The children, too, do not wish to listen to the old tales, the folk stories and harvest songs that gave meaning to life. They want new

> **There is no chance to sit with others, reflecting on the past**

articles of clothing, trainers and jackets, and games that buzz and chirp electronically, until you want to tear them from their hands and stamp on them.

Here, holidays are formal, and even the festivals have become less sacred, celebrations of buying things rather than commemorations of the significant moments of tradition and custom. A day off means a trip to the sea in a shaking bumpy bus with no glass in the windows, or, if you are better off, a child's birthday in McDonald's, a visit to the zoo to look at animals whose confinement you view with indignation and sadness, because it reminds you of your own sense of captivity in the city. Even the people's pleasures are captive, transformed into items for sale.

Certain amenities have also become necessary. A television set is now indispensable (why?); otherwise, the children will spend all their time with friends who do have one. Although television also speaks to them of what they do not yet own or possess, they appear tirelessly avid for such negative instruction. Without a television set, they cannot share in the fate of common heroes or discuss the football game or sing the most recent songs. And then, equipping them for school – how expensive it has become! Whoever would have imagined that preparation for learning could involve such an outlay! A teacher's voice and a pupil's ear, surely that is all that is required. But they must have satchels, uniforms, books, pens, colored crayons. And if you want them to be taught properly, they ought to go to English-medium schools, because without English their prospects are dim. In any case, the teachers in government schools often do not turn up, and when they do, they make the listless children copy pages from text-books, or they place their heads on arms folded on the desk in front of them and shamelessly sleep in front of the whole class, who get up and walk away without the teacher even noticing. The rain beats on the metal roof and drowns the voices in the room. Sometimes the teachers go on strike because they haven't been paid for three months. And the school wants money for outings and educational visits. The head teacher even sent a note asking for a contribution to the upkeep of the school building which leaks in the monsoon.

After years of work, life becomes materially easier; but instead of allowing you to relax in comfort, even the visible improvements are accompanied by unforeseen anxieties and stresses. Rumors are circulating that the house which was built with the help of neighbors is to be demolished for a new government office or a shopping complex. It is confirmed that the land was sold illegally; and there are several claimants that this was part of their ancestral land. The government is fighting them in the courts since they say it belongs to the Ministry for Railways, and anyway, they are determined to build a high-tech park to attract inward investment. Does this mean that you may return home one fine day and find the whole community reduced to rubble?

Every day, when you turn onto the causeway that leads to home, between the two swampy ponds full of bedsprings and plastic bags, your heart is beating until you are reassured that it is indeed still standing, and you catch sight of the smoke rising from the cooking fires. The children run towards you, their eyes shining as though you had been absent for a month. In spite of your exhaustion, you lift them onto your shoulder, past the lines of fruit and vegetable vendors, and stop to buy them a slice of watermelon, before going home to where the domestic fires burn, little celebratory bonfires to mark another day's survival; and as you eat the fresh vegetables and rice with the family, in the silence, you are aware of a fragile moment of well-being, a glimpse of what peace and security might mean.

Even in this money-driven world, there are still spaces for mutual help

Living with uncertainties

You also discover that even in this money-driven world, there are still spaces for mutual help, not only between families and kinspeople from the same villages, but also between neighbors and working companions. Their support and comfort temper the rigors of urban life. A woman who remembers country herbal remedies brings from the informal market behind the cathedral the leaves that must be infused, the roots to be ground to powder, fruits churned to paste, which will cure worms or fever or diarrhea. There is another woman – it seems that the memory of women is longer and more tenacious than that of men – who knows how to get rid of unwanted pregnancies; and yet another who has been present at the birth of countless children, and none of them has died. When the scaffolding collapsed on the construction site, there was a collection in the neighborhood for the family whose only earner had been killed; and when the mother on the fourth floor of the tenement block died of TB, the children were taken in by others who, although poor, managed to absorb them and bring them up as their own.

And everyone remembers the day when the police and municipal workers arrived to clear the area. The government had announced its intention to remove all slums which were an eyesore and an embarrassment in the capital city. They said, to the anger of the people, the slums were breeding grounds for criminals, gangs, a haven for purse-snatchers and drug-dealers. They wanted to send everyone back to the villages. But the policy was challenged in the high court, which found the government was acting legally, but was bound to rehabilitate those whose houses it demolished and provide them with alternative sites.

On the day of the proposed demolition, word went round that something was afoot. The men were called home from work; groups from other slums assembled on the road. By the time the bulldozers and the police reached the area, as many as 10,000 people were waiting for them. The devastation was halted. The police and officials retreated. But it was only a temporary victory. Any day they could return, and next time they will surely give no prior warning of their intention. The insecurity remains. Sometimes, mysterious fires break out, destroying hectares of dwellings. The people must move, and within no time, the area is enclosed with barbed wire, and a new building comes up.

But you have to live with such uncertainties. And within a few years, many people have improved their houses, added an upper storey, with a terrace on top to dry chilies and keep firewood, and even sit from time to time in the tepid winter sunshine and sleep in the hottest nights when the electricity fails. Such houses change hands at high prices – who can say what easy life might not be possible with such sums! But the price of land in the village has now risen, and you cannot get half a hectare with the price your modest house in the city might command.

Eventually, the two-wheeler is sold and an old car takes its place. You return in triumph to visit relatives in the village. They look at you with admiration, and send for all the neighbors, who finger your smart clothes, and hold up with delight the second-hand garments you bought for them in the market, washed and ironed so they look good as new to the unpractised eye of poor villagers. You hold them spellbound with stories of the strange and wonderful things that happen in the city; and you answer their questions with the amused superiority of a parent speaking to a child, even though many of them are older than you are. Are there really people in the city who can go to a hotel and spend more on a single meal than we earn in half a year? Is it true there are places of entertainment where young women will dance wearing almost no clothes? Relatives and friends look at the presents you have brought, the digital clock and the shiny china horse, and they think you must be very rich. They are also thinking of selling their land; in any case, builders are said to be interested in buying up farmland for development – new houses for rich people who, strangely, seem to want to get away from the city, the very

Are there really people who can spend more on a meal than we earn in half a year?

place which provides prosperity and freedom. It is very confusing. But one thing is sure – it is becoming more and more unprofitable to grow the staple crop. Prices continue to fall; the expense of fertilizer and pesticides for the new seeds makes it scarcely worthwhile. No one now grows the old strains; do you remember the fragrance of the special festival rice as it grew in the fields, the sweet smell of the mango flowers? All gone now.

Tugging at the heart

It takes at least a generation before people become truly urban; and even then, the countryside continues to tug at the heart. As a consolation, you now have a proper house, small but adequate, a single storey concrete building with a verandah and a little garden, where you can grow some lemons and chilies; the hibiscus and scented creeper remind you of another home, more distant in time than in place.

And yet, the children who have grown up in the city are not contented, and they have somewhere shed the gratitude owed to parents, that intense feeling of thankfulness you always felt towards your own mother and father, although they could provide you with so little. It seems the children have inherited the restless dissatisfactions which drove you here in the first place. They want to go to parties all the time, they must have clothes which bear this mark or this emblem of a transnational company which you have never heard of. They need a watch and a little machine which they plug into their ears, so that they do not so much walk as dance through the streets with their friends.

Nearly all shopping is now done in the supermarket. The choice of goods is wider. The fruits and vegetables are identical, without blemish, and if they have less taste than you remember, at least they can be prepared more easily. In any case, the young people will not eat *longans* or *rambutans*, but will greedily munch big red apples from America or oranges from Australia. The diversity on the shelves of the supermarket is puzzling: the difference between one product and another hard to discern.

Again, you remember the smallholding or the little farm. There is nothing in the city quite like the satisfaction of sitting under the tamarind tree and listening to the buffaloes as they chew the coarse grass in the half-light of evening. Perhaps, you tell yourself, the recalled sense of stillness and contentment is an illusion, a trick of the memory, a sign that you are getting old. How easy it is to forget these troubling thoughts in the hallucinatory light of the TV screen, which opens out onto so many other people's lives, the good fortune of the woman who wins all the objects she can remember after feasting her eyes on them for one minute, the tearful victor of the quiz show, the nationally televised lottery draw; which bring new kinds of hope into lives of struggle.

There is no rest. You buy goods on credit – a ceiling fan to help you sleep in summer, a refrigerator so the shop-bought food doesn't go bad. Every month eats more deeply into your money. There are stories that the local factory is to close because wages have become too high. The company is moving production to an Export Priority Zone, a neighboring country, or a rural area, where costs are only a fraction of those in the city. Some children from the neighborhood have been sniffing solvents in the new underpass beneath the main road. One of them suffered brain damage, and the parents are trying to raise a loan to pay the hospital bills. A little girl was abducted, her mutilated body found on the rusting rails of a disused track. You just pray that such events will not touch you; strange new disturbances, yet oddly reminiscent of the storms and cyclones that used to rush in from the coast and blow themselves out over the huts sheltered by an ancient stand of trees. Then, too, you prayed and hoped those other storms would pass over you.

At least the women do not have to labor as they did in the fields. They do not have to walk all day to return at sunset, knees sinking under a head load of fuel or fodder for the animals. There is no need to travel three kilometers for drinking water.

And yet, even here, the work of women is never finished, the job in the garments factory, sitting at a machine 10 or 12 hours a day as well as preparing meals, keeping the house clean, listening to the children's prayers before sleeping. Sometimes there is compulsory overtime, and the workers are locked in all night so they cannot leave. There have been fires. In one, 15 young women were asphyxiated by the fumes, unable to escape because the door was padlocked. The bodies were laid out on the pavement in the humid summer dawn. The factory owner had gone abroad for an operation.

> **And yet, even here, the work of women is never finished**

Money skill

As the market economy enfolds us more completely, all earlier ways of self-provisioning – not only growing food and making clothes but also building a shelter, telling stories after dark, reflecting on the meaning of life in the embers of a collective fire – are forgotten. Skill in earning money has superseded all other skills. Just as the cash earned daily, or increasingly, weekly or monthly, now procures everything needed, so the making of money makes you forget old competences and abilities. At last, it causes you to set aside even the memory of an existence outside of the market. When the old recall some of the things they did, they smile with a condescending pity for that former self – looking at the sky and knowing the monsoon would not break yet, reading signs and portents for our own lives in the flight of a bird or the behavior of an animal, going out to look for herbs that soothed fever instead of running to the doctor. The self-reliance which you had taken for granted now seems pitiable. It is as though you had become another person; as indeed you have, a person who is more knowing, wise in a different way from when wisdom meant dealing with the sorrows and afflictions of life. You have become more calculating, more cunning; you know how to make a bargain, how to take advantage of others. When you found money trodden into the mud, you kept it, although it would have been quite easy to find out who had lost it.

You have become more cunning; you know how to make a bargain

You do not admire what you have become; but you know this is the way things are now.

Instead of dependency upon land and seasons, you find you are now totally dependent on money. And by a strange paradox, within market culture, those who have become the most dependent – the very rich – are referred to as people 'of independent means'. You hear your own children complain: 'You can't do anything without money'; an assertion which, however true, arouses their grandparents to an obscure anger, for they can remember a time when they could do so many things in spite of their poverty – celebrations and singing, comforting the sick, helping with births and washing the dead, sustaining the weak and vulnerable, making sure the young men did not take advantage of the simple-minded girl; controlling the behavior of those who offended the sometimes harsh rules of the community; amusing and entertaining one another, the joy of harvest, the shared pleasures and sorrows at weddings and funerals, when kinsfolk arrived from all over the neighboring countryside. Now, birth is a medical condition, and those you love are seized from you as soon as they breathe their last. Even death has become a costly business; and they say, with a laugh touched by bitterness, that they can't afford to live and they can't afford to die either.

If the family was scattered across the countryside, it is now dispersed in different ways. Some have left to work in another city, to study in a distant town; others have moved on, regularized their migrant status, as it were, in America or Australia. And those who remain in the city have to travel to work, and when they come home they are so tired, all they want to do is sit in front of the TV, a bottle of beer in one hand, an instant meal in the other, until they fall asleep, and then drag themselves to bed in the early hours, ready for another day's labor in the cool steel-colored city dawn.

That it was possible to provide for many needs without cash and not be poor has been long forgotten. And even those who are making a good living, earning well above the average wage, still feel strangely impoverished. They are always talking about, brooding over what they can't afford, rather than enjoying what they have. Desire and discontent bring new torments that have nothing to do with poverty, except that it always comes down to not enough money. But what has happened has happened. You cannot even think of going back. The farm is in ruin. The fields have been enclosed for agribusiness. The price of land has soared. There is no one left. Best not to remember. This is where our life has led us and this is where we must try to lead it. This is the future.

The market as cosmos

Still, the advantages of the market are there; its promises do not fade, but are perpetually renewed. The richer we become in the market economy, the greater the space for individual self-expression. Sharper differentiation occurs between people. We no longer see our shared social predicament as a common fate. To get out, to be yourself, to locate a self that has become abstracted from place, becomes the aim of the young. Previously unseen barriers and separations divide generation from generation; new, impermeable divisions arise between those who had seen themselves as bound by a shared destiny. Members of the same family, who had always seen one another more or less as an extension of themselves, become aware of their own private, individual needs. They become preoccupied with their own uniqueness. They cultivate features and characteristics that distinguish them from others, rather than submerge these in a common pool of human belonging. And with time, they come to see no reason why their destiny should follow the same road as that of their kin. They follow their own pathways, sometimes in rancor, sometimes pursuing desires and longings that had previously scarcely been articulated, and which, even now, are barely capable of being put into words. But it is felt, in flesh and blood, in heart and spirit, an ache of the broken ligaments of kinship, a pervasive pain from the ruptured bonds, the torn pith of belonging.

This is an inner echo of outer partings and social separations. Just as people in the neighborhood united against landlords and employers and the coercive agencies of the State, now they see no reason to make common cause with each other. The links of shared circumstances now come to appear parochial, irksome, intrusive. The young want to be on the move, taking off for an indefinable elsewhere. They no longer look for identity or roots in the places or the people who had nurtured them. Their version of the expanding space which their parents had sought within the market is a physical and psychic mobility; as though the act of *migration* had been passed on to them, in such a way that they need to re-enact it repeatedly, obsessively, to be on the move all the time.

Little by little the market becomes cosmos; and the natural world is shut out. The glimmer of artificial light eclipses even the sun; the pallor of the moon is no longer seen above the sodium lights of the city. We find we are living within freedoms that have become inexplicably captive, circumscribed. The technology that has ensnared us must now deliver us. Money which has become our life-blood, must circulate faster and faster through the system, while capital, its beating heart, its informing spirit and its quicksilver mind, diffuses its necessities throughout our lives, our relationships, insinuates itself into our imagination and spirit.

While fresh freedoms unfurl themselves, and as riches accumulate, the true terms of that distant wager become clearer: the future is already inscribed in what we have. The time to come has been colonized, used up in advance. The children, early-ripe adults dependent upon drugs, dance their nights away in ornamented splendor. The old are left to whatever residual mercy remains. A terrible loneliness descends upon the aggressive individualism of an economic necessity which has become so entangled with our human need

Our nearest and dearest have become oddly remote and cold

that they appear inextricable. We can no longer explain ourselves to anyone. No one listens, they cannot hear us. Our nearest and dearest have become oddly remote and cold, like the dead. Strange cults arise around goods or objects in the market – motor-cars become symbols of transcendence, bush-fires of desire spread for some intensively promoted item of consumption, celebrities become the focus of strange tendernesses and longings. This expands into a culture of endless wanting; and that means wanting without end. New poverties are conjured out of abundance, and plenty ceases to be enough.

With the deregulation of desire, it is only to be expected that other, less acceptable forms of desire are released; strange fantasies haunt the imagination of the people, addictions to drugs, alcohol, gambling, shopping, money, entertainment, escape; obsessions, stalking, one-way love affairs with shadows, pedophilia; curious forms of regression and infantilization are uncovered; a need for heroes and super humans to replace the fallible, diminished flesh and blood who are our increasingly unsatisfactory and reluctant companions.

We dread coming home and finding the door kicked in and our precious possessions, the engagement ring and the necklace, the gold watch and the banknotes, looted from their place in the upstairs drawer, the new furniture ransacked, the video gone, the children's computer games destroyed. The old are afraid to open their doors; behind the scraping of bolts and the door on its chain, a wraith-like face wonders if the official from the utility company is an impostor and will bludgeon her to death for the sake of her pension. Women fear the streets after dark, lest the overwrought desires of strangers, kindled for profit by anonymous others, should drag them into the piece of unlighted wasteland beside the canal. The children can no longer walk to school, but have to be delivered everywhere by car because who knows who may be lying in wait for them round the next corner, not only the perverts and weirdos with whom the world is now inexplicably filled, but even other

The world is full of enemies. . . people bent on vengeance

children, who will extort, bully, and who knows, even torture them and leave the beloved body in some derelict house. The TV is never without its images of police and grimfaced neighbors searching every inch of long grass for a teenager who disappeared after an innocent night at the disco. The lessons are swiftly learnt. The world is full of enemies, those we have slighted, people bent on vengeance; you wait for the stone to shatter the glass, the rags soaked in petrol to come through the letterbox – the revenge of this wasted relationship or abandoned lover, some cheated partner or business associate, the retaliation of trashed and used-up relationships.

Bankruptcy of the soul

The familiar neighborhood is full of terrors, peopled with malignant strangers; at best competitors and rivals, at worst, predators, muggers, kidnappers, robbers, addicts, crazies, attackers; an incomprehensible mutation of humanity, which is now declared to be the incarnation of our rapacious, greedy, selfish human nature. When we open our mouths to protest that we know of generosity and self-denial as well, the words stick in our throat. Someone else always knows best, knows more. And when they die, the lonely, the misanthropic, the isolated and the misfits, neighbors are alerted, not by their absence, but by a strange smell in the hallway; and the police must be called to break down the door to find the decomposing body among the chintz and ornaments, with the gas-fire still hissing quietly, and the picture of the grandchildren with their perfect faces against a background of cerulean blue on the little table beside the empty cup and the faded image of the long-dead husband.

But still the promises keep pace with these disorders. Longevity increases, immortality is promised. We shall live to be 150. Spare-part surgery will come with new organs grown on mice, pigs or cows. We can be regenerated, renewed, we can go on into an unimaginably distant future, the elderly riding in observation coaches staring forever at the wonders of each other's capital cities, a diversionary occupational therapy so absorbing as to render inaudible even the crack of doom. Plastic surgery and remodeling can eliminate imperfections we no longer have to live with. The genetic structure of all living organisms will be modified to serve us. Custom-made genes will design faults out of humanity. All the resourcefulness of the existential hypermarket will be deployed to eliminate aberrant characteristics in a more stringent quality control of human production. And if our fouled and spoiled planet becomes uninhabitable, we can colonize outer space, live elsewhere, in a cosmic extension of the mobility that is now our birthright.

We become property owners; exulting in the freedom not to pay rent, even though we go into perpetual debt; the gilded bondage which leases to us the necessities and amenities of life. If only we can keep up the mortgage repayments for 25 years, our children will become the inheritors of a house the value of which rises beyond our wildest dreams.

That they may also be the heirs to other, less desirable legacies is something we prefer not to dwell upon. Strange poisonings are discovered; certain foodstuffs have become inedible. The advanced market economies can perform miracles of wealth-creation, but they are losing the art of delivering our daily bread or clean drinking water. Terrible revelations are made about the denatured processes by which we are fed; cows have been raised on infected animal remains; bovine spongiform encelopathy (BSE) spreads to human beings; and television shows us the skeletal bodies of young women and men, tended by distraught parents stroking the wasted faces and atrophied limbs. No wonder eating disorders have become so significant, when food has been turned against nutrition.

New diseases appear all the time – allergies, respiratory and heart ailments – the ills of excess, obesity, anorexia, strange psychic afflictions that have no name; a sickness of the spirit, a violence of the sentiments, fevers of the emotions, injuries to the soul; above all the numbness of a willed unknowing, and a desperate effort to believe that everything is for the best, that we are going somewhere, and someone knows, not only the destination, but that it is also good.

The value of money supersedes all other values, and the economic calculus invades our inner life, areas of our existence which we had thought proof against its intrusion. There is a price on the value of life; the worth of a lost limb can be accurately assessed; litigation will establish the cost of a betrayed relationship, the amount required to restore a lost reputation, the sum required to raise a child – all these are now regularly costed in the exhaustive inventories of the market. As a reason for not having children, people are heard to say 'Oh we can't afford it', as though a baby were a superior species of consumer good, and the renewal of humanity too expensive to be contemplated. And the world grows older, peopled with the survivors of some distant and unremembered catastrophe.

A political economy of the sentiments has developed in mimicry of all the sacralized marketings elsewhere. When interrogating our profoundest relationships, we ask: 'What's in it for me? Is it a good emotional investment? What do I get out of it? What is the pay-off? Where is the bottom line?' 'I gave you everything', cry the debtors of psychic economics, 'and I was conned, swindled, taken in, cheated.' A language of pecuniary fraud is deployed to describe our broken bonds and ruined attachments. Will it pay dividends? Will I get a good return for love or friendship? How high is my stock right now? I staked everything, and I came away empty-handed. A bankruptcy of the soul and heart that is filed in no courts.

We picture our own funeral, the meaninglessness of life mocked by the significance of death, the crematorium with its handful of mourners at a perfunctory farewell, a few paltry wreaths as the coffin slides behind the blue curtains into the fire beneath: we shall be consumed even as we have consumed, the ashes indistinguishable from the wreckage with which we have strewn our lives, our only trace some fading Polaroids of ancient Christmasses,

I staked every-thing, and I came away empty-handed

smudgy beach-games and archaic fashions. Even our own memories have been expropriated, and in their place only fragments of commerce remain – words of popular songs, images of forgotten films, bits of old TV programs, objects we bought which fell apart: this is what we recall. Is it any wonder that a culture which has expunged history should be haunted by the wispy hair and empty eyes of dementia? And we remember an earlier generation who knew what to expect of life, elderly, fiercely stoical women who knew what to do in a crisis, how to deal with any emergency, who were not afraid to wash the dead or get into bed with people as they lay dying, so they should not die alone.

Spectres at the feast

Confronted by the elegant savageries wrought by a real world reshaped to the contours of market necessity, we find it impossible to distinguish any longer between existential suffering, inseparable from being human, and suffering that could be remedied by collective or social action. We are confused: why did I grow old? Who is guilty of imposing loss and death upon us? Why was I bereaved? Why did sickness strike my child? On the other hand, rich and poor have always existed, injustice is part and parcel of human society, inequality is a force of nature, wealth is distributed by providence. Who can think of interfering with such arrangements?

The dependent freedoms which appeared so empowering as we stood on the threshold of the market, now reveal their limits. We can have more ingenious ways of shopping: we can stroll in acclimatized malls and gallerias, we can shop by computer, buy in by telephone, order by mail, purchase by catalogue without stepping out of our door, but we cannot change the way in which need is answered. Women may become executives and newspaper editors, legislators or senior administrators, but they are not free to alter structures of injustice that create widening gulfs between rich and poor. People may live longer, but the fate of ageing populations in the low-watt penumbra of old-age homes provides them with no reason to do so. We become richer, but more locks and grilles and security guards must provide a security which perishable flesh and blood no longer can. We are free to be alone; one in three persons in the US lives alone, without partner, companion or relative. And what of an increasingly fragile livelihood, the market whose caprice has summoned us into employment for the moment, only to evict us as unceremoniously next year? How can we become worthy, not only of the images of perfection inscribed in the ubiquitous consumer market, but equally of a labor-market so flexible that no one can foresee its future outline, and the skills we shall need tomorrow have not yet been called into existence by divisions of labor that none can foretell?

Other spectres, too, come to haunt the banquet of the perpetual feast; unperceived when the market economy was at first imposed upon the self-reliant peoples of the world, with their modest demands and sustainable management of their sacred resource-base. The capacity of the earth to bear this ever-expanding entity was never questioned. Yet suddenly, the finiteness of the world is asked to bear the infinite nature of human desire; or rather, the boundless necessities of a system that knows nothing of limits.

The displacement of creation

A contemporary American economist writes that: 'Few articles in the econo-mist's creed [sic] outrage non-economists more than the pure, imperturbable belief that human wants are insa-tiable. Yet that belief has long been shared by other disciplines. Man's pre-eminence over the brutes lies solely in the number and in the fantastic and unnecessary character of his wants, physical, moral, aesthetic and intellectual. Had his whole life not been a quest for the superfluous, he would never have estab-lished himself as inexpugnably as he does.'

Nothing must change, but everything must change

The idea that it must all go on for ever like this confronts the certainty that it cannot go on like this. Nothing must change, but everything must change. No wonder the will is paralyzed and the capacity to act frozen.

It is true that the present threat could not have been foretold in the early industrial era, when the dogmas of free markets held people captive, and the faith in the laissez-faire of minimal government was accompanied by such coercive terrorizing of the poor. Critics of the internal contradiction were articulate enough, those who foresaw social catastrophe arising out of social injustice and intensifying dispossession of labor. And although poets, moralists and novelists detested the desecration of nature, industrialism was then seen only as a blot, a stain upon the face of earth; not as a source of terminal subver-sion of the life of the planet.

The position has now been reversed: the dispossessed no longer pose a threat to global order, but the damage to the wounded resource-base is plain for all to see. The poor want only to be included in a market system that has become autonomous, all-embracing, promising everything, beyond human control, and therefore the object of superstitious veneration. For it has not only usurped society, but has displaced creation itself.

The market economy, source of all our freedoms, focus of all our hopes, repository of our faith in progress, now threatens to crush us. It has annulled all alternatives to itself, thereby destroying one of the most fundamental of the human needs it purports to answer – the freedom to change, to find other forms of social and economic organization, to discover fresh ways of answering need, to imagine another future, the better world which this one *could have been*. The journey through the landscapes of altered sensibility has obliterated all other ways of giving freely of our own resources, all other means of consoling one another for the unanswerable riddles of our existence – this has been enclosed and driven to market; and even the memory of self-reliance is lost. The cost of the leashed and diminished freedoms of the market, its celebrated 'freedom of choice', can now be seen as a consolation for our own incarceration within it.

And still the procession of uprooted humanity makes the long, restless journey towards a vague destination, like some vast medieval pilgrimage trudging towards the shrine of a saint with miraculous healing powers; while all the time, they are pursuing the instrument that has robbed them of their capacity to survive by their own efforts, to live in symbiotic peace with the earth, to eat and to clothe themselves as a consequence of their own labors in the places where they must live; towards freedoms that beckon with the irresistible shimmer of a light in the darkness, but which at last only unveil further epic dispossessions, inconceivable to those people on the road to the city, with their carts and bundles, their battered suitcases and their heads full of hope and dreams.

Selective reading list

Books

Achebe, Chinua *Things Fall Apart*, Heinemann 1958

Ali, Tariq *The Clash of Fundamentalisms*, Verso 2002

Benedict, Ruth *Patterns of Culture*, 1934, Mentor Books, New York, ed. 1951

Berry, Wendell *The Unsettling of America: Culture and Agriculture* San Francisco, Sierra Book Club, 1977

Bookchin, Murray *The Modern Crisis*, Black Rose Books, Montreal, Canada, 1987

Chomsky, Noam *World Orders Old and New* New York, Columbia University Press, 1994.

Cobbett, William *Rural Rides*, 1830, ed. Penguin 1967

Davis, Mike, *Late Victorian Holocausts: El Niño famins and the Making of the Third World*, Verso 2002

Dube, Siddharth *In the Land of Poverty: Memoirs of an Indian family 1947–1997* London, Zed Books, 1998

Fromm, Erich *Fear of Freedom*, The Sane Society, Routledge & Kegan Paul, London 1956

Gott, Richard *Land Without Evil* London, Verso, 1993

Hines, Colin *Localization – A Global Manifesto* Earthscan, London 2000

Huntington, Samuel *The Clash of Civilizations and the remaking of world order*, Simon and Schuster 1996

Illich, Ivan *Shadow Work*, Marion Boyars 1981

Illich, Ivan *Tools for Conviviality*, Calder and Boyars 1973

Klein, Naomi *No Logo*, Flamingo Books (HarperCollins) 2000

Korten, David *When Corporations Rule the World*, New York, Kumarian Press 1995

Kovel, Joel *The Enemy of Nature*, Zed Books 2002

Ladurie, Emanuel Le Roy *Montaillou* Penguin, 1980

Malinowski, Bronislaw *Magic, Science, Religion and other essays*, Waveland Press 1992 (originally published 1925)

Mander, Jerry and Goldsmith, Edward *The Case Against the Global Economy: And for a Turn towards the Local*, Sierra Club Books 1996

Max-Neef, *Manfred From The Outside Looking In: Experiences in Barefoot Economics*, Dag Hammerskjöld Foundation, 1981

Mead, Margaret *Coming of Age in Samoa*, 1928, Penguin Books 1943

Monbiot, George *Age of Consent: A manifesto for a new world order* Flamingo, 2004

Morris, William *News From Nowhere*, 1888, ed. Lawrence & Wishart 1977

Mumford, Lewis *The City in History*, Penguin Books, 1961

Ngugi James *A Grain of Wheat,* Heinemann, 1967

Norberg-Hodge, Helena *Ancient Futures: learning from Ladakh*, Sierra Club Books 1991

Roy, Arundhati *The Ordinary Person's Guide to Empire*, Flamingo, (HarperCollins) 2004

Sachs, Wolfgang *The Development Dictionary: A Guide to Knowledge as Power* London, Zed Books 1992

Said, Edward *Culture and Imperialism*, Vintage 1993

Shiva, Vandana *Protect or Plunder*, Zed Books 2001

Sivanandan, A *When Memory Dies* London, Arcadia Books 1997

Thompson, E P *The Making of the English Working Class*, Penguin Books 1991

Tuchman, Barbara, *A Distant Mirror* London, Macmillan, 1979

Woodham-Smith, Cecil *The Great Hunger* London, Hamish Hamilton 1962.

Acknowledgements

I would like to thank Nikki van der Gaag for her help and support in producing this book. I am grateful to A Sivanandan and the staff at the Institute of Race Relations, in whose publication, *Race and Class*, a version of Chapter 15 first appeared. I am grateful to all the friends from other cultures, many of them refugees in Britain, who have generously shared their wisdom and insights.

I should like to acknowledge the help of Survival International, which, for more than a quarter of a century, has worked tirelessly for the rights of small cultures and indigenous peoples to live on in a world which increasingly occludes the rare spaces that remain to them. I have been much influenced by writers like Erich Fromm, Lewis Mumford, to anthropologists such as Margaret Mead and Ruth Benedict in particular, who tried to instruct us in the true meaning of pluralism. I am indebted to peoples everywhere who resist the impositions of cultural dominance and universalism.

Index